WITHDRAWN FROM
MACALESTER COLLEGE
LIBRARY

Cambridge Studies in French

READING REALISM IN STENDHAL

Cambridge Studies in French

General editor: MALCOLM BOWIE

Recent titles in this series include:

For a list of other titles in this series, see p. 263

READING REALISM
IN STENDHAL

ANN JEFFERSON

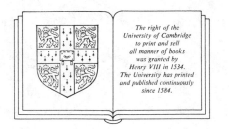

The right of the
University of Cambridge
to print and sell
all manner of books
was granted by
Henry VIII in 1534.
The University has printed
and published continuously
since 1584.

CAMBRIDGE UNIVERSITY PRESS

CAMBRIDGE

NEW YORK   NEW ROCHELLE

MELBOURNE   SYDNEY

Published by the Press Syndicate of the University of Cambridge
The Pitt Building, Trumpington Street, Cambridge CB2 1RP
32 East 57th Street, New York, NY 10022, USA
10 Stamford Road, Oakleigh, Melbourne 3166, Australia

© Cambridge University Press 1988

First published 1988

Printed in Great Britain at
the University Press, Cambridge

British Library cataloguing in publication data
Jefferson, Ann
Reading realism in Stendhal. − (Cambridge
studies in French).
1. Stendhal − Criticism and interpretation
I. Title
843'.7   PQ2441

Library of Congress cataloguing in publication data
Jefferson, Ann.
Reading realism in Stendhal / Ann Jefferson.
p.   cm. − (Cambridge studies in French)
Bibliography.
Includes index.
ISBN 0 521 26274 7
1. Stendhal, 1783−1842 − Criticism and interpretation. 2. Realism
in literature.   I. Title.   II. Series.
PQ2443.J44   1988
843'.7 − dc19   87-17206 CIP

ISBN 0 521 26274 7

For Geoffrey

Un roman: c'est un miroir qu'on promène le long d'un chemin.

SAINT-REAL

Le Rouge et le Noir

Un roman est comme un archet, la caisse du violon *qui rend les sons* c'est l'âme du lecteur.

Vie de Henry Brulard

CONTENTS

Contents

PREFACE

Until very recently realism has appeared as a rather tedious topic on the critical agenda, and there has been little in either contemporary literature or critical thinking to enhance or enliven a view of literature as 'the objective representation of contemporary social reality' (to use René Wellek's neat definition of the term).[1] The hatred of realism which Flaubert claimed as the inspiration of his own writing has continued to flourish in the fiction of the twentieth century, from Gide's self-conscious questionings of the relations between life and art in *Les Faux-Monnayeurs* to the *nouveau roman*'s promotion of the adventure of writing at the expense of the writing of adventures.[2]

Support for this shift of emphasis away from objective representations has come from a variety of critical camps. The history of European fiction has been recast in order to downgrade the great tradition of nineteenth-century realism, and to make way for a rehabilitation of fiction in its largely playful and self-conscious guise; this new tradition begins with *Don Quixote*, proceeds via the eighteenth century (with Sterne, Fielding and Diderot), goes into an eclipse in the nineteenth-century age of realism, and is finally revived and belatedly recognised in the twentieth century with Virginia Woolf, Joyce, Gide, Proust and Nabokov, etc., etc., etc. This, at least, is the story told in Robert Alter's prestigious and persuasive *Partial Magic*.[3] The only fiction that critics find critically interesting is *metafiction* (to take the title of Patricia Waugh's account of the phenomenon), fiction 'which self-consciously and systematically draws attention to its status as an artefact in order to pose questions about the relationship between truth and reality'.[4] The novelist who merely seeks to provide an objective representation of contemporary social reality is a decidedly dull dog; and worse, a creature of bad faith whose lack of self-consciousness permits an unspoken and ideologically undesirable connivance with the forms of bourgeois culture − the point made by Robbe-Grillet when he argues that character and plot are simply the inherited forms of outdated bourgeois certainties.[5]

Preface

The more abstract thinking of contemporary critical theory has only served to support and endorse these views. Saussurean linguistics helped to put writing at the centre of the critical stage, displacing the notion of representation by defining language as the product of a self-sufficient differential system, not as the sum total of words that refer to things. It is not a promising conceptual basis for a constructive theory of realism. Saussure's structuralist and post-structuralist inheritors continue to define the position of speakers and writers as one inside a linguistic system in which reality appears only as an illusion produced by trickery with words – an 'effet de réel' (to use Roland Barthes's phrase)[6] rather than mimesis proper. The mirror that guarantees the representational authenticity of nineteenth-century realism can now only be conceived as a fairground contraption that makes reality an effect that's all done with mirrors. This conception makes of language the prison-house (as Fredric Jameson has so aptly described it)[7] from which the only avenue of escape is into even greater self-consciousness and more play. The system of linguistic differences by which we are constructed and through which the world appears as an encoded mirage may possibly be outplayed: but definitely not discarded.

These, then, are the two components of the deadlock in which realism is bound to appear as theoretically uninteresting, and self-consciousness as incompatible with mimesis. The reading of Stendhal proposed in this book is an attempt to loosen the constraints imposed as a result of seeing things in this light; by showing, first, that there was nothing remotely unself-conscious about the realism of Stendhal's novels; and, second, that mimesis as practised by Stendhal (and no doubt by others too) may take a different form from the one that provides objective records of material and social reality. Reading Stendhal in the light of twentieth-century literary and critical concerns, I could not help being struck by the way that he too seemed to see his own position as being determined by a kind of prison-house of language in which cliché and repetition were more or less inevitable. This view was not, of course, the fruit of a Saussurean theory of language *avant la lettre*, but is ascribable, rather, to Stendhal's perception of the social environment of early nineteenth-century France as a world in which any utterance and any representation was liable either to be a repetition of previous utterances and existing representations, or to become the model for future ones. In short, it was a world in which imitation in the sense of mimesis was constantly under threat of sabotage from imitation in its other sense of plagiarism or emulation. This difference in historical position means that there is also a necessary and significant difference between Stendhal and post-Saussurean criticism, but I have nevertheless found it consistently illuminating to read Stendhal in the light of, and alongside, modern critical thinking, and (for reasons which will perhaps emerge as I go along) especially the work of Roland Barthes. The comparison reveals Stendhal to be as metafictional and as self-conscious a writer as any twentieth-century novelist.

Equally, though, living in the age of positivism, it could never have occurred to him to doubt the reality of reality, and to abandon the attempt to capture it in representational form. The pleasures he himself derived from the arts (of all kinds) depend on mimesis being regarded as the linchpin of all aesthetic enterprise. In his own case, the pitfalls laid in the path of representation by the platitudinising practices of his Parisian contemporaries meant that his writing tended to concentrate on the reader as the focus of literature's mimesis. In some senses, this was a highly anachronistic solution, since it harked back to literary conceptions of an earlier era. But it is a solution which suggests that we have perhaps been defining realism too narrowly in our haste to replace it with a literature construed as a more playful and sophisticated affair. Stendhal's two main metaphors for fiction (the novel is a mirror; the novel is a bow that plays upon the reader's soul) seem, on the face of it, to belong to two totally different conceptions of fiction. The one implies an objectivism that fits nicely with what realism has conveniently been conceived as being; the other presupposes a subjectivism that seems to have no place in the conception of realism as a mirror. Yet, by focussing so intently on the reader, Stendhal's writing makes each metaphor reliant upon the other for its proper working, and so demonstrates that realism is not incompatible with literary self-consciousness, and that mimesis is a vital counterpart to metafiction.

My book is not an exhaustive study of Stendhal's writing. Wilfully partial in its angle of critical approach, it is also partial both in overall design and in its choice of texts. The opening chapter seeks to lay the ground for the critical readings in the subsequent ones by placing Stendhal in his literary-historical context. It chronicles changes in fictional forms from the reader-oriented pragmatics of the eighteenth century to the mimetic preoccupations of the nineteenth; it sketches out the cultural ethos of Stendhal's Parisian readership in the 1820s and thirties; and it draws on Stendhal's own aesthetic writings in order to pinpoint the particular problems that presented themselves in his fiction as a consequence of the configuration of those changes and that readership. Readers who are wearied by this kind of exposition

Preface

(as I suspect Stendhal himself would have been) are advised to skip it and take my historical justifications on trust, for the argument of the remainder of the book adopts a somewhat different tack, and is largely based on readings of four texts by Stendhal: I have concentrated (with varying degrees of thoroughness) on *De l'Amour*, *Le Rouge et le Noir*, the *Vie de Henry Brulard* and *La Chartreuse de Parme*, first because these are the works I like best (a justification not without its basis in Stendhal's thinking, as I hope to demonstrate); and second because, through them, I have been able to explore the aspects of Stendhal's writing which seemed most relevant to my main concerns. I have used the rest of Stendhal's work in a much more eclectic and *ad hoc* way, bringing in discussions of *Armance*, *Lucien Leuwen* and 'L'Abbesse de Castro' where they seemed apposite, and turning my attention from time to time to some of Stendhal's non-fictional writing on literature, painting and music in order to comment more fully on the writing practice of the more literary texts. The result is an approach which I should like to think gave scope for further readings of the texts which I have overlooked or short-changed.

In writing about the importance of readers and the role of the cultural context in Stendhal's work, I have become more acutely aware than I might otherwise have been of how important the context and the readers of even academic critical writing can be. It is therefore a pleasure for me to make the following acknowledgements. I am very grateful to have had the opportunity to rehearse and discuss some early versions of parts of this book with colleagues at the Modern French Critical Theory Group, at a conference on Modern French Autobiography organised by the University of Kent, and at research seminars at Queen Mary College and the Universities of Kent and Oxford, where people asked questions and offered insights which have made a material difference to what I decided to say and how I decided to say it. Equally, I owe a good deal to other colleagues who have provided information and comments in more *ad hoc* and informal ways, but particularly to Christopher Thompson, a Stendhalian of long standing whose expert guidance has illuminated the scholarly field for me. I am also grateful to students past and present whose perceptions and resistances have helped me on my way to a better understanding of Stendhal. Earlier versions of chapters 2 and 5 appeared in *Poétique* and *French Studies* respectively; and parts of chapters 6 and 7 were published in *Romance Studies* and *Stendhal Club* (no. 107, 1985). I gratefully acknowledge permission of the editors of these journals to reproduce them here.

Preface

I owe a very special debt of gratitude to Malcolm Bowie, Terence Cave, Ruth Harris, Diana Knight and Ian Maclean, whose friendship and whose interest in my work have been enormously sustaining and who have contributed invaluably to it by being such wonderfully sharp and generous readers of various parts of the draft at various stages of its development.

Particular thanks are due to the President and Fellows of St John's College, Oxford, my base for more than ten happy years. They not only provided a congenial social and academic working context but made an extremely practical contribution to the production of this book, first by granting me premature leave from teaching for a term, which enabled me to complete the writing, and second, by making it possible for me to buy a word processor, an item that made revising drafts a manageable and occasionally almost pleasurable task. Technology notwithstanding, I have also had invaluable secretarial help from the college office, for which I am immensely grateful — as I am for the expert help of Pamela Mayo in the final preparation of the manuscript.

On the home front I have to thank Liz Painton and Heidi Derry for doing an excellent job in caring for my children. And finally, I should like to record my appreciation to my husband Anthony and the children themselves for being both such tolerant supporters of my work and such effective distractions from it. In spite of Stendhal's horror of progeny, the book is dedicated to Geoffrey, who was born in the middle of it and has remained consistently and consolingly indifferent to its progress.

Part One
INTRODUCTION

1
MIMESIS AND THE READER: SOME HISTORICAL CONSIDERATIONS

Rien n'est plus difficile en fait de romans que de peindre d'après nature et de ne pas copier des livres.
                    Stendhal, 'Projet d'un article sur *Le Rouge et le Noir*'

Le réel, image fabuleuse sans laquelle nous ne pouvons pas lire.
                    Barthes, Preface to Antoine Gallien, *Verdure*

Founding fathers and bachelor uncles

If one looks at the nineteenth-century realist tradition as if it were a family with its own ancestry and descendance (and this is a habit that critics are prone to adopting when confronted with literary movements), Stendhal tends to appear as a member of a collateral line, not as a central figure in the realist dynasty. Although he was nearly two decades older than Balzac, it is nevertheless the younger novelist who is regularly assigned the role of founding father. This recognition of paternity has been conferred on Balzac not just by the critics, but by his literary successors, who have seen in him — rather than in Stendhal — the precursor whose influence their own writing has to reckon with and revise. It was not Stendhal but Balzac whom Flaubert was seeking to unwrite in his *Education sentimentale*, it is Balzac whose name is given to the realist tradition which the *nouveau roman* was trying to oust from twentieth-century fiction, Balzac who is commemorated with quasi-filial affection by Proust in *A la recherche du temps perdu*. Stendhal, in contrast, has been deemed to be, so to speak, without issue in a tradition which nevertheless nobody doubts that he helped to found. The reason for the absence of any Stendhal legacy in the realist tradition has frequently been ascribed to the excessive intrusiveness of the eighteenth-century literary ancestry in his fiction; and on this score he contrasts noticeably with the image of Balzac as the product of his own century and his own century alone, obsessed with its values and apprenticed in the popular fictional forms that emerged for the first time in the post-Revolutionary period.

3

Introduction

In the following pages I shall be seeking to explore and challenge these assumptions, though not so much with the aim of discovering a disinherited line, nor yet to question Balzac's paternity, but in order to evaluate more closely the effects of the eighteenth-century ancestry on Stendhal's writing, and to demonstrate that they did have a positive contribution to make to the realism of the nineteenth. More particularly, I shall be trying to show that if one is to give equal weight to the two rather different metaphors which Stendhal has bequeathed to the dictionary of critical discussion of the novel (the novel as a mirror of reality, the novel as a bow playing upon the reader's soul), then one is necessarily obliged to grant the eighteenth century its dues. For, although a nineteenth-century aesthetic seems to offer a satisfactory explanation of the mirror, the resonances of the bow metaphor can only be picked up by including aspects of eighteenth-century aesthetics as a sounding board. Moreover, I shall be suggesting that the two metaphors do not simply represent alternative or competing conceptions of the novel, but that they are mutually defining: it is not possible to describe the novel as a mirror without seeing at the same time how the mirror might also be a bow. The repercussions of this dual definition can be seen to affect not only Stendhal's own fictional writing, and its place in the realist tradition, but the entire tradition itself. The family characteristics of the realist dynasty may not be quite those that the genealogists have previously described them as being; and reading Stendhal seriously as a realist may mean ending up by seeing realism as a more self-conscious and sophisticated phenomenon than it has hitherto been conceived as being.

In the meantime one might begin by looking at Stendhal as if he had a similar role in the house of realism to the one that his bachelor uncle Romain Gagnon occupied in the Beyle household, for this is certainly the kind of role ascribed to him by critics and theorists of realism as diverse (but also as distinguished) as Erich Auerbach and Georg Lukács. Gagnon was disapproved of by both his father and his brother-in-law (Stendhal's grandfather and father respectively), because this thoroughly likeable, charming, but distinctly unreliable family member proved a little too disinclined to take the serious things in life – like money or a career – seriously, and a little too willing to let himself be seduced away from these concerns by the pleasures of female company.[1] Like his uncle, Stendhal belonged to the libertine world of the *Liaisons dangereuses* and his faults were those of the eighteenth century. Or at least, so they are in the eyes of his critics; and Auerbach's discussion of the novels in *Mimesis* adopts the same sort of tone that one can imagine Gagnon *grand-père* using on the

4

occasions when he would meet his errant son in society, wearing elegant clothes it was obvious he couldn't have afforded himself and which had usually been paid for by his lady friends: although Auerbach recognises the contribution that Stendhal made to what he calls 'the serious realism of modern times',[2] he finds that Stendhal doesn't quite have the staying power to see the project through. He accuses him of being erratic and arbitrary in his presentation of ideas, and of lacking the solid virtues of 'inward certainty and continuity' (p. 405). These are faults that Auerbach quite categorically attributes to Stendhal's eighteenth-century turn of mind, and his Enlightenment conceptions of *esprit* and freedom. In short, he appears as 'a man born too late who tries in vain to realise the form of life of a past period' (p. 410) – ill-suited, by implication, to claim rights of paternity to such a solid and serious dynastic enterprise as the nineteenth century was supposedly to be.

Auerbach is not alone in this assessment, for in Lukács's essay on Stendhal one finds the same mixture of praise and reservation about Stendhal as a founder of realism.[3] Stendhal is praised for the historical typicality of his characters, but when weighed in the scales with Balzac, it is Balzac who emerges decisively as 'the greater realist of the two' (p. 83), because Stendhal's world view proves itself to be at bottom an anachronistic extension of 'the ideology of pre-revolutionary Enlightenment' (p. 77). In other words, Auerbach and Lukács seem to concur (albeit from their rather different perspectives) in their belief that what prevented Stendhal from being a completely convincing realist in the nineteenth-century mould was the legacy of his eighteenth-century education – social, ideological and literary.

Born in 1783, Stendhal was already thirty-two when the nineteenth century began, as he himself dates it in his preface to *Armance*, in the year 1815. Unlike Balzac, who was born in 1799, he could remember a world where Voltaire was considered the greatest literary figure (Stendhal's grandfather kept a bust of the famous *philosophe* on an ebony plinth in front of his desk), where one could meet the original for Laclos's Mme de Merteuil (Mme de Montmaur used to spoil him with candied walnuts when he was a child),[4] when France was still 'gaie, amusante, un peu libertine' and a model for the rest of Europe. The difference between this world and the 'France grave, morale, morose'[5] created by nineteenth-century society and government was one that Stendhal repeatedly refers to and of which he was profoundly and sometimes very uncomfortably aware. It is true, therefore, that, as Auerbach and Lukács say, Stendhal was unlike most of his literary contemporaries: he saw nineteenth-century France through an eighteenth-century optic, or at least against an eighteenth-century ground, and this gave him a very distinctive vantage point from which to interpret and evaluate what he saw in the nineteenth. The contention of this book is that this vantage point not only determined the particular form of his own realism, but also gave him a unique perspective in which to assess the emergent criteria of the particular brand of realism which for many has tended to represent the absolute incarnation of the practice. This catch-all concept of realism is in fact a less than all-embracing affair, for in its insistent foregrounding of the content of fictional representations, it fails to consider their linguistic medium and above all ignores all questions of the readers' reception and response to the text. It is these omissions that Stendhal's eighteenth-century optic brings into focus; and it shows that, far from being a handicap to the realist project (as Auerbach and Lukács would have us suppose), the eighteenth-century viewpoint is essential for an understanding of the nineteenth century that the nineteenth century itself refused the wherewithall to undertake.

The eighteenth century and the pragmatic model

Stendhal himself certainly regarded the relationship between the two centuries as one of discontinuity rather than continuity and progression, and whenever he writes about the eighteenth century it is in order to evoke a lost world of gaiety, elegance and sublime melancholy that contrasts in every way with the dreary *arrivisme* that he saw as characteristic of the nineteenth. Where Hugo revels in the new dawn created by the discontinuity (opening his *Feuilles d'automne* by proclaiming the coincidence of his birth with the beginning of an admittedly less than perfect century when 'Rome remplaçait Sparte', and 'Déjà Napoléon perçait sous Bonaparte'), Stendhal repeatedly testifies to a cultural divide. In his remark that, 'En musique, comme pour beaucoup d'autres choses, hélas! je suis un homme d'un autre siècle' (*Haydn*, p. 399), the interjected *hélas!* suggests that being a man of another century was an attribute that set him apart from his own. For the changes that took place between 1780 and 1825 were not just the enormous political and social ones. More importantly, there was also a complete transformation of mental habits, of the way that people perceived their world and made sense of their experience; what altered, therefore, wasn't just the content of the perceived world, but the very shape and form which that perception took. Michel Foucault has argued that this transformation was so thoroughgoing that it amounts to what he calls an 'epistemological break', by which he means something that is so fundamental that 'les choses ne sont plus perçues, décrites, énoncées, classées, sues de la même façon', and knowledge in the very broadest sense of the word is totally re-formed and recast.[6]

Already, in the simplest biographical terms, it is clear that this break intervened significantly in Stendhal's career: his literary education took place before it, and his writing career, particularly his career as a novelist (which didn't begin until 1827 when he was forty-four), took place after it.[7] Yet it was a career which has earned him a place alongside Balzac and Flaubert in the house of nineteenth-century realist fiction, that is to say, the house which Auerbach himself (in spite of his reservations about Stendhal as a serious realist) named the Hôtel de La Mole in honour of *Le Rouge*, and whose construction is generally held to date from after the break.[8] But what were the consequences of this straddling of the break? Could the two epochs be linked or integrated in some way? Did the eighteenth-century education have to be ditched if Stendhal was to face the changed realities of the nineteenth-century world? Did it survive anachronistically, cutting off Stendhal from the new sensibilities? Or was it capable of being mobilised to provide a valid basis for an understanding of a very different era? And if so, what might that basis be, and what kind of understanding might it yield?

In the eyes of both Lukács and Auerbach there is no doubt that there was a split and that in the case of Stendhal its effects were largely debilitating. For them the eighteenth-century education must necessarily go against the grain of the nineteenth-century world, however intelligent and perceptive Stendhal's understanding of it may on occasion be. But in discussing the impact of this split on Stendhal's fictional writing it is important to realise that it is a very specific conception of realism that brings this rift into view, a conception that emphasises the objectivity of fictional representations and the transparency of their linguistic medium. In such a view Stendhal himself, with his anachronistic values and beliefs, is bound to appear as too obtrusive an authorial presence within the world that he portrays for it to be compatible with this notion of what fictional realism is and how it functions.[9]

And in addition to the complicating issue of authorial intrusion into the conception of representation as objective transparency, there is yet another factor to be taken into consideration when assessing Stendhal's realism, namely the reading context and the reception of works of art in general and fictional works in particular. This concern with effect and response was an aspect of aesthetic thinking that prevailed in one way or another right up to the end of the eighteenth century, and is an element one cannot ignore in considering what Stendhal's legacy from that century might have comprised. In his study of the emergence of the Romantic aesthetic from the preceding critical tradition M. H. Abrams uses the term 'pragmatic theories' to refer to conceptions of art that evaluate art in terms of its effects, and conceive of it primarily as 'a contrivance for affecting an audience'.[10] The criteria of pleasure and instruction were those that were most frequently invoked during the long history of the dominance of this view, which had its origins, says Abrams, in classical rhetoric and in Horace, and continued right up to the end of the eighteenth century. The modern conception of art as mimesis and/or expression (whose emergence it is the purpose of Abrams's book to chart) tends to overlook the fact that the pragmatic view 'has been the principal aesthetic attitude of the Western world' (p. 21).

In the eighteenth century Abrams cites its survival mostly in the neo-classical precepts to be found in Pope, Dryden and Johnson, but in France this neo-classical aesthetic was complemented by the cultural theory contained in Montesquieu's *De l'esprit des lois*. Although pragmatic theories lost ground to the emerging mimetic and expressive theories in the nineteenth century, French Romanticism was, none the less, built on Montesquieu's ideas, justifying its existence by relating artistic practice to cultural and geographical context, and arguing for the need to evaluate different literary styles in relation to different geographical contexts. In particular, Montesquieu's views about the role of climate and other material conditions in the formation of different societies and cultures were co-opted by defenders of the new Romanticism such as Mme de Staël, and were used in particular to support arguments about the difference between the northern and the mediterranean temperaments which figured so prominently in the polemical rhetoric of Romanticism.[11] Stendhal himself, therefore, was the inheritor of a doubly pragmatic tradition, a neo-classical one that emphasised the importance of pleasure (and instruction) in the response to works of art (the idea behind most of the pragmatic theories discussed by Abrams), and a Montesquieuvian one that concentrated on the cultural conditions in which works of art were both created and received.[12]

More than anything else it is this preoccupation with reception and response in Stendhal's Enlightenment inheritance that marks him off from his realist contemporaries and successors: the reader's pleasure in fiction (instruction mattered not at all to Stendhal) and the effects of the cultural conditions of its reception were paramount in his thinking about the novel – not an afterthought or a footnote to it. The concept of cultural relativism penetrated his views on all aspects of cultural and social behaviour. He goes much further than most of his pre-Romantic contemporaries in that he doesn't just use these ideas to defend a northern Romanticism against a southern classicism (as Mme de Staël does), but integrates the effects of cultural reception into his analyses both of social behaviour and of works of art. In his comments on Greek sculpture, for example, he argues that the artistic preoccupation with the naked body and the tendency to represent physical force are the necessary correlates of a society that depended on physical strength and physical skills for its survival. After the invention of firearms, he says, these physical qualities became largely redundant, with the result that modern societies have gradually become indifferent to them. Twenty centuries of civilisation have instead shifted the emphasis on to concern with 'la force de l'âme, l'esprit et la sensibilité',[13] and these now form the stuff of artistic creation. Survival in the modern world is no longer a purely physical matter, but a social one, and this social survival depends on one's ability to amuse – hence the modern admiration for artistic incarnations of these spiritual qualities. For Stendhal, then, aesthetic value always had to be related to the context in which it was produced, since 'la beauté dans chaque siècle, c'est donc tout simplement *l'expression des qualités qui sont utiles'*.[14]

Indeed, for Stendhal, the cultural climate determines not only the overall preoccupation of works of art (force, wit), but the very forms of art that are produced. He claims, for instance, that painting is incompatible with absolute monarchies and cold climates, a theory that explains why England, despite its constitutional monarchy, had – at least in Stendhal's view – no really outstanding painters (*Histoire de la peinture*, I, p. 56). And in a slightly different vein, he uses a similar sort of idea to justify in retrospect the failure of his own youthful attempts to write comedies, which he attributes to the fact that 'la comédie est impossible en 1836', impossible partly because of the character of the nineteenth-century French outlook, and partly because of the rise of the *nouveaux riches*, who constituted an audience unversed in the conventions and style of the genre.[15]

Stendhal's view of the mechanism by which these cultural determinants operate takes as its starting point not the perceptions and insights of the author, but the tastes and values of the audience. His definition of Romanticism, for example, was based not on any notion of literature as the expression of different national temperaments (as it was for Mme de Staël), but on the need for literature to satisfy contemporary cultural and critical conditions:

Le *romanticisme* [*sic*] est l'art de présenter aux peuples les œuvres littéraires qui, dans l'état actuel de leurs habitudes et de leurs croyances, sont susceptibles de leur donner le plus de plaisir possible. (*Racine*, p. 71)

Similarly, if Mozart's music was melancholy (as it was commonly perceived to be at the time), and Cimarosa's more passionate and energetic, it wasn't so much that these differing styles were expressions of their contrasting artistic temperaments, but that they corresponded to the different tastes and temperaments of the audiences for whom they wrote:

Mozart, né à Salzbourg, a travaillé pour des âmes flegmatiques, mélancoliques et tendres comme lui; et Cimarosa, pour des âmes ardentes, passionnées, sans repos dans leurs passions. (*Racine*, p. 184)

Or again, to take the comparison between Racine and Shakespeare: the difference between them is also largely to be explained by the differences between the audiences they were writing for. In the case of Shakespeare, his audience had lived through 'cent ans de guerres civiles et de troubles presque continuels, une foule de trahisons, de supplices, de dévouements généreux', and therefore the drama that pleased them was one which, like Shakespeare's, represented these 'catastrophes sanglantes', yet also provided pleasurable relief and respite from them in the form of 'une foule de peintures fines des mouvements du cœur, et des nuances de passions les plus délicates' (pp. 71–2). Racine's audience, by contrast, far from deriving pleasure from such spectacles, would have been horrified by them, being, as Stendhal rather disparagingly describes them, '[des] poupées sentimentales et musquées qui, sous Louis XV ne pouvaient voir une araignée sans s'évanouir' (*ibid.*). Racine's plays are thus a product of the court for which he wrote, Shakespeare's of the tough people who had had to survive a century of violence and civil war. In short, when it comes to explaining the character of their works, Stendhal is much less interested in what Shakespeare and Racine were like themselves than in the character and temperament of the audience for whom they were writing.

Moreover, the determining influence of the audience is not limited just to the expressive style of a work of art – Mozart's melancholy or the robust quality of Shakespeare's drama – for it also determines its representational scope. What is represented in a play has to be evaluated in relation to what its audience would have been prepared to tolerate. This obviously rules out spiders for the courtiers of Louis XV; but more seriously it means that, for example, if one had a complete record of everything that had been said and done in connection with the death of Iphigenia in Aulis, 'la plupart des choses dites par Agamemnon et par Calchas seraient complètement inintelligibles aujourd'hui, ou si nous les comprenions, nous feraient horreur'.[16] In other words, Stendhal sees even representation as being determined more by the mental habits and the cultural expectations of the audience for whom it is constructed than by fidelity to the original events which it supposedly portrays.

Although most of Stendhal's remarks on the subject were made in the course of the battle over Romanticism, and although they appeared to be primarily concerned with genres other than the novel (notably tragedy), or indeed with art forms other than literature altogether (namely painting and music), they are none the less deeply pertinent to his conception of the novel. In attributing to 'pragmatics' (in Abrams's sense of the word) so vital a part of the representational process, Stendhal was building on the tradition of Aristotelian poetics in which drama was the principal focus of interest; he was also, however, building on the extension and adaptation of that tradition to the increasingly popular (though less respectable) genre of the novel, which was largely preoccupied with its function in relation to its readership. But he was doing so in a way that was to graft the pragmatic concerns of the eighteenth-century novel on to the emergent representational forms of nineteenth-century realist fiction. As a number of critics have said,[17] the realist perspective of the nineteenth century is not the most appropriate one for appreciating a fictional tradition which had quite other concerns, most of them being related in one way or another to the question of their readership. It is therefore the eighteenth-century novel's concern with its readers which I shall be discussing in the next section.

Reading eighteenth-century fiction

A genre which had had to begin by gaining itself respectability achieved its purpose not by asserting the sort of mimetic accuracy that its nineteenth-century successor prided itself on, but by claiming a moral function for itself. At the same time it had also to make itself appealing if it was to find a place with the reading public amongst the more established genres. The desire to please and the intention to instruct both presuppose the reader as the focus of the text's activity in a way that a mimetically oriented writing does not. This pragmatic bias is very clearly demonstrated in the following claim made on behalf of the novel by the Homme de Qualité in his preface to Prévost's *Manon Lescaut* (first published in 1731):

Outre le plaisir d'une lecture agréable, on y trouvera peu d'événements qui ne puissent servir à l'instruction des mœurs; et c'est rendre, à mon avis, un service considérable au public, que de l'instruire en l'amusant.[18]

This formulation is little more than the familiar topos of neo-classical poetics which Prévost is repeating in possibly less than a wholly serious way, since the instruction offered by *Manon Lescaut* is largely blocked by the emotional effects of its sensibility. Nevertheless, the comment does suggest that the content of the novel, its narrative 'événements' have to be evaluated primarily in terms of the effect (be it pleasurable or improving) that they will have on the book's readers. And it is significant, therefore, that the novel is presented in the 'Avis' not as an accurate representation of a certain state of affairs (psychological or social), but as a 'public service' dispensing pleasure and moral instruction to its readership. Furthermore, Prévost suggests that the reader is more likely to be persuaded of the moral rightness being promulgated by the novel if the events within it succeed in affecting his or her sensibility through their emotional impact. Prévost's justification for the narrative content of his moral treatise is that 'il n'y a que l'expérience ou l'exemple qui puisse déterminer raisonnablement le penchant du cœur',[19] a remark which implies that his ultimate purpose in writing the novel is to manipulate the human heart rather than to depict it. The world represented in the novel is therefore designed not so much for the realism of its social and historical portraits, as for the response it will evoke from its readers.

Diderot's *Eloge de Richardson* (1762) makes the same sort of point, except that in discussing the significance of the emotional effects of the text it puts rather more emphasis on the role of the represented world of *Clarissa*. In identifying with the characters who are so exhaustively depicted in the novel, and by being plunged into the physical detail of their world, Diderot suggests that the reader automatically undergoes the moral improvement which he takes to be Richardson's ultimate goal. Like Prévost, he thinks that abstract moral precepts are ineffectual, but believes that the moral dimension comes into effect only when the reader can grasp a living character who performs real actions that the reader can see:

on se met à sa place ou à ses côtés, on se passionne pour ou contre lui; on s'unit à son rôle, s'il est vertueux; on s'en écarte avec indignation, s'il est injuste et vicieux. Qui est-ce que le caractère d'un Lovelace, d'un Tomlinson, n'a pas fait frémir?[20]

The reader's involvement with the represented world unconsciously schools her – or, on this occasion, him – in virtues that he would not otherwise possess:

O Richardson! on prend, malgré qu'on en ait, un rôle dans tes ouvrages, on se mêle à la conversation, on approuve, on blâme, on admire, on s'irrite, on s'indigne ... Mon âme était tenue dans une agitation perpétuelle. Combien j'étais bon! combien j'étais juste! combien j'étais satisfait de moi! (*ibid.*)

In other words, whether one is considering the moral value of a novel, its capacity to amuse, or its emotional effect on the sensibility of its readers, the conception of the role and purpose of serious fiction in the eighteenth century places its audience, and not its represented content, at the centre of its concerns. Any progress the novel seems to have made in the development of the kind of realism associated with the nineteenth century (and both Prévost and Richardson would theoretically be amenable to this kind of interpretation)[21] has to be assessed primarily in the light of the pragmatic aims that the novel set for itself in this period. This factor is a very far cry from the nineteenth-century notion of representation, which invites a comparison with the world it depicts, and leaves to the reader only the role of acknowledging or admiring the accuracy and truth of that representation. So that if one were to put the difference in a nutshell, one could say that the eighteenth century subordinates representation to reading, and the nineteenth century reading to representation.

A second major tradition in the eighteenth-century novel – although one that has received rather less serious critical attention than the first – is the novel of worldliness, whose prime exponents are Crébillon *fils* and Duclos (whom Stendhal frequently refers to), and which leaves profound traces in the novels of Marivaux, Rousseau and Laclos.[22] The concern of the novel of worldliness was with man's social existence and with man as a social creature. Its aim was less to describe the society which is seen as giving significance to individual existences – not, in other words, to offer the set *tableau de mœurs* that the nineteenth-century novel promises to deliver – than to celebrate and reinforce the values of the worldly society which author, reader and characters are all presumed to share. As Peter Brooks succinctly puts it, the novelist of worldliness 'need not reproduce the world in his novel, *he rather situates his novel in the world*' (p. 35, my italics). That is to say, in so far as there is a real world represented in this type of fiction, that world also provides the context

13

for its own representation. The representation thus mediates between the real world of worldliness and the worldly reader in a circular process that makes the reading public the operative factor within the text: first by invoking the standards of worldliness of that public; and second, by seeking in turn to re-impose those standards upon its readership.

Finally, if one looks at a third major fictional tradition in the eighteenth century, namely the self-conscious comic novel as exemplified by Sterne, the Diderot of *Jacques le fataliste*, and Fielding,[23] one finds that here too the reader remains central to the operations of the text; for the self-conscious games that their authors play require the reader − at least in the form of a represented reader in the text − to play a role that gives shape and purpose to everything else in the novel. This reader's imagined responses are used to provide a touchstone encapsulating the tradition and conventions of existing fiction, against which the ploys and innovations of the novel in question may be measured. In this sense the reader becomes the focus around which a context of literary traditions and assumptions is concentrated, and is the means whereby the text can show awareness of its own situatedness within a specific literary tradition (or set of traditions).

In all their manifestations − 'serious', worldly, self-conscious − novels of this period presented themselves to their public as texts whose function depended primarily on context − be it moral, social, literary − and as constructs designed to produce effects within that context. This, then, was the tradition that Stendhal was raised in, and whose suppositions formed the climate in which his own youthful reading took place. It is not, therefore, entirely fortuitous that, in describing the reading habits of his youth and his passion for books like *Séthos* '(lourd roman de l'abbé Terrasson), alors divin pour moi', *Félicité ou mes fredaines* and other examples that he describes retrospectively as 'de plats romans de 1780', Stendhal comes up with the metaphor of the novel as a bow: 'Un roman est comme un archet, la caisse du violon *qui rend les sons* c'est l'âme du lecteur' (*Brulard*, p. 699, Stendhal's italics). So that although the bow image − in which the reader is central − occurs at a later stage in Stendhal's own writing than the mirror definition (1836 as opposed to 1824−30), it actually harks back to a model of reading and a conception of fiction that significantly predates the one implied by the mirror metaphor.[24]

It may seem crude to polarise a discussion of the development of the novel between an eighteenth-century and a nineteenth-century model, but there does seem to be a striking break in the continuity of the fictional tradition between the two centuries, that is to say, between the publication of *Les Liaisons dangereuses* in 1782 and the first perceptible stirrings of a coherent nineteenth-century tradition (the realist one) in the mid-1820s. What intervened between these two dates was, of course, the Revolution and all that followed, but to correlate formal changes in the novel with the political and social changes brought by the Revolution, the Empire and the Restoration in any exact or causally explanatory way would call for ambitious speculation. That the two are linked is undeniable: how they are linked is altogether a more complicated and problematic issue and one that I do not intend to pursue. One also needs to bear in mind that fiction continued to be written and read in the intervening limbo period, but during that time the genre became highly diversified and fragmented in the sense that there had ceased to be any shared conception of what fiction was or ought to be.[25] Its exiled and disoriented heroes and heroines (René, Adolphe, Corinne, Oberman) could be seen as an indirect expression of the novel's own sense of exile from its previous social and cultural position; equally, their physical, social and emotional isolation could be read as an echo of fiction's own loss of contact with a stable and clearly identified reading public, since reading itself was undergoing profound changes of organisation and social character.[26] Once a coherent conception of the nature and purpose of fiction does begin to emerge with the appearance of a new kind of writing towards the end of the twenties, it is a very different one from its eighteenth-century predecessor, and it is to a more detailed consideration of what was at stake in this new writing that I shall now turn.

The realist model

Historical purists might argue that it is jumping the gun to call this new conception 'realism' because, in the strict historical sense of the word, realism became a widespread critical concept only in the late 1840s and 1850s.[27] Indeed one could claim that the term was not properly consecrated until 1856 when a journal of that name appeared (Duranty's *Le Réalisme*), or even 1857 when Champfleury's essays in defence of the concept were published under that title. Strictly speaking, the true realists were writers who now only have a secondary status in our picture of the nineteenth century, such as Murger, Duranty, Feydeau, and later on the Goncourt brothers, all of whom tended to regard Balzac and Stendhal more as precursors than as the exemplary exponents of the movement that the modern critical tradition tends to see in them. However, in practice, most literary historians date the beginnings of realism from 1830, the year after the publication of Balzac's first major success, *Les Chouans*, and the year in which *Le Rouge et le Noir* and Henri Monnier's fictional portrait of the bourgeois character Joseph Prudhomme appeared in his *Scènes populaires*. (The end of the realist period is variously dated at the end of the Second Empire, or 1868, with the publication of *Thérèse Raquin*.)[28] But what matters for this discussion is not which authors or works qualify for inclusion in the realist category, but what conception of fiction was at stake − what, in other words, the realist model comprised.

The earliest documented use of the word in 1826 already indicates the direction in which the trend was to go and points quite clearly to the kind of model for the novel that was in the process of being elaborated. It appeared in the *Mercure français* and the key passage runs as follows:

Cette doctrine littéraire qui gagne tous les jours du terrain et qui conduirait à une fidèle imitation non pas des chefs-d'œuvres de l'art mais des originaux que nous offre la nature, pourrait très bien s'appeler le *réalisme*: ce serait suivant quelques apparences, la littérature dominante du xixᵉ, la littérature du vrai.[29]

In the 1820s the concept of a 'littérature du vrai' of this kind was not exclusively confined to the novel; for much of the defence of Romanticism, particularly as it applied to the theatre, where the tyranny of existing models was perceived to be specially oppressive (much more so than in the fictional sphere), used arguments that ran along these lines. Hugo's *Préface de Cromwell* of 1827 (the year, incidentally, that saw the publication of Stendhal's *Armance*) defended new dramatic forms precisely in the name of 'le réel', and campaigns for an art whose aim is to reproduce 'la réalité des faits'.[30] In the end, however, it fell to the novel to make this new realism, and the reality of facts, its own privileged domain. The newly found 'réel' certainly called for a mirror as the most appropriate metaphor for artistic reproduction, but in the case of the Romantic drama Hugo specifies that it must be a 'miroir de concentration', not a 'miroir ordinaire, une surface plane et unie [qui] ne renverra des objets qu'une image terne et sans relief, fidèle, mais décolorée' (p. 436). Yet the mirror that drama rejects is precisely the kind of mirror that Stendhal seems to have in mind when he defines the novel (in 1830) as 'un miroir qui se promène sur une grande route, [qui] tantôt ... reflète à vos yeux l'azur des cieux, tantôt la fange des bourbiers de la route' (*Le Rouge*, p. 342). And the muddy facts of 'le réel' became the property − if not, as Stendhal goes on to point out, the responsibility – of the novel.

The critical rhetoric associated with the novel in this period (that is, from the mid-twenties on) tends to assimilate the mirror's function to a 'peinture de mœurs' based on observation, and these are the features that critics both seek and admire. Walter Scott's historical novels, which were first translated in 1822 and were very widely read in France during this decade, set a precedent for a view of the novelist as a 'historien de mœurs' whose portrait of his own society was based on contemporary observation. Stendhal claims for his *Armance* that it was an attempt to 'peindre les mœurs telles qu'elles sont depuis deux ou trois ans' (*Correspondance*, 3 Jan. 1826), subtitles *Le Rouge* 'Chronique de 1830' and says of *Lucien Leuwen* that he had 'copié les personnages et les faits d'après nature',[31] all signs that he had at least assimilated the vocabulary of the new realism necessary for the 'promotion' of his novels. Whether or not these are actually the most important aspects of Stendhal's fiction is, for the moment, irrelevant, since the prime significance of these statements is that they testify to the rhetoric of the self-presentation of fiction at the time he was writing. It is this rhetoric that reveals most clearly what the commonly shared conception of fiction as representation was.

Certainly the critical reception of Stendhal's own fiction reveals that these were the criteria in terms of which the genre was praised or condemned. *Le Rouge* was not much liked by the critics when it first appeared, but those who did like it singled out the fidelity and penetration of its depiction of society as the book's chief merit (Weinberg, pp. 10–12). In the course of the decade these criteria for critical assessment emerged even more strongly and consistently. A belated comment on *Le Rouge* by Amédée Duquesnel in 1839 praises it for being 'singulièrement remarquable par la profondeur des observations', and admires its 'peintures de la haute société parisienne et de cet égoïsme brillant qui la ronge' (quoted by Weinberg, p. 13). Balzac, who described his own fictional principles in the 1842 'Avant-propos' to the *Comédie humaine* as being those of 'un peintre plus ou moins fidèle' devoted to the 'reproduction rigoureuse ... des types humains' and to the construction of an 'histoire ... des mœurs',[32] invokes the same principles in his 1840 article on Stendhal. In particular he emphasises Stendhal's gift for observation, calling him 'cet observateur de premier ordre' and remarking on 'la finesse de l'observation' in *La Chartreuse*.[33] He prefaces his comments on Stendhal with a general disquisition on what a novel is or ought to be, making the by now entirely familiar and standard point that a

17

novel is 'une représentation du monde comme il est' (p. 1152) and a 'peinture de la société moderne' (p. 1156). More interestingly, though, he goes on to say that the conventions of the literature of the seventeenth and eighteenth centuries (or what he himself calls 'le procédé sévère de la littérature du xviiᵉ et xviiiᵉ siècles' [*sic*]) are fundamentally ill-suited to this portrayal, thus incidentally revealing that he himself was conscious of the extent of the break that had taken place in the literary tradition, and implicitly supporting the view that Stendhal was caught between two deeply incompatible models of fiction.

The notion of art as a painting 'd'après nature' has a long and respectable history in neo-classical poetics, and the value put on La Bruyère's *Caractères* as the observation of 'les mœurs de ce siècle' (its subtitle) suggests that observation too had its role to play in the painting of nature. But in the first decades of the nineteenth century the significance of these terms was radically altered by the changed cultural and social context in which they were used. Observation was now the key to a new scientific era exemplified in Comte's positivist mission to base all knowledge — from mathematics and chemistry to what he called 'la physique sociale' — on the principle that 'il n'y a de connaissances réelles que celles qui reposent sur des faits observés'.[34] The fruits of observation were not to be a confirmation of the known world, but the discovery of invariable natural laws (an idea that Balzac adapts for his own purposes in the 'Avant-propos' to the *Comédie humaine*). Where La Bruyère's observations had sought to confirm the worldly values that he shared with his readers, the 'scientific' procedures of Balzac followed Comte's general principles in seeking to reveal hitherto unknown truths (or laws) to their readers. Even at the surface level of the representation of *mœurs*, novels were not necessarily describing a world which their readers recognised or were familiar with: it was a society whose shape and direction remained to be discovered, whose values still needed to be explicated, and whose system of rewards and punishments still needed to be deciphered. In some ways contemporary French society was as much of an unknown to its inhabitants as the fifteenth-century world of Walter Scott was to its nineteenth-century readers. The nature painted by art in the age of realism was a new world, and observation the means of orientating oneself within it.

From this account it should now be clear how little the eighteenth- and nineteenth-century models had in common with each other. For, with the advent of the realist aesthetic, representation had become an end in itself rather than a means to a readerly end, and as such constituted the central focus of the novel's new concerns. The skills required of an author were no longer the ability to manipulate readerly sensibilities, but the powers of observation that contribute to the accuracy of social and historical portraiture. The role ascribed to the reader in the realist model is virtually non-existent in that readers no longer have an explicit function in the critical rhetoric that defends and promotes the novel as a genre; at most the reader may be permitted passive exclamations of admiration for the accuracy of the author's representations, as instanced in the response of Alexis de Saint-Priest to *Le Rouge*: 'Voilà de la vérité! voilà de l'exactitude!' (quoted by Weinberg, p. 12).

The only dispute about this model concerned the lengths to which representational accuracy should go. As Stendhal himself puts it in his essay on Walter Scott and *La Princesse de Clèves*, 'Je … sais bien, morbleu! qu'il faut imiter la nature; mais jusqu'à quel point? voilà toute la question' (*Mélanges II: Journalisme*, p. 223). This issue was one that Stendhal himself had fallen foul of in the first reviews of *Le Rouge*, several of which accused him precisely of having gone too far. Jules Janin complains that Stendhal directs his attention only to the base and ugly side of life (a complaint commonly voiced about realist writing in the period, and, ironically, one which Stendhal himself made about many of the paintings in the exhibition which he reviewed in the 'Salon de 1824').[35]

Those who sought to resist the lengths to which realism (both in painting and in fiction) seemed liable to go did so in the name of an opposition between truth on the one hand, and reality on the other, arguing against the simple representation of reality and for some kind of transcendental significance in a work of art.[36] In his 1827 preface to *Le Cinq-Mars*, for instance, Vigny draws on the early nineteenth-century revival of Platonism in order to oppose 'la VERITE de l'Art' to 'le VRAI du fait', and demands the freedom 'de faire céder parfois la réalité des faits à l'IDEE que chacun d'eux doit représenter aux yeux de la postérité' (Vigny's capitals).[37] Even some of those who defended the realist credo apparently based on 'la réalité des faits' began to backtrack a little when they saw how far the trend was being taken. In her 1832 preface to *Indiana* George Sand describes the novelist as a mirror which reflects the social inequality that happens to exist, and as a machine that merely reproduces it, 'et qui n'a rien à se faire pardonner si ses empreintes sont exactes, si son reflet est fidèle';[38] but by 1846 she is defending the view that 'L'art n'est pas une étude de la *réalité positive*: c'est une recherche de la *vérité idéale*.'[39] Similarly, Balzac, who defends fiction as a faithful history, nevertheless criticises Stendhal for having reproduced his world too faithfully, and remarks that, 'En voyant un paysage un grand peintre se gardera bien de le copier servilement, il nous en doit moins la lettre que l'Esprit' (p. 1208). The servility involved in 'mere' copying is a theme that recurs frequently in the debates about realism, and it shows that in so far as realism was seen to have a problematic aspect, the opposition between letter and spirit, fact and transcendence, reality and truth, *le vrai* and *le vraisemblable* constituted the only terms in which the problem could be perceived and discussed. The pragmatic concerns of the eighteenth-century model were not seen as relevant to an argument whose ground had decisively shifted elsewhere.

The model shared by both defenders and detractors of the new realism was largely constructed so as to exclude any functional role within it for the reception and reading of the texts produced in accordance with it. Yet the realist—idealist opposition frequently gets translated into moral terms in a move which, if only by implication, does bring the issue of readerly reception back into play. For the critics of realism repeatedly accuse it not just of misrepresentation (concentrating exclusively on the base and the ugly), but also of immorality. Realism was perceived by its opponents as offending the morality of the society within which it was produced, an offence which Stendhal in particular was often charged with.[40] For example, in 1839, Théodore Muret condemns Stendhal for 'sa moquerie pour les choses saintes, pour les idées que, sans distinction d'opinion, chacun est tenu de respecter'.[41] And in a more general perspective, as the term 'realism' gradually became assimilated into the critical currency during the forties and fifties, it acquired a distinctly derogatory connotation, and ended up as more or less synonymous with 'immorality' – an association of ideas by which Flaubert's *Madame Bovary* was particularly affected.[42]

Although the indignation caused in certain quarters by the faithful representations of realism cannot have escaped the attention of most of its practitioners, Stendhal is unique in building this awareness into his conception of the novel and into the very substance of his own representations. For these representations are always placed by Stendhal's authorial commentary in relation to an anticipated response, a response that is characterised as one of deep disapprobation and outrage. Stendhal's mirror metaphor, which is usually taken as the guarantee of mimetic accuracy, is also frequently associated with the offence that it is liable to cause. Stendhal expects the gentleman reading *Le Rouge* to take umbrage at the novel's depiction of Mathilde's behaviour as described at the point in the narrative where the metaphor makes its appearance. And it is supposedly in order to counter the reader's outrage that Stendhal adduces the mirror argument. The passage in question quite explicitly links specular representation with anticipated accusation:

Eh, monsieur, un roman est un miroir qui se promène sur une grande route. Tantôt il reflète à vos yeux l'azur des cieux, tantôt la fange des bourbiers de la route. Et l'homme qui porte le miroir dans sa hotte sera par vous *accusé d'être immoral*! Son miroir montre la fange, et *vous accusez le miroir*! Accusez bien plutôt le grand chemin où est le bourbier, et plus encore l'inspecteur des routes qui laisse l'eau croupir et le bourbier se former. (p. 342, my italics)

In exculpating himself and his mirror, Stendhal demonstrates that representations, because or in spite of their documentation of the real world, are inevitably bound up with that world, and in far more numerous ways than that implied by the neutral fidelity of quasi-historical observation. He sees, in other words, that representations necessarily and always have a pragmatic orientation.

This perception on Stendhal's part is, however, not just an anachronistic hangover from his eighteenth-century education, for it is inseparably linked to his view of contemporary French society as a whole. In his eyes, it was a question not just of seeing that particular literary practices are related to broader models and traditions (realism to a pragmatic concern with readers), but of seeing that models and traditions must themselves be related to the audience whose reading serves to endorse them. Nor was it a question of asking what readers might learn from novels (history, etc.), and in what way novels might serve to instruct them; rather, Stendhal saw the necessity of asking what interests, particularly social and cultural interests, the reading of novels might be reinforcing. Whose cause might novels find themselves co-opted into supporting? Whose interests would they be made to benefit? And the very disingenuousness of realist writing made it far more vulnerable on this count than the worldly novel of the eighteenth century, whose complicity with the cultural values of its readers was fully explicit and whose social function was openly acknowledged and accepted by readers and writers alike.

The century of platitude

In discussing Stendhal's realism one needs to remember, therefore, that the society about which he wrote was also — and indeed perhaps first and foremost — the society within which, for which, and often against which, he wrote. Leaving aside for a moment the question of the mimetic function of the novel, this factor already gives the genre a social significance which positivist models tend to ignore: from the moment that one regards the genre as owing its very existence to the society within which it is produced, it can no longer be conceived as a purely transparent medium for the depiction of that society. Certainly, for Stendhal, novels were not so much the most faithful means of recording social reality as the product of the particular culture they were hailed as representing. Just as the social and political conditions of Renaissance Italy tended to favour painting, so – in Stendhal's eyes at least – those of nineteenth-century France promoted novels.

In the first instance, novels are seen by him as both a symptom of and an antidote to the boredom generated by the stultifying mores of contemporary French society. Reading novels is the only consolation that women, in particular, have in a social world dominated by the 'sotte pruderie qui ... est venue attrister la France, et lui faire perdre des droits au titre de *gaie* qu'elle méritait si bien avant la Révolution' ('Projet', p. 713). In a gay society like the one that Stendhal, admittedly rather utopianly, attributes to pre-Revolutionary France and modern-day Italy, amusement is built into the fabric of daily social life, and opera is the dominant form of artistic entertainment. Amusement and entertainment in these forms make novels unnecessary as a source of either consolation or distraction. Furthermore, although the era of the novel of worldliness is over, Stendhal regards his contemporary Parisians as being more desperately reliant on a model of worldliness than their eighteenth-century predecessors, whom this particular form of fiction was designed to satisfy. The extreme dependence of his contemporaries on such a model may be explained by the fact that, in losing a monarch, the French had lost the single 'patron convenu' which the courtier had traditionally modelled himself on; and in the ensuing social fragmentation, the monarch's role in this respect had been taken over by that elusive and amorphous entity, '*l'opinion de la majorité*', elsewhere referred to by Stendhal as 'l'opinion publique' (*Racine*, p. 204). The modern Parisian is perpetually occupied in seeking out correct models for his behaviour and in making sure that he manages to conform to them. In Stendhal's view, he is an entirely worldly being, whose existence is wholly devoted to 'cette civilisation si avancée, qui pour chaque action, si indifférente qu'elle soit, se charge de vous fournir un modèle qu'il faut suivre' (*Armance*, p. 151).

Conformity is the keynote in a society that breeds a pervasive uniformity. Stendhal sees Paris as the capital of fashion, not for aesthetic reasons (indeed he positively disliked the skinny appearance of French women, which he compared unfavourably to the natural and healthy looks of their Italian counterparts), but because fashion is one of the most powerful means whereby conformity can be imposed and maintained. Stendhal thought that the further up the social ladder you go, the greater this uniformity becomes, so that the Faubourg Saint-Germain is populated largely by '[des] jeunes gens parfaitement généreux [qui] se croiraient perdus s'ils n'étaient pas tous la *copie exacte* les uns des autres' ('Projet', p. 722, Stendhal's italics). The 'opinion toute faite' tends to be the only form that opinion takes in Paris. Everyone copies everyone else in the hopes that they will succeed in conforming to the elusive but all-powerful 'opinion publique'. And in this 'siècle ... si adonné à la platitude' ('Testaments', *Romans*, I, p. 1397), repetition governs every aspect of behaviour and discourse, so that as Stendhal himself says: 'La figure de rhétorique la plus puissante chez les Français [est] la *répétition*' (*Mélanges III: Peinture*, p. 93, Stendhal's emphasis).

In a society like this it seems inevitable that novels will be read for the model of social behaviour that they are assumed to be proposing, rather than for the accuracy of the social history that they claim to be documenting – a tendency confirmed by Stendhal's comment in *Le Rouge* that Mathilde's suitors in the de La Mole salon are all perfect copies of Chateaubriand's René. Whatever the intentions of the novelists themselves, novels are in danger of being turned by their readers into models which they then set about adapting themselves to, rather than being appreciated as the record of particular facts or truths. Benjamin Constant remarks in his 1824 preface to the third edition of *Adolphe* that a suspiciously large number of his readers claim to have had the experiences he portrays in his unfortunate hero, a statistic he is inclined to ascribe more to the vanity of these readers than to the universality of the phenomenon depicted in his novel:

Presque tous ceux de mes lecteurs que j'ai rencontrés m'ont parlé d'eux-mêmes comme ayant été dans la position de mon héros. Il est vrai qu'à travers les regrets qu'ils montraient de toutes les douleurs qu'ils avaient causées perçait je ne sais quelle satisfaction de fatuité; ils aimaient à se peindre comme ayant, de même qu'Adolphe, été poursuivis par les opiniâtres affections qu'ils avaient inspirées, et victimes de l'amour immense qu'on avait conçu pour eux. Je crois que pour la plupart ils se calomniaient, et que si leur vanité les eût laissés tranquilles, leur conscience eût pu rester en repos.[43]

The sting in this last sentence is something that one can readily imagine Stendhal savouring.

What is disquieting in this situation for Stendhal is not so much that realism may go unnoticed or be misperceived by a Parisian reader-ship more intent on finding socially effective models of behaviour, but that realism itself is in danger of becoming caught up in this pattern of conformity, repetition and fashion. Already by 1830 the realist imperative '*imitez la nature*' is being reduced by 'les gens du monde' to a mere fashionable slogan in a way that threatens to undermine the whole validity of the enterprise ('Walter Scott', *Mélanges II: Journalisme*, p. 223). The authenticity implicit in realist representation is vulnerable to the threat of absorption into the Parisian process of repetition and platitude. In a century devoted to platitude, anything is grist to the mill of this process and there is no intrinsic reason why the closely observed social histories of realism should be any exception. In Stendhal's view, there is nothing to stop realism from becoming simply a reproducible style, nothing to prevent an imitation of nature (*mimesis*) being reduced to the imitation of a certain style (*imitatio*).[44] The Parisian passion for the conformities of 'l'opinion publique' can succeed in removing representations from their connection with the real by turning them into a model for the kind of imitation on which Parisian society – as Stendhal sees it in any case – clearly thrives. Indeed, he believed that the tenets of nineteenth-century realism actually encourage this kind of imitative corruption, because he regarded the detailed descriptions of material reality popularised and exemplified by Walter Scott as a fairly unchallenging stylistic trick that more or less anyone could learn and repeat. As he puts it in the essay on Walter Scott: 'L'habit et le collier de cuivre d'un serf du moyen âge sont plus faciles à décrire que les mouvements du cœur humain' (p. 221). And he makes the same point about the David school of painting, which in Stendhal's eyes had simply copied the style of its founder, patiently and mechanically learning accurate drawing like 'une science exacte, de même nature que l'arithmétique, la géométrie, la trigonométrie, etc.', which would allow them to 'reproduire avec le pinceau la conformation et la position exacte des cent muscles qui couvrent le corps de l'homme' (*Mélanges III: Peinture*, p. 26).

In fact Stendhal tends to see artistic tradition in general in terms of this cycle of imitation and platitudinisation of artistic or literary achievement; and in his view, it requires the courage of genius to bring about progress through a rejection of the tyranny of a given style or set of conventions. (His *Histoire de la peinture en Italie* and his *Racine et Shakespeare* are very clearly based on this assumption.) But although this is a fairly widely accepted conception of artistic tra-dition, it is not normally seen as having any relevance to realism, whose documentary basis is, on the contrary, commonly seen as removing it from the snares of this kind of cycle of imitation. But there is no intrinsic reason why this should be so, and in his recurrent engagements with the question, Stendhal is drawing attention to the essentially problematic nature of realism at the very moment of its inception, by showing that representations have their own stylistic momentum as well as a mimetic veracity, and by indicating that the copying of nature cannot easily be safeguarded from copying of the plagiarising kind, nor the imitation of the real preserved from imitations of style. Stendhal's apparently aristocratic disdain for the everyday in the arts is not just pre-Revolutionary snobbery (although there may well be an element of snobbery in it); it is also, and more importantly, related to his feeling that the everyday in the arts is 'common', 'vulgar', 'prosaic' (all recurrent words in his critical vocabulary), for the reason that the accessibility of the everyday offers a certain sort of easy reproducibility. Words like 'vulgar' and 'prosaic' refer not just to a reality, but to the over-familiar style which that reality elicits and promotes.

The survival of the reader-oriented model of fiction in Stendhal's thinking would seem therefore to be far more than an idiosyncracy or an anachronism. The implications of the pragmatic aspect of Stendhal's conception of the novel in the realist era are obviously very far-reaching, for, by problematising the most basic presuppositions of the genre, they invite a thorough reappraisal of the realist model.

Copying and the 'déjà-dit'

Stendhal's eighteenth-century legacy colours his conception of nineteenth-century realism in such a way as to create another potential anachronism through its similarities with more topical, twentieth-century discussions about realism. In their structuralist and post-structuralist guise these discussions are apt to construe mimesis entirely as a question of style and convention.[45] Facts and observation become irrelevant to a view of language as a thoroughly and inescapably coded affair. Tzvetan Todorov, for example, illustrates a certain kind of modern critical viewpoint when he argues that language has no necessary link with the real, and that what we take to be a reflection of reality is actually mere verisimilitude, *le vraisemblable*. *Le vraisemblable* is a product of language and the conventions of discourse, a trick played by literature when it seeks to make us believe that 'elle se conforme au réel et non à ses propres lois', a 'masque dont s'affublent les lois du texte, et que nous sommes censés prendre pour

25

une relation avec la réalité'.[46] There is, moreover, something distinctly Stendhalian about his claim that *le vraisemblable* can be defined as a relation to 'l'opinion publique' (though the term harks back to Aristotle's notion of the *doxa*), as conformity to a particular set of generic conventions, and a style that seeks to deny that it is one (p. 94). Similarly, when Barthes says in *S/Z* that the descriptions that form the basis of fictional realism are always implicitly related to an artistic model and not to reality, and that representation 'consiste à copier une copie (peinte) du réel',[47] one hears a striking echo of Stendhal's complaint that most of the modern paintings one saw in the Louvre were not based on genuinely observed scenes, but simply reproduced the already encoded histrionic gestures of the famous actor Talma. Equally, his charge that 'Au lieu de s'attacher directement à la nature et de la copier, *on imite une imitation*' (*Mélanges III: Peinture*, p. 92, Stendhal's emphasis) anticipates Barthes's remark almost verbatim. (What for Stendhal is a complaint or a reproach is, however, for Barthes an accepted and inevitable state of affairs.)

If they do nothing else, these parallels at least lend support to Stendhal's claim that he would not be understood until after his death, although he never mentioned a date as late as 1970 (the year in which *S/Z* was published): 1880 or 1935 are usually the dates that he envisages. But despite the apparent appropriateness of twentieth-century concepts of writing to Stendhal's nineteenth-century practice (and, let it be said, it is an appropriateness that this study will draw on extensively), one should not allow it to blind one to a fundamental dissimilarity between the two; crucially, what Stendhal does not share with the twentieth-century critical theorists is the degree of their mimetic pessimism. However elusive, and however vulnerable to banalisation, the real remains the touchstone of Stendhal's aesthetic theory and his fictional practice. Paintings, plays, novels are in Stendhal's view either bound to the real or they are not: Shakespeare's plays were, Racine's were (or at least they were sometimes: Stendhal is apt to change his mind about Racine), but those of their imitators definitely were not. And a key moment in Stendhal's own awakening to aesthetic experience took place on the day he discovered that painting wasn't just an exercise in stylistic imitation, but a representation of reality (*Brulard*, pp. 751–2). The real for Stendhal is the 'holy real', the 'saint-réal', cited as the source for the mirror metaphor in *Le Rouge*.[48]

So rather than introduce anachronism again, and subject Stendhal to a reading that would inevitably bracket out the mimetic aims that are central to his enterprise, the comparison should be used as a basis for a reconsideration of nineteenth-century realism itself. If Stendhal has been perceived as a reluctant or less than whole-hearted realist (viz. Lukács, Auerbach and also Zola, who complained that his famous mirror showed only the heads and not the bodies or the physical environment of his characters),[49] it is not so much that he was too steeped in the eighteenth century to enter into the spirit of the realism of the nineteenth, but rather that he was peculiarly aware of the problematic nature of the trend that he also helped to found. The vulnerability of realism to its own conventions and linguistic procedures is something that Flaubert, writing a quarter of a century later, was highly sensitive to as well; but in his case he sought to solve the problem by recourse to an aestheticism which is quite alien to Stendhal's way of thinking and writing. (Certainly, Flaubert himself saw no resemblance between his own preoccupations and those of his precursor Stendhal, whom he found 'mal écrit et incompréhensible comme caractères et intentions'.)[50] The vulnerability of realism to stylistic banalisation, of imitation (mimesis) to imitation (plagiarism) is endemic to the whole realist project, as we shall see, first, in an analysis of the rhetoric of realism and, second, in a comparison with the other arts and techniques of mimetic reproduction in the period.

The key words in the rhetoric of realism are 'copier', 'copie', 'imiter', 'imitation', 'reproduire', and 'reproduction'; and they are all equally double-edged, lending themselves simultaneously to the sense of 'faithful representation' and to that of 'plagiarised repetition'. (Indeed the ambivalence is so fundamental that it is hard to find synonyms that distinguish clearly between the two senses, even though conceptually they are quite antithetical.) For example: Balzac describes himself as '*copiant* toute la Société' ('Avant-propos', p. 14), whereas Stendhal criticises contemporary painters because 'ils *copient* les tableaux de David' (*Mélanges III: Peinture*, p. 7, my emphasis). And in the same passage he speaks of David as having found 'une nouvelle manière d'*imiter* la nature', yet goes on to dismiss his successors as mere '*imitateurs*' following slavishly in their master's footsteps. The ambivalence of the term 'reproduction' is less immediately obvious, but in practice its ambiguity is brought out by the way in which it tends to be associated with contemporary forms of mechanical reproduction – particularly printing and photography – whose very existence is enough to problematise the distinction between the two senses of copying and imitation.

George Sand's definition of her function as a novelist is as a kind of printing machine, 'une machine qui *décalque* [la réalité], et qui n'a

27

rien à se faire pardonner si ses *empreintes* sont exactes' (*Indiana*, p. 6). The 'calque' metaphor was fairly extensively used in the critical literature on realism (see Weinberg, p. 127). In defending artistic truth against factual reality, Vigny continues the same metaphorical associations when he asks, 'A quoi bon les arts s'ils n'étaient que le redoublement et la *contre-épreuve* de l'existence?' ('Réflexions', p. 144); and a critic of realism, Elme-Marie Caro, condemns 'l'imitation brutale de nos mœurs' as 'une sorte de *contr'épreuve daguerrienne* de la vie de chaque jour'.[51] These metaphors all implicitly relate fidelity of mimetic replication to procedures of reduplication: George Sand's printing machine provides an exact record of an image, but it is also a means of making an infinite number of copies of that image. So that the two senses of the word 'imitation' become blurred in a single process.

The mention of the daguerrotype (a technique that was introduced to the public in 1839) is indirectly linked to the same association of ideas. Although the image of reality that imprints itself directly on to the daguerrotype plate only yields one copy, the multiplication of photographic images from a single imprint had been envisaged as an aspect of photographic technique ever since the first experimental attempts to develop it. And with the advent of photography proper, a technique that had been pioneered by the English photographer William Fox Talbot and which eventually supplanted the daguerrotype, a photographic image was theoretically infinitely reproducible.[52]

It is a striking feature of the rhetoric of realism that it should have borrowed so heavily from the sphere of printing, whose most significant developments from the first decade of the nineteenth century onwards were in the area of productivity rather than representational accuracy. At the beginning of the century the average rate of production for a printing machine was 300 sheets per hour. With the invention of the steam-powered Koenig press in 1811 the figure increased by a third to 400, then to 1000 by 1814, and 2000 by 1820, an improvement which enabled the London *Times*, who were the first to use the press, to maintain and expand their large circulation.[53] The further development of the Koenig press introduced in France in the 1820s by Cowper and Applegarth soon pushed these figures up to between 4000 and 5000 per hour. In other words, the printing industry saw a sixteen-fold increase in production in the space of little over two and a half decades. Subsequent technical refinements allowed the figures to go higher still in response to increasing demands from the newspaper industry, itself expanding rapidly to take advantage of the growth of the reading public (but also in order to promote that growth).[54] The machines used to produce *La Presse*, for example (*La Presse* being one of the first newspapers designed for a mass readership), made possible the production of 60,000 copies per hour when they were adopted in 1847. And the invention of the rotary press in the 1840s led to changes which meant that by 1865 *Le Petit Journal* had a circulation of more than 250,000. This astronomic increase largely benefited the newspaper industry, where it served to create the idea of a 'circulation war', a phenomenon which started in a serious way in 1836 with Girardin's introduction of *La Presse*, selling at half the price of existing newspapers to a greatly enlarged readership. Although the development of a scale of production that aimed at generating what one would now call a mass readership only took place in the latter part of the realist period, it is clear from even the briefest of historical accounts that the introduction of the new machines in the 1820s and the massive increase in productivity that they quickly proved capable of in the decade between 1814 and 1824 cannot have failed to produce an association between printing and reproducibility in the cultural imagination. It does, therefore, seem very remarkable that printing, which in reality was an instrument for mass reproduction, should nevertheless have appealed primarily to that imagination as a source of images for accurate mimetic representation in literature and the arts.

This is all the more curious when one considers that the printing process has also provided a slightly later age with the vocabulary to describe imitation in its other, pejorative sense. In its strict technical sense, the word 'stereotype' is used for the printing process whereby a single solid plate is made from a forme of type according to a technique that was originally developed at the beginning of the eighteenth century but which took a few decades to become established. The word is already used in its modern figurative sense by Balzac in *Le Père Goriot*, which is cited as an example of such usage by *Robert*. Similarly, the word *cliché* was introduced around 1785 to refer to the imprint of the page composed of individual characters on the soft surface, over which the hot metal for the solid plate (the stereotype) can then be poured. Its more familiar sense is fairly widely attested by the end of the nineteenth century.[55] French, of course, still keeps an active non-figurative meaning of the word for a photographic negative, but the figurative meaning of both words, *stereotype* and *cliché*, has become the dominant and more widespread one.

In both strings of association, the role of printing in the linguistic and literary imagination of the period indirectly supports the view that realism was a problematic concept from its very inception, claiming commitment to a representation of the real that is implicitly undermined by the potential reproducibility of that representation. However, the novel was clearly not alone in this ambivalence, which it shared with the very arts and techniques from which it drew its metaphors, photography and printing. Indeed, all three − photography, printing and realist fiction − can be seen as products of the passion for the real that began to emerge in the early years of the century. This passion had clearly taken hold by the mid-twenties, when it is acknowledged by writers such as an anonymous contributor to *Le Globe* in 1824, who writes that what he calls 'le besoin du vrai' has become 'le trait de caractère du siècle', or Sainte-Beuve, who speaks in 1825 of 'ce besoin presque unanime de vérité qui se proclame hautement dans les arts de notre époque'.[56] Evidence of this passion, or what both the above writers call a *need*, can be documented from the Restoration in 1814, the year in which Joseph-Nicéphore Niepce began the work that, with the collaboration of Louis-Jacques-Mandé Daguerre, was to culminate in the appearance of the first daguerrotype in 1839. The first 'photograph' by Niepce himself dates from 1822. (Roland Barthes reproduces it in his essay on photography, *La Chambre claire*.)[57] It was in this year too that Daguerre opened his Diorama in Paris, a sort of box construction capable of creating, by its exploitation of depth and perspective, what Gautier, in his novel *Fortunio*, called 'l'illusion la plus complète'. Coincidentally, Stendhal records a visit to the Diorama in his journal for 1826, and later recalls − apparently erroneously − having had a portrait of himself made by a painter who lived opposite the Diorama.[58] This slip creates a suggestive association of ideas between portraiture and the daguerrotype technique, whose development drew in part from the experimentation with light involved in the construction of the Diorama − despite the fact that the appearance of the daguerrotype did not take place until seven years after Stendhal's misremembering in *Souvenirs d'égotisme*. The incident can, however, be seen as a symptom of the felt need for the real alluded to by Sainte-Beuve and his anonymous colleague, which predates the invention of the techniques designed to satisfy it. When photography was finally established, what it was appreciated for was precisely its ability to 'établir les *faits* [that ubiquitous word in the writings of the period] avec la précision et l'impartialité que … seule une machine qui ne raisonne pas peut atteindre'.[59] It was this aspect of photography, however, that provoked Baudelaire's famous attack on it: photography's capacity to pander to the French public's 'goût exclusif du Vrai' was leading to what he called the industrialisation of art. Although he had in mind the mechanism that permitted exactitude of representation rather than multiple reproduction, he nevertheless saw this industrialisation of art as a response to the philistine demands of the public ('Notre public ne cherche que le Vrai. Il n'est pas artiste') which photography then reinforced. It was the public, in other words, who had called for the mechanical exactitudes of photographic realism.[60] Photography, as good or ill, represented an achievement against which realism was always measuring itself, either in order to claim it for its own, or in order to distinguish itself from it.[61]

1814 was an important year for the press too, because the abdication of Napoleon in that year brought with it a relaxation of the laws of censorship governing newspapers, which consequently gained significantly in scope and importance. Although the press during the Restoration was predominantly a press of opinion rather than of brute fact,[62] it did increasingly become a source of information and was not always primarily subordinated to political ends. Indeed, the desire to present itself in these terms – as fact rather than opinion – is strongly implied by the increasing tendency for newspapers to take the mirror metaphor as their title, a phenomenon which began earlier in France than in other countries.[63] The press's reputation for the reliability of its information was such that Napoleon's decision to return is said to have been based on what he read in the papers about the political situation in France (with consequences that no doubt dented that reputation for a while). Foreign affairs and the economy provided newspapers with a substantial factual content, and agencies like the Agence Havas were set up and used as a source of pure information on these subjects.

Furthermore, this period saw the emergence in the press of the *fait divers*, purely factual accounts of everyday events without obvious political implications or national repercussions, such as crimes, murders, acts of bravery or mishaps of various kinds. Stendhal's *Le Rouge* is, of course, based on just such a *fait divers*, involving the murder by a private tutor, Antoine Berthet, of his former mistress and employer. His trial was reported at length in the *Gazette des Tribunaux*, which was set up in the twenties precisely in order to satisfy the curiosity of readers about 'the facts' in cases like this.[64] Under the July Monarchy as much as 10 per cent of the big-circulation newspapers consisted of these *faits divers*, a figure which makes another telling link between the factual and the reproducible. All in all, then, it would seem that the development of newspapers like *La Presse* and *Le Siècle* (both founded in 1836) tended to promote

31

information over opinion, a priority which is exemplified in the slogan of *La Presse*'s owner, Girardin: 'Publicité des faits et non polémique des idées' (quoted in Varin d'Ainville, p. 205). So, with this increasing emphasis on fact and information of all kinds in newspapers that were simultaneously aiming for mass circulation, there appears yet again substantial testimony to that association between the passion for the real and multiple reproducibility which seems so characteristic of the period.

The association cannot be regarded as coincidental, for it appears to be part of a wider cultural phenomenon that Walter Benjamin discusses in his essay 'The work of art in the age of mechanical reproduction'.[65] In this essay he explores the parallelism of the two trends, 'Namely,' he says, 'the desire of contemporary masses to bring things "close" spatially and humanly, which is just as ardent as their bent toward overcoming the uniqueness of every reality by accepting its "reproduction"' (p. 225). The conjunction of these two desires testifies to the decay of what he calls 'aura', or the uniqueness of the placing in time and space of a given object or work of art. He is primarily interested in film as the art form engendered by the age of mechanical reproduction (but also in the consequences that it has for the arts in general) and he does not specifically mention the realist novel. Nevertheless, his account of the way in which the mechanical reproducibility of works of art goes to the very heart of their relation to the real does have some significant implications for realism.

Moreover, it confirms once again that Stendhal's sensitivity to the problem wasn't just a personal quirk, but that he was already aware in his own day of something which did not enter into critical discussions of realism until quite some time later. It is true that Stendhal's perception of the issue was not specifically derived from a preoccupation with the mechanical component in the reproduction of reality, which are the terms in which Benjamin sees it. But even so, there is a distinctly Benjaminesque quality in his comment that the growing popularity of prints encouraged by the recent invention of lithography (yet another reproductive technique dating from the early part of the nineteenth century) was not only threatening to oust painting (*Mélanges III: Peinture*, p. 15), but was encouraging painters to paint for immediate lithographic reproduction: 'tant de jeunes peintres semblent travailler uniquement pour donner des sujets aux graveurs lithographiques' (p. 68). Indeed, in his (relatively rare) mentions of the topic, he seems to see the mechanical arts as a depressingly characteristic product of a society entirely lacking in energy. For instance, comparing the cultural circumstances that produced the masterpieces of Fra Bartolommeo in fifteenth-century Italy with those of nineteenth-century France – which seems able to produce only steam-powered cannon capable of firing twenty times per minute over a distance of three miles – Stendhal notes with sorrow:

Nous triomphons dans les arts mécaniques, dans la lithographie, dans le Diorama; mais tous les cœurs sont froids, mais la *passion* sous toutes les formes ne se trouve plus nulle part. (p. 67, Stendhal's italics)

He sees the arts of mechanical reproduction as the characteristic and inevitable product of a world whose social organisation was based on the replication or imitation of models: what painting was to the passionate energies of Renaissance Italy, lithography and steam-powered cannon were to the century of platitude. It is because of the platitudinising predisposition of contemporary France that, for Stendhal, realism has to start from the initial premise that imitation in the sense of mimesis always takes place in a context involving imitation in the other, pejorative sense.

Reading and the reproducible

Since the two senses of imitation, antithetical though they are, cannot be separated, Stendhal's realism is best conceived primarily in relation to the problem of reproducibility, rather than as a more or less accurate record of the reality of his time. Not, of course, that it isn't also a record of this kind; it is, but above all as a strategic element in this relation. It is only when Stendhal is defending Romanticism that he allows himself occasionally to write as if faithful mimesis and sincerity of observation were sufficient antidote in themselves to imitation, and argues that to be Romantic one has simply to drop the precepts and conventions of classicism, and set about copying reality instead of one's predecessors. His sketch for a 'comédie romantique' entitled *Lanfranc ou le poète*, in *Racine et Shakespeare*, qualifies for entry under the rubric 'Romantic' because

les événements *ressemblent* à ce qui se passe tous les jours sous nos yeux. Les auteurs, les grands seigneurs, les juges, les avocats, les hommes de lettres de la trésorerie, les espions, etc., qui parlent et agissent dans cette comédie, sont tels que nous les rencontrons tous les jours dans les salons; pas plus affectés, pas plus *guindés* qu'ils ne le sont dans la nature. (p. 102, Stendhal's italics)

Although the kind of play that Stendhal seems to have in mind, with its novel-like emphasis on the representation of the everyday aspects

33

of social life, does not correspond very closely to the practice of his Romantic contemporaries, he seems to have been sufficiently infected by their rhetoric to repeat their beliefs in the possibility of a drama entirely free of the constraints of precedent, convention and audience expectation.

When it comes to other forms of writing, however, he will much more frequently, and much more characteristically, draw attention to the way in which even the most carefully observed truths are liable to become platitudes with the passage of time. Thus, after a discussion of the British class system in the *Souvenirs d'égotisme*, he remarks: 'Cette *vérité*, si paradoxale aujourd'hui, sera peut-être un *lieu commun* quand on lira mes bavardages' (p. 489, my italics). It would take merely the three decades that he envisages as the time-lapse between the moment of writing and the date when he expects these 'bavardages' to be read, for truth to be transformed into common-place. And he defines the classicism which Romanticism was seeking to oust as precisely the corruption of faithful representations by repeated imitations, whose effect was, so to speak, to empty them out and render them platitudinous. Representations have, therefore, always to be calculated in relation both to existing platitude and, more problematically perhaps, to anticipated imitations.

One particularly important device in Stendhal's strategic dealings with the problem of imitation is the *petit fait vrai*, an item which other critics have tended to treat as the linchpin of a more traditional, objectivist view of Stendhal's realism. However, rather than regard the *petit fait vrai* as the stamp of authentication guaranteeing the veracity of a whole scene, one could see it instead as a device designed to resist or explode the banality that threatens to engulf the representation in which it appears. Facts in Stendhal's fiction can't be seen as minimal units of mimesis which, when taken collectively, would fill out a whole canvas of representation, because in his eyes, facts had value only as single entities; en masse they appalled him, to such an extent that he wrote: 'L'artiste sublime doit fuir les détails' (*Histoire de la peinture*, II, p. 94). This was largely because, in the mass, detail transforms mimesis into platitude, and connotes banality by spelling things out in a way that can be grasped by 'le vulgaire'. He claims, for instance, that Rossini's music lacks the sublimity of the great eighteenth-century composers because it has too many 'détails', and that 'par l'effet de cette foule de détails, il est parfaitement compris du vulgaire et fait les délices de la canaille des cœurs' (*Journal*, 11 December 1829, *Œuvres intimes*, II, p. 35). It would therefore have been only for the people he called 'les demi-sots' that he would have revised *Le Rouge* by providing 'la description physique des personnages à la scène du salon', and by mentioning that 'le canapé … avait cinq pieds dix pouces' (Notes on the Civita-Vecchia copy of *Le Rouge*, p.495 and p.501). Factual accuracy is consequently irrelevant to truth, or even, at times, thoroughly incompatible with truth, as witness Stendhal's remark that: 'Le vrai sur les plus grandes comme sur les plus petites choses me semble presque impossible à atteindre, du moins un vrai *un peu détaillé*' (*ibid.*, p.493. Stendhal's italics). As witness too, perhaps, the extraordinary number of factual errors in his biography of Napoleon, where as many as two thirds of the minor matters of fact that he mentions (dates, figures, titles, etc.) are wrong.[66] Facts in the mass are not a matter for serious consideration – that is to say, the way to resist the banalising potential of facts in the mass is either to treat them with this cavalier disdain for accuracy, or else to take them seriously only in the singular, where the very singularity of a fact can be used to distinguish it from the vulgarity of the mass.

When Stendhal's *petit fait vrai* is made to serve the purpose of inimitable truth rather than that of reproducible facts it does so in a way that has remarkable similarity to Barthes's concept of the 'troisième sens', or what, in his essay of that title, he also calls 'le sens obtus';[67] and Barthes's concept can be used to illuminate some of the aspects of Stendhal's strategic use of small facts. The obtuseness in Barthes's phrase refers to the way in which a material detail in a representation can be used to stymie more obvious, nameable meanings, and so confront interpretative conventions with their own limitations. Barthes returns to this notion in *La Chambre claire*, where he calls it the *punctum*. Although he has a broadly mimetic view of photography – a photograph reproduces what once existed – Barthes sees certain photographs as being composed of two elements: the *studium* and the *punctum*. The *studium* is the nameable, and therefore conventional and coded aspect of the photograph; the *punctum* (and not all photographs have it) is a detail that resists the already-known that is associated with the *studium*. A very similar idea is to be found in Walter Benjamin's 'Little history of photography'. In his discussion of photography he speaks of 'the tiny spark of contingency … with which reality has so to speak seared the subject'.[68] For Benjamin it is not the representation as a whole which ties the photograph to the real, but the chance spark whose heat may even put the entire image under the threat of destruction. In both Barthes's and Benjamin's conception, then, the realism of a photograph lies in the way in which a single spark or detail resists the coded or reproducible whole, a conception which seems to tally in its broad outlines with the view that I am tracing in Stendhal's writing.

Barthes and Stendhal in particular are very revealingly in agreement in the way they define realism in terms of its effect upon the reader or spectator, as opposed to measuring represented facts against a verifiable reality. The *punctum* is not just a spark of the real which burns the image, but that which 'part de la scène comme une flèche, et *vient me percer*' (my italics), the chance element in a photograph 'qui ... me *point*, mais aussi me meurtrit, me poigne' (*Chambre*, p. 49, Barthes's italics). The searing trace of the spark is as much an effect felt by the spectator as it is marked on the image, though Barthes and Stendhal differ in the scope of the response ascribed to the reader. In Barthes's account the *punctum* resists encoding so totally that it is not the photographer or the photograph that determines what the burning detail will be, but the spectator: a *punctum* is only ever a *punctum* for a particular individual. Stendhal's views are less exclusively dominated by the response of the reader, since for him veracity depends on the authenticity of the input by the author, though it can be gauged only by its effect upon the indivdual reader or spectator.

Stendhal even goes so far as to argue that mimesis as accurate representation is an impossible ideal and one that readers and spectators never seriously expect to encounter. The pleasure that one derives from a theatrical representation, for example, comes precisely from one's knowledge that it is an illusion and not the real thing, and it is for this reason that one can be delighted in the theatre by things that, if they were real, would be too horrific to contemplate:

Si, pour un instant, cette illusion ... existait au théâtre, la tragédie la moins ensanglantée deviendrait *horrible*, et tout le plaisir que donne l'art ou la perfection de l'imitation disparaîtrait. (*Racine*, p. 160, Stendhal's italics)

Artistic illusion works not so much by recreating the real thing, but by 'représentant à l'auditeur ce qu'il aurait senti lui-même si les choses qu'il voit se passer sur la scène lui étaient arrivées' (p. 159). The real is registered in the reader's response through which she or he imaginatively recreates it, and the representation on the stage is just a means to this ultimate mimetic end.[69]

It is, nevertheless, possible, Stendhal admits, to come across occasional moments of perfect illusion in the theatre, but he describes them much more in terms of a *punctum* effect on the spectator than as instances of exemplary mimetic accuracy. Their fleeting nature makes them the temporal equivalent of the photographic detail that constitutes the *punctum*. But more important by far is their poignant effect upon the members of the audience. Stendhal calls them 'ces instants délicieux et si rares d'*illusion parfaite*' (*Racine*, p. 59, Stendhal's emphasis), a phrase which includes an emphasis on both their punctual character ('instants ... si rares') and the spectator's emotive response ('instants délicieux'). The latter aspect is brought out particularly clearly when he links the pleasure of a theatrical performance with these moments of perfect illusion:

Tout le plaisir que l'on trouve au spectacle tragique dépend de la fréquence de ces petits moments d'illusion, *et de l'état d'émotion où dans leurs intervalles, ils laissent l'âme du spectateur.* (p. 60, Stendhal's italics)

According to these criteria, the reader's response will be the only sure way of telling whether the real has succeeded in leaving its burnt trace upon the image of a theatrical representation.

This interdependence of representation and response in Stendhal's thinking presupposes a view of reading not normally asociated with the realist model, and which, through its implicit evocation of musical theories of representation in the Enlightenment, harks back once again to an eighteenth-century conception of an emotional engagement with the arts in general and literature in particular. Reading for information or out of sheer intellectual curiosity (motives that a notion of fiction as a history of 'mœurs' might be thought likely to presuppose on the part of its readers) has only a very marginal value for Stendhal. The function of literature is only incidentally to satisfy that curiosity, since its prime purpose is to make its mark upon the reader's soul. '*Faire un livre*' is not a question of '*faire comprendre une idée*', but 'faire sentir, donner quelque nuance d'émotion' (*Souvenirs d'égotisme*, p. 466, Stendhal's italics). The quality of a representation cannot be assessed unless the representation is set in the context of the response it evokes. For this reason, then, the mirror metaphor for the novel can have validity in Stendhal's eyes only when it is aligned with that of the bow; the only authentic mirror will be one that is also a bow.

The mirror: reflections, models and responses

If we return to the question of Stendhal's mirror metaphors in the light of the problems outlined above, it should now be clear that although he may be the most frequent user of the metaphor in the period, the concept is not actually the key to his aesthetic value system. Moreover, Stendhal's mirror does not constitute a single and stable entity; it appears in a number of different versions according to the context and response it is associated with. Even the classic metaphor of the mirror as the emblem of representation is dependent upon its reception by a world prepared to authenticate it as such. And in any case, although it is the sense that is usually ascribed to his use of the metaphor, the conception of the mirror as guarantee of mimetic veracity is only one of the mirror's manifestations in Stendhal.[70]

It appears in this simple specular sense in a review that Stendhal wrote in 1825 for the *New Monthly Magazine*. He describes Picard's novel *L'Honnête homme ou le niais* as a history of 'les mœurs françaises' that concentrates particularly on hypocrisy as a social phenomenon (*Mélanges II: Journalisme*, p. 130). The idea of a social history leads quite naturally to a mirror simile: 'Dans ses romans ... M. Picard rend ce qu'il voit comme un *miroir*' (this is Stendhal's emphasis), and more specifically a mirror that reproduces 'la vérité des *habitudes sociales*' (again Stendhal's emphasis). But in Stendhal's opinion this is an achievement '[qui] donne peu de *plaisir* aux personnes qui habitent le pays' (my italics), a remark which suggests that specular reflections are not enough in themselves to produce the pleasure which he sees as the chief value of reading. This is not, in short, a rave review of Picard's book, and it offers a telling indication that Stendhal's priorities lie elsewhere.

The second version of the mirror metaphor associates specular representation with readerly vanity in a way that gives the notion of the mirror a different and rather sharper twist. In his preface to *Armance*, Stendhal compares his novel with a comedy by Mazères and one by the same Picard who wrote *L'Honnête homme ou le niais*, and writes of these two authors: 'Ils ont présenté un miroir au public; est-ce leur faute si des gens laids ont passé devant ce miroir?' (p. 267). This rhetorical question implies a readership or audience whose vanity is offended by the faithfulness of portraits of contemporary social mores, and recalls the touchy response of the gentleman reader of *Le Rouge* when confronted with the mirror's version of Parisian behaviour as exemplified by Mathilde. The implication is made again by the fable Stendhal includes in the third preface to *Lucien Leuwen*, written nearly ten years after the *Armance* preface (suggesting that the idea was a constant in Stendhal's thinking):

Il y avait un jour un homme qui avait la fièvre et qui venait de prendre du quinquina. Il avait encore le verre à la main, et faisant la grimace à cause de l'amertume, il se regarda au miroir et se vit pâle et même un peu vert. Il quitta rapidement son verre et se jeta sur le miroir pour le briser.

Tel sera peut-être le sort des volumes suivants. (p. 762)

Stendhal seems to be saying that what readers want from mirrors is not the faithful documentation that the rhetoric of realism so earnestly promises them. Instead, a mirror is for them something much more like what it is for the young bishop of Agde in *Le Rouge* whom Julien catches unashamedly practising his benedictions before a portable mahogany looking glass in the abbey at Bray-le-Haut. The mirror is here quite unequivocally associated with the Parisian practice of imitation and imitativeness: the young bishop repeats his gestures of benediction 'en nombre infini, et sans se reposer un instant' (p. 100), thus aligning his reflected movements with 'la figure de rhétorique la plus puissante chez les Français ... la répétition' (already quoted above). Similarly, his concern to get his mitre placed in exactly the right position on his head is a concern to match his reflection with a social model: tilted too far back, 'cela aurait l'air un peu niais', but equally, 'il ne faut pas non plus la porter baissée sur les yeux comme un shako d'officier' (p. 101). For the ambitious cleric the mirror is the means whereby he can adjust his appearance to fit a socially consecrated, and therefore thoroughly stereotyped, image of a bishop, and be sure of distinguishing it from that of an army officer or the 'niais' in the title of Picard's novel.

The third and final metaphor is the only positively valorised one in Stendhal's repertoire, and he treats it much more like a bow playing upon the violin of the reader's soul. The violin effect is one that Stendhal particularly appreciates in certain schools of landscape painting (though in Stendhal's eyes this was a style that was definitely not in the same league as the painters whom he most admired, namely Raphael and Correggio). For instance, in his review of the Salon of 1824, he singles out Constable's 'Haywain', and writes of it that 'son délicieux paysage, avec un chien à gauche, est le *miroir de la nature*' (*Mélanges III: Peinture*, p. 47, my italics). The mention of the word 'délicieux' immediately gives a clue as to the evaluative angle at which the mirror is being set within Stendhal's aesthetic system. The charm of the mirror works because truth is an effect and not a fact: 'la vérité *saisit* d'abord et *entraîne* dans ces charmants ouvrages' (p. 47, my italics). The paintings of Constable and of other 'peintres-miroirs' that Stendhal mentions (such as Gaspard Poussin and the Flemish school) draw the spectator through the looking glass into a world recreated by his or her subjective response to the specular representations of the singular and sublime aspects of nature (*Racine*, pp. 178–9). It may also be that there is a slight *punctum* effect in the mention of Constable's dog on the edge of the picture, as also in the 'aspects *singuliers*' and the '*contrastes* sublimes' that Stendhal admires in these landscapes. But in this context the main point is, first, that these 'mirror-painters' stand out from the imitators – Constable from the David School, and Poussin from the 'gens communs qui veulent suivre Raphael' (*Racine*, p. 179) – so that the mirror serves here to break the debilitating cycle of imitations that the bishop's use of it served, by contrast, to sustain. And the second, and possibly the more significant, point is that the validity of the specular representations of these painters is gauged entirely by the affective response that they evoke in the souls of their individual spectators.

In all three versions of the mirror, the reader proves to be the key to how it operates: the *amour-propre* of the grimacing fever victim means that he takes umbrage at the specular reflection of the way he is; the vanity of the bishop means that he uses the mirror to make his reflection coincide with the model that Parisian mores require that he copy. Both these responses are deeply egocentric reactions to mimesis, and may be contrasted on this score to the third, where (perhaps partly because of the content of the representation, in which recognisable and socially defined human figures barely appear) the reader makes no imitative connection between him- or herself and the represented world, and projects himself instead through the reflection into that world in a manner that can be validated neither by mimesis nor by emulation.

These various conceptions of the mirror all point to the complexity of the workings of representation in Stendhal. And although the third version emerges fairly unequivocally as its only acceptable manifestation, it nevertheless cannot be achieved without some reliance on the sort of mimetic documentation instanced by the first, and without taking into account the threats posed by the readerly strategies exemplified by the second.

If Stendhal's place in the history of realism is to be distinguished from that of his contemporaries and from contemporary critical notions of what realism was, it is because, by including response and context in his own conception of the topic, his was a far more complex and problematic idea of representation than theirs. His apparently eccentric view of fictional realism may set him apart from the tradition in which it is Balzac and not Stendhal who has consistently appeared as the figurehead. But it also offers an implicit and highly illuminating comment on it, reminding twentieth-century readers, for whom realism really has become a cliché, that it is a far more complicated issue than modern accounts and debunkings of it have been inclined to give it credit for. The 'era of suspicion' that Nathalie Sarraute – in a phrase borrowed, tellingly, from Stendhal − [71] identified in 1950 as the successor to realism, and as a product of its overworked conventions, was already the era in which the realist novel emerged and the context in which it evolved. Stendhal's fiction can therefore be seen as being designed both to provide a portrait of the era of suspicion and to offer an antidote to it, a mimesis devised with a view to bypassing the twin snares of imitation and emulation.

Part Two
DE L'AMOUR

2
LOVE AND THE WAYWARD TEXT

Il y a des gens qui n'auraient jamais été amoureux s'ils n'avaient jamais entendu parler de l'amour.

La Rochefoucauld, *Réflexions ou Sentences et Maximes morales*

Bookish passions

De l'Amour was written seven years before Stendhal began his career as a novelist with *Armance,* and nearly a decade before he consolidated that career with the publication of *Le Rouge et le Noir.* Given the chronology of Stendhal's literary output, which places his 'physiology of love' between the *Histoire de la peinture en Italie* (1817) and *Rome, Naples et Florence en 1817* on one side, and *Racine et Shakespeare* (1823) on the other, *De l'Amour* lends itself to being considered either as a thinly disguised autobiographical response to his unhappy and one-sided affair with Mathilde Dembowski, or as a theoretical treatise on human passion, which the later novels will duly exemplify in narrative form. However, one could equally well – and in my opinion, more profitably – read it as a kind of anticipation or rehearsal of the problem that Stendhal was to confront in the writing of the novels proper. This is because, as conceived by Stendhal, both the lover and the novelist share the same vulnerability to the repetitions and imitations of the century of platitude. In the face of a culture of imitation it is as hard for the lover to guarantee the authenticity of his passion as it is for the novelist to keep his hold on the real. Both aspire to an originality and an authenticity of feeling and expression in a context which is saturated with already-spoken and already-written versions of love and of reality; both the lover and the novelist have to reckon with the possibility that their desire and their representation may not be spontaneous and original, and that passion and realism might, even if unwittingly, be merely a copy or a derivative of somebody else's book or somebody else's emotions. In exploring the lover's predicament Stendhal could be seen to be exploring his own future predicament as a novelist; so that the problems that the lover encounters and the solutions that he finds for them can be read metaphorically as warnings and guidelines for the novelist-to-be.

The link between literature and love may not immediately strike one on a reading of *De l'Amour*, but it is a connection that is repeatedly encountered in the novels, suggesting that Stendhal's worry about the effects of books extends to the question of love as well. Love in Stendhal's fictional world is frequently depicted as imitative, and more specifically, as imitated from books and writing. For instance, in *Le Rouge*, the strategy used by Julien to seduce Mme de Rênal comes (somewhat bizarrely, it is true) straight out of the *Mémorial de Sainte-Hélène*; he makes an easy conquest of Amanda Binet in the café at Besançon by quoting a few lines from *La Nouvelle Héloïse* at her, a strategy he tries to repeat with Mathilde de La Mole; and he gets Mme de Fervaques to fall in love with him by using a sequence of ready-written love letters borrowed from his friend Prince Korassoff. More disturbingly, even his feelings for Mathilde prove eventually to have been fundamentally unserious, part of what he calls the 'novel', which ends with his entry into the army. In other words, the anxious desire not to copy from books that Stendhal voices in his article on *Le Rouge* would seem to apply just as much to the lovers depicted in those books, and to be just as well founded.

But to return to *De l'Amour*: the problem is implicitly construed in these terms from the very first page, where Stendhal opens his 'cours d'anatomie morale' (p. 401) by classifying love according to its different types, a procedure that is designed primarily to distinguish the authentic from the counterfeit versions of the phenomenon. Of the four kinds that he lists, only the first, *l'amour-passion*, is the real thing. This is the love exemplified by 'la religieuse portugaise', Eloïse and Abélard, 'le capitaine de Vésel', 'le gendarme de Cento', Werther and Saint-Preux. (These are the cases cited by Stendhal, and beyond that he says nothing more about such love at this stage.) The fourth and last on his list is the largely unproblematic but ultimately trivial *amour-physique*, which, he says, is the form in which everybody first experiences love, and is of little intrinsic interest: 'quelque sec et malheureux que soit le caractère, on commence par là à seize ans' (p. 7). It is the two other forms, *l'amour-goût* and *l'amour de vanité*, that are problematic, because they are entirely derivative. Of the two, *l'amour-goût* is decidedly the lesser evil because, although it models itself through and through on a worldly formula, it never pretends to be anything other than what it is. The reader of Duclos and Crébillon *fils* will know from these and other novels of their kind which describe the heyday of *amour-goût* in the Paris of the 1760s that, 'c'est un tableau où, jusqu'aux ombres, tout doit être couleur de rose, où il ne doit entrer rien de désagréable sous aucun prétexte, et sous peine de manquer d'usage, de bon ton, de délicatesse, etc.' (p. 5). Love in this rose-tinted mode is a game whose every move is known in advance by its worldly practitioners, and where the demands of social protocol and good manners mean that the formula must always be faithfully respected and punctiliously repeated.

L'amour de vanité, however, is a much more disquieting affair since it is a love which mistakes itself for authentic *amour-passion*. Like *amour-goût*, it is copied from books, but unlike the worldly counterpart, which places enormous value on the fidelity of the copying, it tends to suppress all consciousness of its imitative status: 'les idées de roman vous prenant à la gorge, on croit être amoureux et mélancolique, car la vanité aspire à se croire une grande passion' (p. 6). Whereas the difference between *amour-goût* and *amour-passion* is that between 'une froide et jolie miniature' and 'un tableau des Carraches' (p. 5), and is thus entirely unmistakeable, *l'amour de vanité* takes itself to be an instance of the *amour-passion* on which it models itself. Unlike the elegant Parisians of the 1760s, whose *amour-goût* merely confirms the model which it repeats, the essential quality of *amour-passion*, its authenticity, is lost through its imitation as *amour de vanité*. When Julien Sorel draws on Rousseau's authentic text to further the interests of his vanity, his imitation is a debasement of the model from which his behaviour is inspired. And he is not alone in this, for *l'amour de vanité* is the most widespread of all the forms that love takes, particularly in the nineteenth century, and particularly in France (or at least in French-speaking countries); for 'A Genève et en France ... on fait l'amour à seize ans, pour faire un roman, et l'on se demande à chaque démarche et presque à chaque larme: Ne suis-je pas bien comme Julie d'Etanges?' (p. 255). The sixteen-year-olds, whose apprenticeship in love would normally begin with the un-pretentious pleasures of *l'amour-physique*, operate with one eye on the text and the other on the mirror, and demonstrate how easily vanity can transform readers of a novel into imitators of a model.

These classifications and their definition suggest that the would-be novelist is indeed in a closely analogous position to the would-be lover, and furthermore, that fiction itself is specifically responsible for the predicaments of the lover. It is, after all, chiefly fiction which mediates the models with which the lover's vanity will seek to tempt him. Through literature, passion finds itself beset by fictional representations of itself; and this is just as true of the supposedly authentic forms of love as of the avowedly bogus ones. The rites of passage undergone by the sixteen-year-old in his encounter with physical love are placed under the aegis of a distinctly pastoral style when Stendhal illustrates it with the following injunction: 'A la chasse, trouver une belle et fraîche paysanne qui fuit dans le bois' (p. 6). These purely physical frolics are being incited by a highly literary example.

Curiously, however, this entanglement with literature applies just as much to *l'amour-passion*, and Stendhal illustrates it almost exclusively with literary cases. Rousseau is the literary source which provides the example of Saint-Preux, just as his is the text from which *l'amour de vanité* derives some of the major roles in its repertoire. The exemplary nun comes out of the pages of the *Lettres portugaises*, the seventeenth-century novel which was still widely read in Stendhal's time, and is one of the staples of Mathilde's reading in *Le Rouge*. Abélard, Eloïse and Werther are self-explanatory references; but even the obscure allusion to the 'capitaine de Vésel' has a literary origin in the *Mémoires* of Besenval that were published in Paris in 1805–6. The 'gendarme', it would appear, refers to a documented case that occurred in the early years of the nineteenth century in Ferrara, but it has the ring of the most literary of fictions: imprisoned at the request of the parents of the girl whom he had seduced, the 'gendarme' took poison brought to him by the girl and they died together on either side of the barred window of his prison cell, in a manner that seems to echo the deaths of Romeo and Juliet in one of Stendhal's favourite Shakespeare plays.[1]

If literature provides examples of every form of love, good and bad, high and low, true and false, the question is then raised as to whether any form of love can be genuine and untainted by imitation. What is the difference between the passionate lover like the 'gendarme de Cento' whose story resembles that of Shakespeare's hero, and the Parisian girls whose every tear has its counterpart in Rousseau's heroine? Love of any kind in Stendhal's world would seem to be a very bookish thing, and a product of literary and cultural example rather than of natural instincts.

This is a problem that has already been addressed by one of the most illuminating of Stendhal's critics, René Girard, who argues in his book *Mensonge romantique et vérité romanesque* that all desire is imitative, always copied from someone else's desire, and is never original. Spontaneous desire is a myth, or, as the title has it, 'un mensonge romantique'. Authenticity and spontaneity may represent an ideal (an ideal that certainly matters very much for both the lover and the novelist in Stendhal), but, says Girard, this ideal is purely conventional; and in his view, fiction fails when it does not show this to be so. Loving necessarily means loving *like* Eloïse and Abélard, or *like* Saint-Preux and Julie, and 'la vérité romanesque' (the other half of the title) consists in revealing these models as the sources, or what Girard calls the 'mediators' of desire. This means that truth in fiction does not consist of dispensing with models in order to paint direct from nature, but of revealing the models which have constructed that painting. As Girard says in the English version of his book, 'great writers apprehend intuitively and concretely, through the medium of their art, if not formally, the system in which they were first imprisoned together with their contemporaries'.[2] By representing the systems which produce desire, the novel outlines and uncovers the conventions and discursive ideologies which constitute the *déjà-dit*.

In other words, fiction should be seen as necessarily working from inside the system which it appears to be trying to free itself from. What counts, then, is the stance taken towards conventions and models, not some futile determination simply to wish them away. Although Girard does not spend very much time discussing the realist aesthetic, his argument reinforces the similarity between desire and realist fiction that emerges from Stendhal's writing, and helps to explain why love might have such a privileged place in fiction, and fiction such a crucial role in desire.

Werther and Don Juan

Stendhal's account of *amour-passion* in *De l'Amour* makes it clear that he sees it as a phenomenon that is thoroughly grounded in social and cultural convention. There is no doubt that this, the highest form of passion, is the product of a particular culture – even though that culture is one that tends to define it as natural – and that it is inconceivable outside the sophisticated conditions of European civilisation. 'Dans une société très avancée l'*amour-passion* est aussi naturel que l'amour-physique chez des sauvages' (p. 276). If Stendhal values what he calls 'le naturel', it is precisely as a certain manner of respecting conventions, and not as an escape from them back to the natural world of the savage: 'On appelle *naturel* ce qui ne s'écarte pas de la manière habituelle d'agir' (p. 98). *Le naturel* is an integral part of the most civilised forms of behaviour, and in particular, it is the 'condition nécessaire du bonheur par l'amour'.

If Italy is the homeland of *amour-passion* (as one might say that France is the homeland of *amour de vanité*), it is not because the Italians are freer from convention than the French, but because their attitude towards convention is more 'natural' (in the sense that Stendhal defines the word). *Le naturel* of advanced civilisation is deeply respected and explicitly acknowledged in Italian civilisation in a way that it is not in France. A sign of this explicit respect is the fact that love itself is the subject of endless public discussion in Italy and is constantly translated into a body of highly codified maxims and formulae: 'l'on entend citer tout haut dans les salons les maximes générales sur l'amour. Le public connaît les symptômes et les périodes de cette maladie et s'en occupe beaucoup' (p. 147). But far from restricting the possibilities for love, this codification actually appears to favour its development. The knowledge about love that Italian girls pick up from attending their mothers' salons and listening at keyholes (though not from reading novels, be it noted, because Italians don't read them) makes them far better mistresses than their French counterparts. The Italian girl's knowledge of maxims about love promotes love, whereas the French or the Swiss girl's reading of *La Nouvelle Héloïse* distorts and perverts it.

The distinction between these two systems of convention is not so much in their content as in their structure; the French one is closed and hierarchical, whereas the Italian one is open-ended and non-hierarchical:

En France nous cherchons à imiter tous les deux le même modèle et je suis juge compétent de la manière dont vous le copiez. En Italie je ne sais pas si cette action singulière que je vois faire ne fait pas plaisir à celui qui la fait, et peut-être ne m'en ferait pas à moi-même. (p. 170)

The Italian resembles the lover of *amour-passion* through his or her relation to language and convention, a relation that is quite different from the one that the Frenchman and the *amoureux de vanité* share. These latter two regard all systems exclusively as a means of personal advancement, and as a kind of currency which can be traded and exchanged for profit.

Stendhal illustrates this opposition in the contrasting figures of Don Juan and Werther. Don Juan, as the representative of an *amour de vanité* in the French style, is described by Stendhal as both a merchant and a general: a merchant because '[il] réduit l'amour à n'être qu'une affaire ordinaire' (p. 232); and a general because 'il pense ... au succès de ses manœuvres' (p. 233). Both general and merchant see conventions as a means and not as an end in themselves. By contrast, Werther and the passionate lover indulge in neither trade nor manoeuvre; in their hands the conventions of love acquire a kind of autotelic status, since their currency is not for exchange but is spontaneously and autogenically produced: 'L'amour est la seule passion qui se paye d'une monnaie qu'elle fabrique elle-même' (p. 295). The most gain to be had comes from remaining within the code itself and not from attempting to move outside it in order to dominate it. (Though the very concept of gain is, paradoxically, quite inappropriate here because it automatically implies a position outside the system from which one might master it.)

All gestures of domination and manipulation are wrong because they reduce the code to something circumscribable and repeatable, and therefore wholly monotonous. The convert to Italianism is appalled by

les Françaises avec leurs petites grâces tout aimables, séduisantes les trois premiers jours, mais ennuyeuses le quatrième, jour fatal où l'on découvre que toutes ces grâces étudiées d'avance et apprises par cœur sont éternellement les mêmes tous les jours et pour tous. (p. 149)

In Stendhal's world what is repeated is, by definition, also a means of self-advancement. It is only the unbeliever who is capable of reciting the New Testament at length (like Julien at Verrières). The true believer would be like the lover, non-tactical, incapable of repetition, yet firmly within the code. Calculation and repetition always go together, and every stage of *amour-goût* and *amour de vanité* is indelibly marked by their configuration: 'tout [y] est calcul comme dans toutes les prosaïques affaires de la vie' (p. 244). Don Juan's love is a form of *amour de vanité*, designed simply to prove his superiority over others: 'L'idée de l'égalité lui inspire la rage que l'eau donne à l'hydrophobe' (p. 234). As a result he finds himself condemned to inevitable repetition in his loves:

Don Juan me disait …, dans un accès d'humeur noire: 'Il n'y a pas vingt variétés de femmes, et une fois qu'on en a eu deux ou trois de chaque variété, la satiété commence.' (p. 235)

By making of love a means of 'faire sentir son pouvoir', it becomes nothing more than a form of *ennui*. The calculations of self-interest are inseparable from the monotonies of utter predictability.

The characteristics of *amour-passion*, on the other hand, are quite different. The lover manipulates the code within which he finds himself and yields to a passivity that proves to be extremely productive. 'Rien d'intéressant comme la passion, c'est que tout y est imprévu, et que l'agent y est victime' (p. 244). This reverses, term for term, the configuration associated with *amour-goût* and *amour de vanité*. *Ennui* is dispelled by the unforeseen. In 'l'amour à la Werther … l'on ne sait pas où l'on va' (p. 96), and the extent of the lover's necessary lack of control seems to be directly related to the force of his feelings: 'la véhémence et l'imprévu ... sont ... les caractères de la passion' (p. 97). Only love (and, according to Mathilde, a sentence of death) sets one at the mercy of chance in quite this way. Neither can be bought and both involve complete renunciation of power.[3]

The productivity associated with *amour-passion* is attributable not to the happiness which comes from fulfilment (not least because *amour-passion* is rarely fulfilled in Stendhal), but rather to the unhappiness that love brings. Stendhal's lover is by definition unhappy, and the cause of this unhappiness is uncertainty, for he never knows whether his feelings are returned. The anxiety associated with this uncertainty is a powerful source of interest for the fearful lover, since 'l'homme qui tremble ne s'ennuie pas' (p. 239). His imagination is endlessly active, improvising a hundred different interpretations to any given phenomenon. 'Tout est *signe* en amour', writes Stendhal (p. 133), and as a result the lover is absorbed in a never-ending process of interpretation and speculation. The anxious and unhappy victim of *amour-passion* is at least spared that most wretched form of unhappiness, namely the *ennui* that follows inevitably from the predictable monotonies of his counterpart in Don Juan.

The lover's unstable hermeneutic condition is encapsulated in Stendhal's metaphor of *cristallisation*. *Cristallisation* begins at stage five of the seven stages through which love (*amour-passion*) comes into being. It follows admiration, desire, hope, and the birth of love; and is followed in turn by doubt and further *cristallisation*. Contrary to the implications of one set of connotations of the word, *cristallisation* fixes nothing, but instead creates a world in which endless possibilities take shape in the lover's eye:

Laissez travailler la tête d'un amant pendant vingt-quatre heures, et voici ce que vous trouverez:
Aux mines de sel de Salzbourg, on jette, dans les profondeurs abandonnées de la mine, un rameau d'arbre effeuillé par l'hiver; deux ou trois mois après on le retire couvert de cristallisations brillantes: les plus petites branches, celles qui ne sont pas plus grosses que la patte d'une mésange, sont garnies d'une infinité de diamants, mobiles et éblouissants; on ne peut plus reconnaître le rameau primitif. (pp. 8–9)

The beloved is transformed by the lover's desiring gaze into whatever he wants or imagines her to be and she ceases to have any fixed identity:

Vous la voulez tendre, elle est tendre; ensuite vous la voulez fière comme l'Emilie de Corneille, et, quoique ces qualités soient probablement incompatibles, elle paraît à l'instant avec une âme romaine. (p. 31)

In just one woman the 'amant à la Werther' can find all twenty varieties mentioned by the satiated Don Juan; and no doubt he may discover others that Don Juan has never even dreamed of, since his imagination is capable of constructing such illogical hybrids as a tender Emilie.

Cristallisation has all the plural, unpredictable qualities that mark the lover himself. In the description of the 'rameau de Salzbourg' Stendhal speaks of the twigs being 'garnies d'une infinité de diamants, mobiles et éblouissants' (p. 9). The lover cannot possibly hope to control anything so plural, so labile, and so dazzling; *cristallisation* is a phenomenon to which he submits, not a technique (like that of seduction in the case of Don Juan) which he can master; and this is why passion proves to be such an absorbing affair. The lover does not simply pass into another world, he also moves from a single to a multiple perspective:

Du moment qu'il aime, l'homme le plus sage ne voit plus aucun objet *tel qu'il est*. Il s'exagère en moins ses propres avantages, et en plus les moindres faveurs de l'objet aimé. Les craintes et les espoirs prennent à l'instant quelque chose de *romanesque* (de *wayward*) … Une marque effrayante que la tête se perd, c'est qu'en pensant à quelque petit fait, difficile à observer, vous le voyez blanc, et vous l'interprétez en faveur de votre amour; un instant après vous vous apercevez qu'en effet il était noir, et vous le trouvez encore concluant en faveur de votre amour. (p. 32, Stendhal's italics)

The mention of the novelistic in all of this raises an issue to which I shall return below, but it is clear that the lover exists in a world of immense imaginative fertility where things can be both white and black, just as the beloved can be both tender and 'romaine'.

There is, however, a price to be paid for living in such absorbing circumstances, for under them the lover finds himself deprived not only of his reason ('la tête se perd'), but also of all social support: 'C'est alors qu'une âme en proie aux incertitudes mortelles sent vivement le besoin d'un ami; mais pour un amant il n'est plus d'ami.' The lover can have no friends because he no longer sees things the way they are, which is to say, the way that the rest of the world (including, of course, his friends) sees them. An ugly woman becomes beautiful in the eyes of her lover but by the same token his vision passes beyond the reach of social agreement: where others see an ugly woman, he sees a beautiful one. He cannot share his vision with anyone and yet desperately wants to.

Furthermore, in losing a common vision he also loses a common language and becomes unintelligible to the rest of the world: 'les propos des amants semblent si ridicules aux gens sages, qui ignorent le phenomène de la cristallisation' (p. 345). Love is both the cause and the object of this incommunicability. Only the orthodox and the sane share a common discourse expressing common agreement, and the mark of the lover's discursive solitude is precisely this social interpretation of it as 'ridicule'. The lover constantly exposes himself to the risk of society putting its own interpretation on his situation and defining it as ridiculous. Indeed, fear of ridicule is such that many people (especially women, who are supposedly more sensitive than men to *l'opinion publique*) are prevented from ever falling in love at all.

The lover is caught in a paradox whereby, on the one hand, his passion is the product of the society in which he lives, and yet, on the other, he is perceived by that society as belonging to a totally different order. The society which leads him to think of Corneille's Emilie in connection with his beloved is the society which can make no sense of his application of that comparison. Part of the problem is, as I have already said, caused by the difference in attitude towards the conventions by which society operates: mastery and gain in the case of Don Juan and society at large (in society it is not just Don Juan who behaves like a merchant and a general, since all social beings are merchants and generals); and passivity and suffering in the case of Werther and his kind. But another part of the problem has to do with language and the sort of linguistic conflicts that are revealed and provoked by the lover's asocial position, and it is this aspect of the lover's situation which I shall be considering in the following pages.

'Faire trembler le langage'

The lover's social isolation reveals that his predicament is not just a private and emotional one but is also a discursive or linguistic one; the way the lover speaks of his passion and its object is not the same as the way that the society (in which that passion was bred) speaks of them. Moreover, neither party seems very happy with what each perceives as the alien nature of the other's discourse: the lover suffers from the lack of any friend able to share his multiple visions, and society resents the presence of a person who refuses to comply with its accounts of the way things are. The lover, however, appears to be more willing to resign himself to the isolation of his linguistic condition than society is to acknowledge and tolerate that isolation (witness society's use of the term 'ridicule' to describe and dispose of something that it finds as unintelligible as it is intolerable). The question raised for the novelist by this situation is: whom should he follow in describing the lover's condition? The crystallising lover with his perpetually revised views of his beloved and his chances of success? Or the society which can see him only as ridiculous? The problem with following the lover is that the novelist risks losing a language in which to make himself intelligible; and the problem with society is that in seeking to describe something which it cannot understand, the novelist may succeed in saying nothing at all. In depicting passion, he is faced, therefore, with an impossible choice between the unintelligible discourse of the lover and the *doxa* of society's dismissal of him as 'ridiculous', a choice which pitches him into a situation of apparently unresolvable discursive conflict.

This discursive conflict is an issue that is confronted head on by Barthes in his *Fragments d'un discours amoureux*,[4] which takes up many of the same issues as those raised in *De l'Amour*, but deals more extensively and explicitly than Stendhal with the particular question of the lover's discursive situation. As a student of semiology, Barthes makes no claim for the originality or spontaneity of emotions, and he acknowledges from the outset that 'aucun amour n'est originel' (p. 163). Love is a kind of 'contagion affective' which is passed on by language, books and other people, and so is always awaited, and on its arrival, always imitated. Nevertheless, once he loves, the lover finds himself caught within a code that is profoundly at variance with all other codes. The lover's isolation, however codified in itself, creates a conflict between two different sets or styles of convention. His own style cuts him off from society by being profoundly asocial. The lover is incapable of participating in any form of worldliness ('coteries, ambitions, promotions, manigances, alliances, sécessions, rôles, pouvoirs', p. 23). His condition can be neither accepted nor adequately described by any of the major social discourses of our day – Christian, Marxist or psychoanalytic (the particular targets of Barthes's attack) – all of which try to place him back in the world and so cure him of his contagion. Barthes's lover is in the curious position already identified in *De l'Amour*, which on the one hand is produced by social conventions, and yet, on the other, is incapable of being absorbed back into them.

In the Barthesian view, the conflict provoked by the lover's marginal and isolated position is created by the fact that his discourse is structurally and constitutionally incapable of complying with discourses of mastery, those discourses which seek to colonise and contain all alien forms of discourse. The discourses identified by Barthes as instances of this type are all forms of what Stendhal might have called linguistic Don Juanism. The lover's discourse, on the other hand, is a linguistic equivalent of Wertherism, being devoid of all causality, all finality, and in particular being incapable of submitting to the ordering forces of narrative: 'l'amoureux parle par paquets de phrases, mais il n'intègre pas ces phrases à un niveau supérieur, à une œuvre' (p. 11). In Barthes's view, narrative is the literary equivalent of the calculating manoeuvres of the merchants and the generals mentioned by Stendhal in *De l'Amour* as the typical practitioners of *amour de vanité*. The particular form of narrative exemplified by the *histoire d'amour* differs from the *discours amoureux* in demanding that the lover subordinate himself to

[ce] grand Autre narratif, à l'opinion générale qui déprécie toute force excessive et veut que le sujet réduise lui-même le grand ruissellement imaginaire dont il est traversé sans ordre et sans fin, à une crise douloureuse, morbide, dont il faut guérir ...: l'histoire d'amour (l'"aventure") est le tribut que l'amoureux doit payer au monde pour se réconcilier avec lui.   (*ibid.*)

The *discours amoureux* may be thoroughly coded and conventional in itself, but it nevertheless resists the *doxa* through its inability to conform to hierarchically structured and structuring codes. Its figures are highly imitative, but '[elles] ne peuvent *se ranger*: s'ordonner, cheminer, concourir à une fin' (Barthes's italics). Unlike the discourses of mastery mentioned by Barthes, and unlike narrative, the lover's discourse makes no attempt to manipulate and control alien discourses. Where the social discourses work to translate all alien discourses into their own terms (as when society describes Stendhal's lover as 'ridicule'), the lover is content simply to assert his discursive otherness.[5]

Barthes places particular emphasis on the way that the lover's status as a victim extends to the sphere of language: the 'maladie heureuse' (as Stendhal calls love) is accompanied by a kind of linguistic malady, and one of the first effects of the lover's condition is the drastic reduction in linguistic scope that he suffers. The lover finds himself cut off from whole areas of language in a way which contrasts with the expansionist tendencies of social discourse (expansionist both because it refuses to recognise that there may be topics whereof it cannot speak, and also because it seeks to encompass all alien forms of discourse within its own domain). For instance, he finds himself no longer able to name, and the qualities of the beloved defy his expressive capabilities: 'Atopique, l'autre [the beloved] fait trembler le langage: on ne peut parler *de* lui, *sur* lui; tout attribut est faux, douloureux, gaffeur, gênant: l'autre est *inqualifiable*' (p. 44, Barthes's italics). The undecidable nature of the beloved's qualities in the eyes of Stendhal's lover is extended by Barthes to utter descriptive aphasia. So much so that, eventually, even the naming of love itself loses its referential purity; it ceases to be a description or, as Stendhal claims for his account, a 'physiology' of a thing, and becomes itself a form of appeal or verbal seduction: 'tout propos qui a pour objet l'amour (quelle qu'en soit l'allure détachée) comporte fatalement une allocution secrète (je m'adresse à quelqu'un, que vous ne savez pas, mais qui est là, au bout de mes maximes)' (p. 88). Indeed, this shift in the axis of the lover's language from the referential to the 'conative' (to use Roman Jakobson's term)[6] is one that already applies to Stendhal's own text in *De l'Amour*; for in writing about love, he was also offering 'une confession, un plaidoyer, une apologie' addressed to the object of that love, 'Métilde'.[7]

According to Barthes, this disturbance of the referential function affects the pronominal and the adjectival elements of language too. The lover becomes incapable of using the third-person pronoun ('he' or 'she') in connection with the beloved, and all adjectives are erased from his dictionary. The greater the lover's desire for his beloved, the greater the 'échec langagier' he is drawn into: 'plus j'éprouve la spécialité de mon désir, moins je peux la nommer ... le propre du désir ne peut produire qu'un impropre de l'énoncé' (p. 27). The only adjective that remains to describe the particularities of the beloved in this linguistic *débâcle* is the patently inadequate 'adorable'. The lover retreats from a whole sphere of language dominated by gossip, 'le potin', which trades, like Stendhal's merchant, in the 'wicked' and reductive pronoun *he*, and whose merchandise is a product of its 'fabrique immonde d'adjectifs' (p. 263). The lover's enemies are the 'langages reçus' of Marxism, Christianity, psychoanalysis, narrative and gossip, all of which aim to draw him out of his discursive otherness and claim him for their own. If he submits to these enemies, he will mark that submission in the form of a narrative which translates his alien status back into social terms.[8]

In all this, literature is in a highly problematic situation: it is both the means whereby the lover passes out of the social world (it provides him with the lover's repertoire of figures), and the means whereby he is reclaimed by that world (it translates those anarchic figures into a socially acceptable and hierarchically ordered form of narrative). Literature is both the agent of subversion and the incarnation of the *doxa*. While there seems, as yet, no obvious solution for the novelist, Stendhal's discussion of the difference between the French and Italian languages has some illuminating implications in the light of the problem identified by Barthes. What is different about the two languages in Stendhal's view is not just a question of grammar and vocabulary (although these are not without significance), but the difference in discursive practices associated with each of them. It is true, nevertheless, that the Italians are enormously helped by the fact that their language has far greater semantic subtlety and range, especially on matters of love, than French has. Italian is the language of the lover because 'il y a des noms propres en italien pour mille circonstances particulières de l'amour qui, en français, exigeraient des périphrases à n'en plus finir' (*De l'Amour*, p. 169). Many aspects of love defy expression in French because it lacks the lexical richness of Italian, and Stendhal's own recourse to Italian words in his account of love in *De l'Amour* would seem to bear this out: *puntiglio* (p. 117), *pettegolismo* (p. 170), *furia francese* (p. 169), *un porco* (p. 168), *avvicina* (p. 172) and *fiasco* (pp. 335–9).

But this lexical variety is merely a by-product of a far more thoroughgoing difference between the two languages; for where French bears all the imperialistic and hierarchical hallmarks of the kinds of discourse castigated by Barthes, Italian reflects the plurality of Italian society, where different codes and different discourses are allowed to coexist in peace. (Even husbands and lovers coexist in peace in Italy.) If 'le *ridicule* n'existe pas en Italie' (p. 170), it is because such a concept is unthinkable in the a-hierarchism of this plurality; the lover's discourse is respected in society and no attempt is made to translate it back into a different discursive register.

The point is nicely illustrated by the remarks that Stendhal makes about dialect in Italy; whereas in France the same language is spoken throughout the country, in Italy, he says, each city has its own regional dialect, and there is no one master idiom:

On parle français à Lyon comme à Nantes. Le vénitien, le napolitain, le génois, le piémontais sont des langues presque entièrement différentes et seulement parlées par des gens qui sont convenus de n'imprimer jamais que dans une langue commune, celle qu'on parle à Rome. Rien n'est absurde comme une comédie dont la scène est à Milan, et dont les personnages parlent romain.
(p. 170)

It is evident that Stendhal's preferences are for this Italian plurilinguism over French monolinguism; but this preference in itself is not enough to keep the tyrannical effects of monolinguism at bay. For French, being a monovocal, hierarchically structured system, seeks to colonise and annex all other systems, the Italian language included: 'La langue italienne, beaucoup plus faite pour être chantée que parlée, ne sera

Love and the wayward text

soutenue contre la clarté française qui l'envahit que par la musique' (p. 170). The monolinguism of writing has to be countered by resorting to the language of music; and where the plurilinguism of Italian is supported by the open-ended language of music, you get an unmatchable form of expression – Italian opera. This perhaps explains the privileged position that 'the divine Cimarosa' and the Italian operas of Mozart always held in Stendhal's esteem. It also suggests why the opera should be the most characteristic cultural form in Italy, and the novel the one most favoured by the French.[9]

Love and the dialogic

The implications for the novel of this comparison between the French and Italian languages are that there is another choice than the one between the unintelligible and isolated discourse of the lover and the *doxa* (or what Stendhal would call the 'opinion publique')[10] of society: there is a choice between a French discursive practice that hierarchises and 'invades' (to use Stendhal's word), and an Italian one that permits the coexistence of Venetian and Neapolitan dialects, the lover's discourse and that of his friend, words and music. The choice, in other words, lies between what Mikhail Bakhtin calls 'monologism' on the one hand, and 'dialogism' on the other.[11]

In Bakhtin's view, all national languages are composed of a variety of different discourse types or codes, and a single language is actually not single at all, but profoundly 'heteroglot', being made up of

social dialects, characteristic group behaviour, professional jargons, generic languages, languages of generations and age groups, tendentious languages, languages of the authorities, of various circles and of passing fashions, languages that serve the specific sociopolitical purposes of the day, even of the hour. (*Dialogic Imagination*, pp. 262–3)

Given the inherent heteroglossia of language, there are two alternative ways of responding to it: either speakers (whose utterances are invariably drawn from this repertoire of different codes or 'dialects') recognise the existence of discursive difference, and acknowledge the otherness of other 'dialects' (which is *dialogism*); or else they seek to impose their own discourse by silencing others and refusing to acknowledge them in dialogue (which is *monologism*). Stendhal's conception of Italian is remarkably like the discursive practice of dialogism; and his view of French is very close to the monologic pattern of what Bakhtin calls 'unitary languages', which operate by 'reigning over' other languages, 'supplanting' them, 'incorporating'

them, even 'enslaving' them (p. 271). (Remember the way that
Stendhal describes 'la clarté française' as an 'invasion' of Italian
plurilinguism, or what one should perhaps follow Bakhtin in calling
'heteroglossia'.)

The relevance to the novel of this opposition between dialogism
and the monologism which seeks to deny it, is that Bakhtin regards
the novel as a fundamentally dialogic genre whose function is
to condense and heighten the dialogism that characterises all
discourse. A work such as Pushkin's verse-novel *Evgenij Onegin* is
consequently described by Bakhtin as an 'encyclopedia of Russian
life', not because it 'catalogues the things of everyday life', but because
in it 'Russian life speaks in all its voices, in all the languages and styles
of the era' (p. 49). Like every novel (in Bakhtin's view of the genre),
Evgenij Onegin is a 'dialogised system made up of the images of
"languages", styles and consciousnesses that are concrete and
inseparable from language' (*ibid.*). Fiction is – to use another
Bakhtinian term – a thoroughly polyphonic affair which, in citing
the different discourses of its day, seeks to heighten its readers' sense
of those differences.

Bakhtin's conception of the novel as a uniquely and intrinsically
dialogic genre is open to dispute, not least because, as Stendhal himself
shows, novels can easily be used to impose the unitary language of
a highly monologic model upon their readers (viz. the role of fiction
in upholding the Parisian values of imitation). Nevertheless, Bakhtin's
views do offer a double advantage. The first is a conception of the
novel as both a part and a reflection of the discursive practices of the
society in which it is produced, a conception that seems highly
appropriate to a novelist like Stendhal, who has such a strongly
developed sensitivity to the dialogic. And the second advantage is that,
even without adopting the notion of dialogism as the overarching
definition of fiction in general, it remains a useful concept for
distinguishing between different kinds of fiction, the polyphonic
versus the more unitary examples of the genre.

This latter appropriation of Bakhtin would certainly seem to tally
with the ideas about fiction that emerge from Stendhal's remarks on
the subject in *De l'Amour*. Stendhal appears to have two alternative
views of the novel, seeing it in both a positive and a negative guise.
When speaking positively of it he tends not to use the word 'roman'
and thus imply a fixed generic object. The term he uses instead is 'le
romanesque', which is not necessarily confined to formal literary
incarnations. It is (as we have seen above) the word he uses to describe
cristallisation, and in Stendhal's lexicon it contrasts with the word

prosaïque which, in referring to all that is vulgar and calculating, implies an alternative model of fiction. The novel *Don Quixote*, for instance, has (in Stendhal's view) both prosaic and novelistic elements. Don Quixote himself embodies the element of the *romanesque*, being 'toujours rempli d'imaginations romanesques et touchantes; ... toujours nourrissant son âme de quelque contemplation héroïque et hasardée'. Sancho Panza, on the other hand, is the embodiment of the *prosaïque*, being 'tout égoïsme et servilité; ... un modèle d'esprit de conduite, un recueil de proverbes bien sages; ... ruminant quelque plan bien sage' (p. 243). The prosaic is thus associated with the repeated and the prescriptive, imposing univocal models that promote the repetition of proverbial truths, and the calculating hierarchies of plots. The novelistic, in contrast, is associated with contemplation rather than calculation, chance rather than plots, and imagination rather than established opinion.

A prosaic novel predisposes its reader to repetition and imitation. But in the hands of the right reader (one of the happy few) the novelistic novel incites *rêverie*. A plural text evokes a plural response: 'la rêverie ... est le vrai plaisir du roman' (p. 36). The 'waywardness' that Stendhal speaks of in his discussion of *cristallisation* is thus the common feature that links the lover, the novelistic text in which he may be represented, and its happy reader. It is in this sense that *De l'Amour* may be considered a novelistic text. (Barthes says of the lover's discourse that it consists of 'aucun roman (mais beaucoup de romanesque)', p. 11, and much the same could be said of *De l'Amour*.) Stendhal acknowledges that *De l'Amour* is not a novel, because, in his words, it is not 'amusant comme un roman' (p. 321). But by this he means perhaps that it is not teleologically organised in narrative form. On the other hand, Stendhal did suggest in the 'Puff-Article' which he wrote for *De l'Amour* that his book had '*tout le charme du meilleur roman*' (p. 400). If he was right, this is the wayward, novelistic charm that is so deeply incompatible with the narrative finality elsewhere associated with the novel.

Despite Stendhal's claims that this work is 'une description exacte et scientifique' (p. 321), a simple, logical, mathematical account, 'un cours d'anatomie morale' (p. 401), in short, a 'Physiologie de l'Amour', these are negated by almost every aspect of the text. It has no coherent order and was found (according to Stendhal) to be largely unintelligible to the majority of his readers. If his aim was to write 'une description exacte et scientifique d'une sorte de *folie*' (p. 321, italics mine), his project was bound to fail, because, as this chapter has sought to demonstrate, love in particular and *folie* in general cannot be written about mathematically or exactly.[12] As a discussion of love, *De l'Amour* succeeds not by being scientific, but by being novelistic.

In this case its disordered, fragmentary composition acquires a special and a very positive significance. Stendhal claims that his text was written in pencil on little scraps of paper 'pris dans les salons où j'entendais raconter les anecdotes' (p.330), and was even delivered to the printer in this form. The refusal of order implied by this genesis seems to be being offered as a guarantee of the text's authenticity, and it recalls the fact that Barthes's lover also speaks in fragments, 'par paquets de phrases', never transcending the horizontal plane of the *discours amoureux* to arrive at 'une œuvre'. These bundles (Barthes's and Stendhal's) are both placed firmly under the aegis of chance, as if to preserve them from all attempts to impose a teleological (and hence monological) order on them. In Barthes's case, 'les figures surgissent dans la tête du sujet amoureux sans aucun ordre, car elles dépendent chaque fois d'un *hasard*' (*Fragments*, p.10, my italics). In Stendhal's case, the first of these fragments were recorded as the result of a *chance* conversation, and even the events in one of the anecdotes recounted on this occasion were said by its narrator to have been confided in him through 'le hasard' (p.330). Moreover, the fragments were jotted down by Stendhal on the playing cards that had been abandoned by the *faro* players for the greater pleasures of the conversation in question – a perfect emblem of the chance that guarantees the authenticity of the text inscribed upon them. What, then, could be more *wayward*, more novelistic than this thoroughly chancy method of composition?

De l'Amour is also *romanesque* in the requirements it makes of its readers. To read *De l'Amour* it is necessary, according to Stendhal, to have 'l'habitude de passer des heures entières dans la rêverie' (p.323). This, he says, will rule out all businessmen and ninety-six out of every hundred readers of Mme de Staël's *Corinne* (p.321). The wayward text will remain unintelligible to all but the most wayward reader (*rêverie* being one of the most undirected forms of human activity). The reader must have passed through the school of waywardness by having been made unhappy by love ('cette faiblesse des âmes fortes', p.328), and by having acquired 'l'habitude, contre nature, de penser en lisant', a habit that comes through reading 'quelqu'un de ces ouvrages insolents qui forcent le lecteur à penser ... par exemple, l'*Emile* de J.-J. Rousseau, ou les six volumes de Montaigne' (p.328). (The insolent text would perhaps be one that engaged dialogically with its readers, recognising both their otherness, and its own as perceived by them.) *De l'Amour* becomes novelistic when the reader finds that 'à chaque instant on ferme le livre pour penser' (p. 400). The book invites *rêverie* but not imitation: 'N'est-ce pas dire que *l'Amour a tout le charme du meilleur roman*?' (p. 400, Stendhal's italics).

De l'Amour may be regarded as Stendhal's first mature work (as indeed many have), because it is, for the reasons given above, the novelist Stendhal's first novelistic work. In it he found both a topic and a manner of writing through which he could rehearse and explore the novelistic before committing himself to the novel proper. The novelist discovers that he can learn from the lover, first by adopting the tactics of a Werther in the face of the *déjà-dit*; and second by seeing how the lover is treated in the homeland of passion, Italy, and so avoiding the treatment meted out to him in the land of *amour de vanité*. The plurilingual or Italian nature of fictional dialogism allows the novel to accommodate antagonistic discourses without necessarily having to sanction any one at the expense of the others. If the lover's discourse is at odds with all other forms of utterance, the polyphonic novel can represent this state of affairs and not be obliged to see a victor emerge. (In any case, the lover never would be the victor; victory in this sense never even enters his calculations.)

By the same token the lover's discourse is in itself likely to prove an invaluable component of the multilingual novel, because perception of its discursive distinctiveness will promote a general sharpening of dialogic consciousness. Its antagonistic relations with other forms of expression will help heighten awareness of the differences between them. The chief problem for the novelist proper will be how to use these materials in constructing his fiction without at the same time submitting to the unifying and reductive force of the demands of narrative. If *De l'Amour* retains any exemplary function in relation to the fiction, it is not as a theoretical (and therefore monologic) treatise against which all narrative varieties may be measured, but as a superlative instance of the *wayward* or multilingual text.

Part Three
LE ROUGE ET LE NOIR

3

UNEXPRESSING THE EXPRESSIBLE

détacher une parole seconde de l'engluement des paroles premières

Barthes, *Essais critiques*

Trials and the lover's tribute: 'L'affaire Berthet'

In his projected article on *Le Rouge* Stendhal prides himself on being the first to describe a wholly new phenomenon, 'l'amour parisien', and on thus overcoming the major difficulty in writing fiction, 'ne pas *copier des livres*' ('Projet', p. 716, Stendhal's italics). He states quite categorically that, 'Cette peinture de l'amour parisien est absolument neuve. Il nous semble qu'on ne la trouve dans aucun livre' (p. 724). But if Stendhal manages to write without other books, he does so in order to represent a subject that is almost entirely dependent on books – love in general and 'l'amour parisien' in particular. Furthermore, books contaminate not just the subject of the novel, but its very origins; for in composing *Le Rouge* Stendhal relied to a great extent on sources of the most vulgar and platitudinous kind, namely the newspaper reports of two murder trials as contained in the *Gazette des Tribunaux*. The first of these, known as *l'affaire Berthet*, appeared between 28 and 31 December 1827; and the second, *l'affaire Lafargue*, was reported in two versions, one in the *Gazette*, and the other in the *Courrier des Tribunaux*, between 30 March and 1 April 1829, only a few months before Stendhal began working on *Le Rouge*. His interest in this latter case is also revealed by the fact that he copied out large sections of the reports almost verbatim in his *Promenades dans Rome*, which was published in the same year.[1]

Both trials were dealing with crimes of passion. In each case the accused was a young man who had murdered the woman he loved and then tried unsuccessfully to take his own life. If Stendhal's interest in the Lafargue case is attested by his incorporation of it in the *Promenades*, the importance of the Berthet case can be inferred from its extensive similarity with Julien Sorel's story in *Le Rouge*. The son of

67

a blacksmith, Antoine Berthet found himself destined for a career in the Church owing to a combination of his physical frailty (which would have prevented him from taking up his father's trade), superior intelligence and a little learning. After a spell in a seminary in Grenoble, he was hired as a tutor to the children of the Michoud family in the village of Brangues in the Dauphiné, where he fell in love with Mme Michoud, the wife of his employer and the mother of his charges. After leaving his post in the Michoud family (for reasons that are not entirely clear), he was taken on by the comte de Cordon as an 'instituteur'. Here the daughter of the house began to take an interest in the unhappy tutor, who was suffering from jealousy at having seen himself replaced in the Michoud family both professionally and emotionally by a former classmate from the seminary. On being dismissed by M. Cordon, and on failing to get accepted in any other seminary (and thus having to face an end to his hopes of a career as a priest), Berthet thought he detected signs of deliberate obstruction by M. and Mme Michoud, and he decided to return to Brangues and shoot Mme Michoud in the village church before taking his own life. Mme Michoud died of her wounds and Berthet was eventually sentenced to death for 'voluntary murder with premeditation'.

The similarities between the *affaire Berthet* and the plot of *Le Rouge* will be evident even from a brief summary like this. There are, in addition, minor characters (such as the 'curé' who had taken responsibility for Berthet's education) and minor details (such as the pallor of the accused on the day of his trial) that reinforce the overall similarity. But my intention is not to repeat or recapitulate the work that has already been done to establish sources and parallels. Rather, I shall concentrate instead on what, in view of Stendhal's desire not to copy from books, is one of the most striking aspects of his recourse to the Berthet case: the narrative style which the *Gazette des Tribunaux* (and apparently also the protagonists themselves) used to present the material on which Stendhal drew so copiously for his novel.

To eyes that have been sensitised by Barthes's discussion in the *Fragments*, one of the most noteworthy features of the reports is that the purpose of the court proceedings seems to have been the construction of something very like the *histoire d'amour* which society exacts as tribute from the wayward lover. The questions that should interest us, then, are first, why Stendhal should take the risk of basing his novelistic venture on this kind of narrative tribute when everything that he writes in *De l'Amour* should have warned him of its dangers; and second, how he manages to parry these dangers in his own writing.

But before engaging with these issues, I should like to examine the Berthet case more closely to see how the lover's narrative is produced by its narrators and what forms it takes in its various versions. This narrative has to be spoken about in the plural, for the prosecution, the defence, and finally Berthet himself all come up with somewhat different accounts of the events in question. Nevertheless, regardless of the discrepancies between them, the aim of each of these versions is to provide a coherent and plausible explanation for the crime and the passions that inspired it. In these tales one can see violence and passion being recuperated with more or less equal success by the particular forms of the *doxa* involved in the case.

Whatever the terms in which the legal institution may have defined the purpose of the legal proceedings, one may be fairly sure that the readers of the *Gazette des Tribunaux* were primarily motivated by the desire to read an *histoire d'amour*, and this is what they expected the trial to provide. The *Gazette*'s own report certainly implies very strongly that this is what the public who attended the trial in unprecedented numbers were hoping to hear: 'Jamais les avenues de la cour d'assises n'avaient été assiégées par une foule plus nombreuse ... *On devait y parler d'amour, de jalousie* et les dames les plus brillantes étaient accourues' (p. 650, my italics). The presence of these brilliant ladies in the audience is fairly decisive confirmation that the interest of the public is first and foremost in these questions of love and jealousy.

What the court had to decide was whether Berthet's crime (the facts of which he did not dispute) was, in the words of the prosecuting counsel, 'volontaire et le résultat d'une longue préméditation'. That is to say, Berthet's crime was to be evaluated in terms of the sort of calculations that will inevitably put a narrative and worldly construction upon it.[2] Indeed, the prosecution's interpretation consists of just such a worldly narrative, whose worldly component is so pronounced that it barely even qualifies as an *histoire d'amour*: summing up, the prosecuting counsel invites the jury to look into 'les derniers replis de cette âme perverse', and promises them that they will find 'l'ambition déçue, l'amour-propre blessé d'un homme envieux qui s'irritait de voir Mme Michoud favoriser Jacquin [Berthet's successor and rival] plus que lui' (p. 665). And he argues that the more sentimental motive of 'la jalousie de l'amour' must be rejected, since the logical outcome of such a motive would (according to him) have been the murder of the rival, Jacquin, and not that of the beloved, Mme Michoud.[3] In other words, with notions such as 'ambition déçue' and 'amour-propre blessé', the prosecution translates Berthet's case into the worldly vocabulary of 'coteries, ambitions, promotions, manigances, alliances, sécessions, rôles, pouvoirs' that Barthes identifies as the constituent features of the world from which the lover is bound to withdraw (*Fragments*, p. 23); and the tale of passion is largely recast as a tale of ambition.

The defence's tale, on the other hand, is unequivocally a tale of passion. Suggesting that Berthet was the hapless victim of the older and more experienced Mme Michoud, who corrupted his youthful innocence by means of '[une] suite de caresses et d'insinuations' (p. 663), the defending counsel sets out his narrative aims as follows:

Je m'engage à prouver que l'amour a donné la mort; que l'amour est souvent un délire, que la volonté de l'accusé n'était pas en sa puissance, lorsqu'il devint à la fois suicide et homicide.

In this story it is the older woman whose motives generate the causal sequence that forms the basis of the narrative; in it she is cast as the worldly agent, and Berthet the passionate victim. As it turned out, however, the slur on Mme Michoud's character entailed by this version of events (a calumny deliberately concocted by the defence, and, according to Berthet, quite unjustified) proved to be the undoing of the case; for the prosecution won the day and succeeded in establishing beyond any legal doubt the calculated, voluntary and premeditated nature of Berthet's criminal act.

But the prosecutor did not have the final word, and the brilliant ladies in the audience were eventually rewarded with the tale of love and jealousy for which they had obtained their seats, when Berthet himself rounded off the legal proceedings by offering his own tribute to society, and giving an account of his motives and his actions in the words of an *histoire d'amour* of his own making. As another newspaper report put it (in *Le Pirate* of 9 and 16 May 1830): 'Les débats terminés, Berthet lui-même voulut dire à ses juges *l'histoire de ses passions et de ses malheurs*' (p. 669, my italics). In this tale Berthet portrays himself as a creature of delicate physical constitution, endowed with equal delicacy of spirit, '[un] faible et timide enfant, dont le cœur était fait pour les sentiments les plus doux et les plus tendres' (p. 670). His passion for Mme Michoud was a response to the first 'attentions délicates' he had ever been the object of in the course of his entire existence. Overwhelmed by his first experience of such delicacy and touching goodness on the part of a woman, Berthet found himself in the grip of emotions that he confessed to her as the effects of '[un] cœur dévoré de passion, troublé de terreur religieuse et d'effroi pour le sacerdoce' (p. 671). As a result of Mme Michoud's compassion for Berthet's torment, she swore an oath before her crucifix never to forget him and to make him happy for the rest of his life. When this promise seemed to have been broken, Berthet's jealousy reached such a pitch that he eventually decided to remind Mme Michoud of her Christian oath by killing her in church. He concludes his tale by describing the remorse and repentance that followed his terrible crime, addresses himself to God as the ultimate judge of the human heart and begs for divine mercy. The author of the newspaper report (a former companion of Berthet's in the seminary and a witness of both the trial and the execution) adds a brief coda to Berthet's narrative and ends with the sentence: 'Les dames de la Charité ont dit qu'il [i.e. Berthet] était mort en saint' (p.674). This conclusion thus endorses the religious character of Berthet's version of the tale. Although there is the most affecting component of love and jealousy in this narrative, it is a tribute that quite specifically marks Berthet's reintegration into social discourse (if not into society) as a subordination of passion to religion. The discourse of Christianity associates the torments of passion with those of religion, gives special significance to the oath made before the crucifix and the ecclesiastical setting of the murder, and links them all in the appeal for divine clemency, the repentance of the accused and his final conversion.

This, then, is a quasi-hagiographical narrative of misplaced sensibilities and Christian repentance, and differs as much from the defence's narrative of innocence corrupted by worldly experience as it does from the prosecution's narrative of ruthless ambition. But despite these differences, these narratives are all equally effective as forms of social tribute: their differences are only differences in styles of the *doxa*, and do not constitute fundamental differences of kind. In principle, there is no reason why society should not be just as happy with a tale of repentance as with a tale of seduction or of ambition. If the tale of seduction proves to have been misjudged and unfounded, the newspapers seem to hover fairly evenly between the prosecution's version and Berthet's own. Legal and narrative precedent meant that the prosecution's case was bound to cast the socially inferior employee as a fortune hunter and to produce the verdict that it did; but presumably the deliria of love and jealousy as contained in Berthet's narrative will have appealed rather more than the tale of ambition to the readers of the *Gazette* and the audience in the public gallery who had gathered specifically to hear talk of love and jealousy rather than tales of undisguised ambition.

As far as Stendhal himself is concerned, the character of the various versions will not have had any particular significance, since as instances of the *déjà-dit*, they will all have been as abhorrent to him as they were appealing to the readers of the legal press. Whatever interest he found in the Berthet case, he encountered it in these heavily encoded forms and not in the raw state of lived or imagined experience. And whatever the aims and claims of his 'Projet', the *Gazette* and *Le Pirate* between them reveal that his book began with other books, his novel with one of the most 'prosaïque' and platitudinous forms of writing that the century of platitude could produce.

The catechism of the nineteenth century: 'L'affaire Lafargue'

Despite the platitudinous forms in which they were mediated by the press, Stendhal was fascinated by crime and criminal personalities, and became an assiduous reader of the *Gazette des Tribunaux* and of its rival, the *Courrier des Tribunaux* (founded in 1827).[4] In his comments on the Lafargue trial in the *Promenades dans Rome*, Stendhal states that the appeal of cases like that of Lafargue lies in the qualities of energy and passion that they testify to, and which contrast so strongly with the loss of the 'faculté de sentir avec force et constance' amongst the upper classes of Parisian society (*Promenades*, p. 1079). Adrien Lafargue was a wood-carver and cabinet-maker, educated, like Berthet, beyond the requirements of his peasant origins and his professional calling, who fell in love with his landlady's daughter, and when she betrayed him, murdered her and sought to take his own life too. There is no point in analysing in any detail the constructions put on these events (so similar in outline to those of the Berthet case) by the legal proceedings. More worthy of attention are the explicit comments made by Stendhal himself upon them. Liprandi, as a modern commentator, sees in Lafargue's case only a 'vulgaire drame d'abandon' (p. 9) perpetrated by 'un assassin du type courant' (p. 150); but Stendhal hails Lafargue as a man '[qui] a plus d'âme à lui seul que tous nos poètes pris ensemble, et plus d'esprit que la plupart de ces messieurs' (*Promenades*, p. 911). He sees him, that is to say, as the antithesis of the weary preoccupation with 'le modèle à imiter, qui, tel que l'épée de Damoclès, apparaît menaçant sur votre tête' (p. 1079), and as a living contrast to the etiolated Parisian spirit. He admires Lafargue as an example of '[les] âmes tendres et nobles', amongst whom he also numbers Mme Roland and Napoleon (p. 880) (who were for him the highest incarnation of energy and freedom from *convenances*). In short, he unreservedly prefers the knife with which Lafargue cut his mistress's throat to the sword of Damocles represented by the ubiquitous menace of the 'modèle à imiter'.

Stendhal's sympathies and his reasons for them are quite unequivocal: he and the novel that was partly inspired by Lafargue are united
in their allegiance to the qualities of passion and energy and by their
opposition to all that is Parisian. Yet, as I have suggested, there is a
paradox here, because tales like those of Lafargue and Berthet are
brought to the attention of Stendhal as a member of the reading public
through the very medium that supports Parisian conformity – the
newspaper and its narrative forms based on the socially determined
histoire d'amour. (Lafargue's first deposition in court consists of the
orderly narrative of the lover's tribute: in response to questions put
to him by the presiding judge, Lafargue offers '[sa] déclaration tout
entière', and asks permission to 'exposer [sa] vie *avec ordre*', p. 1070,
my italics.) All the violent energies that Stendhal admired in a
Lafargue or a Berthet are contradicted by the platitudinising format
of the lover's tribute and the written journalistic word. This contradiction is not mentioned in his comments on the Lafargue case, but
elsewhere (and not least in the *Promenades* themselves) Stendhal
makes some fairly devastating attacks on newspapers and their
function in society. His major objections to the press were, first, that
newspapers interpose themselves between their readers and reality,
offering a substitute for real observation and independent enquiry;
and second that, as a consequence of this, newspapers promote mere
parrotting of received opinion, both in their own pages and amongst
their readers.

Stendhal accepts that the press is a genuine political necessity, and
that the (relative) freedom of opinion that it defends has a vital
contribution to make to the maintenance of a new-found political
liberty: 'Politiquement parlant, notre liberté n'a pas d'autre garantie
que le journal' (*Mémoires d'un touriste*, I, p. 36). But the price to be
paid for this political liberty is what Stendhal calls a 'charlatanism'
that ultimately works against more fundamental forms of freedom.
Newspapers dispose of reputations in a manner that may have nothing
to do with reality, but their word is taken on trust by their readership
to the point that 'à Paris on voit tout *à travers le journal*' (p. 34).
In the provinces, by contrast, where newspapers are fewer and are held
in rather lower esteem, they have no power to determine the perceptions of their readers in this way; 'le bourgeois de La Charité
[Stendhal's example of a provincial town here] voit par ses yeux, et
de plus, examine avec une profonde curiosité ce qui se passe dans la
ville'. In metropolitan society the charlatanism of the press severs any
link between reality and writing, and seeks to impose standardised and
usually unsubstantiated representations upon its readers. Stendhal

does not say so in the *Promenades*, but it is quite conceivable that there may be more than a little of this charlatanism in the *Gazette*'s account of the Lafargue case. This is a view held by Liprandi who, after comparing the newspapers' version of the trial with other documents and sources, states that the newspapers had produced a highly romanticised portrait of the accused (in reality 'un assassin du type commun'), endowing him quite fictitiously with all the qualities of youth, beauty, sincerity, poverty, passion, sorrow, ardour and sensibility appropriate to 'un héros romantique'.

Before dealing with the implications of this paradox, let us look in a little more detail at Stendhal's other objection to the press. In his view, newspapers also serve the interests of the century of platitude because their Parisian readers turn to them as a source of ready-made opinions which may be repeated with political impunity and positive social benefits. He complains in *Racine et Shakespeare* that '[l]es jeunes gens prennent leurs opinions toutes faites dans *Le Constitutionnel, Le Courrier français, La Pandore*, etc.' (p. 114); and in the *Promenades dans Rome* he claims that 'le *Constitutionnel* est le catéchisme de tous les Français nés vers 1800' (p. 775), a consecrated litany of OK liberal opinions to be learned by rote and intoned on suitable social occasions.

According to Stendhal's own criteria, then, the newspapers from which he drew so much of his material for *Le Rouge* stood at the antipodes of everything that his novels were aiming to achieve: a grasp on the real and an escape from the copying of the written word that would enable him to boast on the novel's completion that 'Cette peinture ... est absolument neuve', and that 'Il nous semble qu'on ne la trouve dans aucun livre.' So, in writing this novel, he not only had to be mindful of avoiding a repetition of the established example of other novelists; he had also to deal with the added problem of how to extricate himself from the particularly pervasive and insidious form of discursive 'engluement' (to quote from the Barthes epigraph at the head of this chapter) that newspapers are.

This is a difficulty that may be regarded as an extreme form of the difficulty that Barthes sees in all literary writing; in his view, what literature has to contend with is not the unnameable, but the over-named (*le trop-nommé*).[5] L'écrivain', he says, 'n'a donc nullement à "arracher" un verbe au silence ..., mais à l'inverse, et combien plus difficilement, plus cruellement, moins glorieusement, à détacher une parole seconde de l'engluement des paroles premières que lui fournissent le monde, l'histoire, son existence, bref un intelligible qui lui préexiste.' The over-named quality of the world means that the writer's task comes to be, in his words, to unexpress the expressible, (*inexprimer l'exprimable*), to unwrite the over-intelligibility of the languages which so cruelly and ingloriously precede him. It is as just such an unwriting of the catechisms of intelligibility that I shall be reading *Le Rouge* in the remainder of this chapter, assuming that Stendhal had perceived values in the content of the two crimes (nobility, energy and passion) that needed to be turned against the very medium of their narration (platitude and repetition). If, as he claimed, Stendhal succeeded in not copying from books in *Le Rouge*, it was perhaps not because he managed to avoid their influence altogether, but because he found ways of unwriting texts whose primary purpose was to incite the very copying that Stendhal so abhors.

The lover's text

In Stendhal's novel everybody, be it voluntarily or involuntarily, starts off from a situation of discursive *engluement*, and none more so than the lovers. Julien begins his sentimental education on the basis of prescriptions culled from Napoleon; Mme de Rênal's discovery of passion is made with (though also in spite of) the proverbial forms of popular wisdom and the precepts of Christian teaching; and Mathilde, the main proponent of the 'absolutely new' phenomenon of *l'amour parisien*, has the entire contents of her father's library in the Hôtel de La Mole at her disposal to help her construct the drama of her noble passion. In describing *l'amour parisien* Stendhal may be setting an example without literary precedent, but it is a phenomenon that is itself peculiarly dependent upon literary precedent and cultural example. However, instead of putting all the emphasis on the new love story (the one that is not to be found in any book), Stendhal manages to turn the discursive *engluement* of the situation to advantage by making the story he has to tell first and foremost a story about this dependency. The result is that it is this dependency rather than love itself that seems to emerge as the main preoccupation of Stendhal's narrative.

In some senses, then, *Le Rouge* remains as silent about love as ever its author was about his own personal experience of it. In *Henry Brulard* Stendhal writes: 'je n'ai jamais dit un seul mot des femmes que j'aimais' (p. 541), and the autobiography does nothing to change this state of affairs. Indeed, *Henry Brulard* is brought to a close by the prospect of having to describe Stendhal's love for Angela Pietragrua and the impossibility of saying anything about it: 'Comment peindre le bonheur fou?' he asks; 'Ma foi je ne puis continuer, le sujet surpasse le disant' (p. 958). And the very last words of the book are: 'On gâte des sentiments si tendres à les raconter en détail.'[6] In *Le Rouge* Stendhal manages not to spoil tender feelings by writing about them directly, but makes his topic precisely the way in which tender feelings are spoiled by the various discourses which undertake both to prescribe and to describe them.

In *Le Rouge* love is shown to be at the mercy of books both in anticipation and in retrospect. Texts (both written and oral) provide normative and interpretative models that are powerful determinants of the outcome of the experiences through which they purport to guide their young readers. I shall begin by discussing Julien and Mathilde as certain kinds of users of the lover's text, before moving on in the following section to examine the case of Mme de Rênal, whose use of her texts is rather different from that of both her lover and her rival.

Julien is a fine example of the kind of person who, as La Rochefoucauld says, would never have fallen in love if he had not read and heard about it first. His seduction of Mme de Rênal is inspired entirely by books and is executed book in hand. His misfortune (but also, as we shall see later, his salvation) is to have read rather inappropriate texts: the *Mémorial de Sainte-Hélène* and 'le recueil des bulletins de la grande armée' (p. 20), Rousseau's *Confessions*, but no novels. From Rousseau Julien acquires a certain sensitivity about his social position in the Rênal household:

Cette horreur pour manger avec les domestiques n'était pas naturelle à Julien, il eût fait, pour arriver à la fortune, des choses bien autrement pénibles. Il puisait cette répugnance dans les *Confessions* de Rousseau. C'était le seul livre à l'aide duquel son imagination se figurait le monde.   (p. 20)

But for ideas on women Julien is entirely — and bizarrely — dependent on Napoleon:

Certaines choses que Napoléon dit des femmes, plusieurs discussions sur le mérite des romans à la mode sous son règne lui donnèrent alors, pour la première fois, quelques idées que tout autre jeune homme de son âge aurait eues depuis longtemps.   (p. 49)

One could imagine more appropriate and illuminating sources of information, but it is these 'ideas' taken from Napoleon that form the basis of the first stage of Julien's campaign to seduce Mme de Rênal.

For the second stage, he supplements his repertoire with the Bible and the stories that Fouqué tells him about his own unhappy love affairs and the failure of his plans for marriage: 'Tous ces récits avaient étonné Julien; il avait appris bien des choses nouvelles' (p. 72). In fact the second stage (whose aim is summarised in the words, 'je me dois à moi-même d'être son [i.e. Mme de Rênal's] amant', p. 75) is actually suggested to Julien by Fouqué's narratives, and is no more 'natural' than his concern about whom he dines with in the Rênal household: 'Une telle idée ne lui fût pas venue avant les confidences naïves faites par son ami' (p. 75). This new knowledge is turned into a specific project by Julien: 'D'après les confidences de Fouqué et le peu qu'il avait lu sur l'amour dans sa Bible, il se fit un plan de campagne fort détaillé. Comme, sans se l'avouer, il était fort troublé, il écrivit ce plan' (p. 77). The dangers of relying too closely on the written word are revealed on the occasion when Mme de Rênal inadvertently provides Julien with a chance to advance his cause (by asking him if he has any other names), which he bungles for want of an appropriate script. The would-be general of passion finds himself caught off his guard, and is struck dumb by surprise: 'Cette circonstance n'était pas prévue dans son plan' (p. 77). Stendhal goes on to suggest that without his written plan of campaign, 'l'esprit vif de Julien l'eût bien servi'. But although a little 'give' in the written prescription might be of some help, Julien's success is achieved not by abandoning bookish models, but by obtaining more relevant ones.

An odd volume of *La Nouvelle Héloïse* found at Vergy advances Julien's knowledge considerably and serves him extremely well, first with Amanda Binet in the café at Besançon ('depuis dix minutes, il récitait *La Nouvelle Héloïse* à Mlle Amanda, ravie', p. 157), and later with Mathilde on the first night he visits her in her bedroom: 'Il eut recours à sa mémoire, comme jadis à Besançon auprès d'Amanda Binet, et récita plusieurs des plus belles phrases de *La Nouvelle Héloïse*', p. 326). The advantage of the new text for Julien is that it matches his new mistress's reading experience, which had been the case neither with Mme de Rênal nor with Amanda Binet. Mathilde's ideas about love do indeed derive from *La Nouvelle Héloïse* (as well as from *Manon Lescaut* and the *Lettres portugaises*, etc.);[7] unlike Mme de Rênal, her expectations about love are largely conditioned by fiction. Mme de Rênal and Julien do not share the same conceptions about love, for she has read neither Napoleon's memoirs nor Rousseau's confessions. Julien and Mathilde share the same reading habits (they both steal volumes from the same set of Voltaire in the de La Mole library), and have acquired the same views on the way a love affair should be conducted. Mathilde's knowledge about the protocols of passion complements Julien's phrases from

La Nouvelle Héloïse. It tells her that she should speak to her lover when he comes to her room: 'cela est dans les convenances, on parle à son amant' (p. 327), that at a certain point she must give herself over to 'transports' and await 'cette entière félicité dont parlent les romans' (p. 328). Having the right text would seem, on the fact of it, to further the lover's cause considerably.

In the event, however, the possession of the appropriate text leads to disaster and disappointment: the lover's text obtrudes too much in the feelings it is supposed to incite, and, on this occasion at least, the leap from page to passion is too much for either party to accomplish. The expectations Mathilde feels that it is legitimate to have of the first physical encounter with her lover mean that her transports 'étaient un peu *voulus*. L'amour passionné était encore plutôt un modèle qu'on imitait qu'une réalité' (p. 327). The total felicity promised by the novels fails to materialise, and the 'N'est-ce que ça?' that, for Julien, followed his role-conscious night with Mme de Rênal is echoed in Mathilde's doubts about her love for Julien that follow her own night of textual imitation. If the episode is a success for Julien it is because his concerns are not for Mathilde, but for his honour; on this occasion he is following his Napoleonic text and is there to prove not his love but his bravery.

The most successful lover's text, and the one most successfully applied, is contained in Prince Korassoff's sequence of love letters. As the consultation with her ex-lover establishes, it exactly conforms to the expectations of its addressee, the Maréchale de Fervaques. More significantly, perhaps, it is adopted in a wholly unserious way by Julien, as a code to manipulate rather than as a model to imitate. Indeed, it seems that the lover's text is always more effective when used like this: Amanda Binet, whose interest in love verges on the professional, is far more impressed by the phrases from Rousseau uttered by Julien than is Mathilde, whose purposes are entirely serious. Julien's success at this stage is that of the worldly lover rather than that of the passionate lover. This is *amour-goût*, in which 'un homme bien né sait d'avance tous les procédés qu'il doit avoir et rencontrer dans les diverses phases de cet amour' (*De l'Amour*, p. 5); and its effectiveness may well depend less on having the right texts than on having the right attitudes towards them.

Mathilde's relative failure in the sphere of love (not only on the night in question, but in the novel as a whole) raises an important issue because, despite the occasional hiccup, she is, in Stendhalian terms, working from the perfect text. It is not just that Rousseau and the *Lettres portugaises* tend to make better texts for the would-be lover than the *Mémorial de Sainte-Hélène*; this is a fairly trivial point when compared with the fact that on many issues Mathilde seems to be working from an implied text that is very like the one that Stendhal himself is writing in *Le Rouge*. Most of what Mathilde demands of love tallies very closely with the values already expounded in *De l'Amour*. Like Stendhal she loathes the vanity and the monotony of the Parisian salons, and her ideal of love is designed to provide both an alternative to them and an escape from them. The young men who have wooed her in the salons have all read *René* and repeat their text to the letter: 'C'était toujours la passion la plus profonde, la plus mélancolique' (p. 294). As a reaction, she demands of love that it be extreme, all-consuming and outside the conventions of society; and the figure she sees in Julien is very similar to the one that Stendhal saw in Lafargue. Between herself and Julien everything is to be 'héroïque, tout sera fils du hasard' (p. 297), words that closely echo key passages in *De l'Amour*. The chief characteristic of their love will be energy; at every stage it will exceed the ordinary and the already-done, and avoid 'l'ornière tracée par le vulgaire' (p. 338). She loves Julien best when, most resembling the noble spirit that Stendhal admired in Lafargue, he nearly kills her with the medieval heirloom that he snatches off the wall in the library. This gesture transports her, in a way that imitating Rousseau never could, back to 'les plus beaux temps du siècle de Charles IX et de Henri III' (p. 332). In Stendhalian terms Mathilde is right both in her criticisms of Parisian society and in the values (such as those of the century of Charles IX and Henri III) that she admires as an alternative. As we have seen, the mediocrity and monotony of life in Paris is a recurrent motif in Stendhal's writing, and the importance of love as a counter to it is extolled on every page of *De l'Amour*. Why then, although she is right, is Mathilde so fundamentally wrong?

One way of answering this question would be to look at another figure in the novel who also, though right, is nevertheless wrong: Count Altamira. His comment: 'Il n'y a plus de passions véritables au xixe siècle: c'est pour cela que l'on s'ennuie tant en France. On fait les plus grandes cruautés, mais sans cruauté' (p. 279) could easily have come from Stendhal's pen. However, Altamira's rightness is made wrong by being put to use. His insights are inspired by, and put to the service of, his political interests, and it is Mathilde herself who notices that 'son esprit n'avait qu'une attitude: *l'utilité, l'admiration pour l'utilité*. Excepté ce qui pouvait donner à son pays le gouvernement des deux Chambres, le jeune comte trouvait que rien n'était digne de son attention' (p. 275). Utilitarianism of whatever kind is, in Stendhalian terms, incompatible with authenticity. Truth is like the love of Don Juan: once it is associated with profit it loses all its value.

Mathilde turns out to have quite a strong streak of utilitarianism of her own, not least in her comments about Count Altamira. Her remark about death sentences that seeing Altamira inspires ('Je ne vois que la condamnation à mort qui distingue un homme … c'est la seule chose qui ne s'achète pas', p. 273) seems to be borne out by the ending of *Le Rouge* itself; and even her scorn for trade and profit is a consistent feature of Stendhal's own writing (as this very argument testifies). But the truth of Mathilde's insight is falsified by being turned to profit when it becomes a pretext for self-congratulation:

Ah! c'est un bon mot que je viens de me dire! Quel dommage qu'il ne soit pas venu de façon à m'en faire honneur! Mathilde avait trop de goût pour amener dans la conversation un bon mot fait d'avance; mais elle avait aussi trop de vanité pour ne pas être enchantée d'elle-même.

There is nothing to preserve truth of any kind from falsification in this way. Although Stendhal's world has positive and negative values that can fairly easily be established, there is no ultimate authority which can prevent the positive values from being corrupted through vanity and utilitarianism. Truth has no inherent distingushing features and can become the object of any bland and self-interested repetition. Thus, when in a moment of weakness Julien allows his feelings for Mathilde to break though his defences, he is able to deny the truth of what he accidentally says by immediately claiming that it was mere quotation, 'des phrases pour vous plaire' (p. 410). A moment of genuine passion is transformed by simple fiat into one of the 'modèles qu'on imitait' which Stendhal's fiction is so sensitive to and which so threaten its authenticity.

In the figure of Mathilde Stendhal profanes some of his dearest truths, even going so far as to allow Mathilde to appropriate his ideal, Mme Roland, as when she indulges in the following fantasy: 'S'il y a une révolution, pourquoi Julien Sorel ne jouerait-il pas le rôle de Roland, et moi celui de Mme Roland? J'aime mieux ce rôle que celui de Mme de Staël' (p. 339). In this way, Stendhal demonstrates that although there is truth and falsehood, good and bad, authentic and inauthentic in his world, truth, good and authenticity are susceptible to betrayal in the very gestures which seek to identify and formulate them.

The affair with Mathilde is a story, then, of a progressive upgrading and improvement of the lover's text. The comic unsuitability of Napoleonic memoirs gives way to an apprenticeship that schools the lovers through books whose content and social currency make them much better reference guides to the passions of the human heart. In Mathilde's anticipation of the values of the novel in which she herself appears, one might think that the lover had reached a kind of apotheosis and found the text to beat all texts. But *Le Rouge* demonstrates at the same time that the disengagement of its own writing from the discursive *engluement* of both its own and its characters' origins is more difficult to achieve than might at first appear. For the hard-won 'parole seconde' of the literary text can be instantly transformed into a 'parole première' which it risks succumbing to afresh. It doesn't seem to take much for the unwriting achieved by the literary text to be recuperated as yet another form of the intelligible. This is the difficult, cruel and inglorious story that Stendhal is also telling in the tale of Mathilde's and Julien's Parisian passion.

Exemplary misprisions

The story of Parisian love is not, however, the whole story in *Le Rouge*, and the chronicle of Mme de Rênal's provincial passion tells a rather different tale. In it it is possible to read a solution to the problems evidenced by Mathilde and her 'amour de tête', as Stendhal calls it in his 'Projet d'un article' (p. 725). But if Mme de Rênal offers a solution, it is a solution that can be emulated neither by the reader of the text which represents it, nor by the author of that text. Mme de Rênal may be exemplary, but she is also inimitable; and the main reason why she is inimitable is that, although she is right in one sense, she is equally wrong in another. She is a kind of inverse image of Mathilde, who is wrong because of the way she chooses to be right: Mme de Rênal is right because of the way in which she allows herself to be wrong.

She is wrong because she is ignorant, provincial and superstitious, and consequently fails either to understand or to interpret correctly many of the things that go on in the world around her. As a convent-educated provincial who regards reading novels as a sin, Mme de Rênal has available to her only a very small repertoire of models as guides both for her own behaviour and for making sense of the behaviour of others. And just because she is so ignorant and superstitious, it never occurs to her to question or to seek alternatives to the framework of interpretation with which she operates; and she draws heavily, repeatedly (and for the reader somewhat comically) on the formulations of 'l'opinion publique' and of religious doctrine to make sense of the situations that she finds herself in. Indeed, with such a patently inadequate stock of wisdom, misprision becomes a kind of leitmotif for Mme de Rênal's whole conduct. Yet it proves, paradoxically, to be her saving grace.

Mme de Rênal's lack of worldly experience and the dearth of cultural models in her environment enable her to behave in ways that no self-respecting, novel-reading Parisienne (or even a *femme de chambre*) would permit of herself. Far from seeing Julien as a potential lover or as a fortune hunter whose ambitions may be a threat to her family's stability, she is unable to make him out at all, since he is quite unlike her idea of preceptor-priests in particular and of the male sex in general. Her idea of a tutor is 'un être grossier et mal peigné, chargé de gronder ses enfants, uniquement parce qu'il savait le latin, un langage barbare pour lequel on fouetterait ses fils' (p. 25). And as far as men in general are concerned,

elle se figura que tous les hommes étaient comme son mari, M. Valenod et le sous-préfet Charcot de Maugiron. La grossièreté, et la plus brutale insensibilité à tout ce qui n'était pas intérêt d'argent, de préséance ou de croix; la haine aveugle pour tout raisonnement qui les contrariait, lui parurent des choses naturelles à ce sexe, comme porter des bottes et un chapeau de feutre. (p. 36)

Nothing, therefore, prepares her to see the combination of Jean-Jacques Rousseau and the young Napoleon, whose examples animate Julien's every thought, so that, for want of the relevant text, she finds in Julien 'l'air timide d'une jeune fille' (p. 27). And with this image in her mind, she is in no position to anticipate the ferocious calculations for seduction that Julien soon undertakes and as a result of which love is eventually – though unexpectedly – born.

Nor is she able to make any sense of these feelings when they do emerge. She relies wholly on her confessor for her knowledge of passion, and as a result she is not equipped to interpret the experience that she encounters with Julien:

Ce n'était guère que son confesseur, le bon curé Chélan, qui lui avait parlé de l'amour, à propos des poursuites de M. Valenod, et lui en avait fait une image si dégoûtante, que ce mot ne lui représentait que l'idée du libertinage le plus abject. Elle regardait comme une exception, ou même comme tout à fait hors de nature, l'amour tel qu'elle l'avait trouvé dans le très petit nombre de romans que le hasard avait mis sous ses yeux. Grâce à cette ignorance, Mme de Rênal, parfaitement heureuse, occupée sans cesse de Julien, était loin de se faire le plus petit reproche. (pp. 41–2)

Unexpressing the expressible

The contrast with her Parisian, novel-reading counterpart (e.g. Mathilde) is striking and proves to have significant consequences for the action itself:

A Paris, la position de Julien envers Mme de Rênal eût été bien vite simplifiée; mais à Paris, *l'amour est fils des romans.* Le jeune précepteur et sa timide maîtresse auraient retrouvé dans trois ou quatre romans, et jusque dans les couplets du Gymnase, l'éclaircissement de leur position. *Les romans leur auraient tracé le rôle à jouer, montré le modèle à imiter*; et ce modèle, tôt ou tard, et quoique sans nul plaisir, et peut-être en rechignant, la vanité eût forcé Julien à le suivre.   (p. 36, my italics)

The possession of knowledge and of models to refer to would disastrously alter the course of the very events for which they provide the interpretation. The joyless imitation of models derived from their nightly representations on the popular stage contrasts dramatically with the happiness that ignorance and misprision bring for Mme de Rênal. In her case misunderstanding and superstition are shown to be the path that leads to *amour-passion,* or what Stendhal in his 'Projet d'un article' calls 'l'amour vrai, simple' (p. 725). Her experience is inimitable, not because it is difficult, but because no one else is in a position to repeat her errors; the sophistication that makes it possible to identify her errors as such is the very thing that makes their imitation impossible. The knowing reader of *Le Rouge* is denied the chance of emulating Mme de Rênal's route to salvation precisely because of the knowledge that enables him or her to be reading the novel in the first place. The exemplary quality of Mme de Rênal's authenticity is due not so much to her ability to do without models as to the inappropriateness of the models that she uses.

The models are brought into play on several occasions in the course of her affair with Julien, and show to what extent, far from being a free spirit, she is bound by the provincial culture in which she lives. She is, for example, suddenly horror-struck at the realisation that she is ten years older than Julien, and is afraid that because of this difference in age Julien will find her unlovable. She is obsessed with the idea which, as Stendhal points out, is an *idée reçue* of popular wisdom:

Quoique Mme de Rênal n'eût jamais pensé aux théories de l'amour, la différence d'âge est, après celle de fortune, un des grands lieux communs de la plaisanterie de province, toutes les fois qu'il est question d'amour.
                                    (p. 86)

It is almost the only concept that she has at her disposal for interpreting Julien's behaviour and, instead of regarding his concern with his role as a sign of his hypocrisy, she can see in it only 'un triste effet de la disproportion des âges'. What makes Mme de Rênal's invocation of these *idées reçues* different from that of Mathilde and Julien is, however, not ultimately their content, but the ungratifying effects that their application has for her. They do not flatter her vanity or bring her honour (in the way that Mathilde would have liked her *bon mot* about death sentences to have done), and Mme de Rênal interprets her models in ways that bring her little but humiliation and suffering. This is primarily because her recourse to them is entirely devoid of calculation, as witness her remarks to Julien on the topic of her age: 'Hélas! j'ai dix ans de plus que vous! comment pouvez-vous m'aimer! lui répétait-elle *sans projet*, et parce que *cette idée l'opprimait*' (pp. 85–6, my italics). The same is true of the occasion when, unable to control her feelings and act with discretion, she goes to listen at Julien's door: 'Cette action lui semblait la dernière des bassesses, car elle sert de texte à un dicton de province' (p. 85). Where Mathilde's recourse to models becomes a pretext for self-congratulation, Mme de Rênal's translation of her own role and actions into the terms of popular sayings and provincial wisdom is perceived by her as being profoundly degrading.

Mme de Rênal's reliance on religious interpretations is equally un-self-interested, and an even more potent source of suffering and imagined disgrace. Her sudden recognition of the fact that her relationship with Julien amounts to adultery causes her an anguish that almost deprives her of her reason. Her conception of adultery itself is entirely provincial and religious – and indeed what other view of it could she have, since she lacks any knowledge either of Parisian life or of literature (bar the few novels which 'le hasard avait mis sous ses yeux' and to which, in any case, her own lack of experience prevents her from attaching any credence)? Realising that her actions make her an adulteress, she pictures that definition in the most literal and traditional terms with herself 'exposée au pilori, sur la place publique de Verrières, avec un écriteau expliquant son adultère à la populace' (p. 64). This image of shame does nothing more than repeat a commonplace of popular mythology which Mme de Rênal makes no attempt to control or manipulate; and the 'écriteau expliquant son adultère à la populace' graphically illustrates the extent to which she instinctively represents herself as a victim, rather than a general, of discourse. But it is precisely because she represents herself as its victim that she can be seen as offering a solution to the problems which Mathilde creates by constantly striving to be the master of the unorthodox images from which she derives such pride.

Perhaps most harrowing of all for Mme de Rênal is her interpretation of her son's illness as a punishment from God. The religious significance of her actions hits her with sudden force, and the resulting agony which she has to endure reveals the existence of a kind of double bind, in which her ignorance and the degree of her suffering are mutually correlated guarantees of her authenticity. This seems to be borne out by Julien's reactions on seeing her grief: 'Julien fut profondément touché. Il ne pouvait voir là ni hypocrisie ni exagération' (p. 108), an assessment whose reliability one may be fairly sure of, for who more sensitive to hypocrisy and exaggeration than Julien? In any case, although the novel is not proposing any religious solutions (unlike Berthet, Julien goes to his death unconverted), Stendhal seems far more anxious not to undermine Mme de Rênal's religious convictions and interpretations in the reader's eyes than he is to endorse Mathilde's elitist and individualistic principles, many of which nevertheless echo his own.[8]

Right up to the end of the novel Mme de Rênal remains a victim of the discourses which so unadvantageously structure her existence, even when the consequences of doing so cease to be purely imaginary. In succumbing to the stratagems of the new curé of Verrières and confessing to him, and, most importantly, in making his religious account of her relationship with Julien publicly known through her letter to the Marquis de La Mole, she fatally alters the course of Julien's life, with consequences that in addition nearly deprive her of her own. In due course she also has to accept the loss of her social position in falling prey to the constructions of public opinion; after the scandal of Julien's crime, she recognises that, as she tells him in prison, 'Je suis à jamais, pour Besançon et toute la Franche-Comté, une héroïne d'anecdotes', a statement that is characteristically uttered with 'un air profondément affligé' (p. 473). Even when all the disgrace that she imagined in connection with the commonplace of provincial 'plaisanterie', the 'dicton de province' and the 'écriteau expliquant son adultère à la populace' is suddenly made real, she makes no attempt to put anything else in their place; and whatever she may or may not think about their truth or their validity, she none the less continues to accept their domination.

Despite their very obvious inadequacy for the experiences that they are required to explain, Stendhal himself seems, curiously, every bit as loath as Mme de Rênal to propose any alternative or improvement to these orthodoxies, a reluctance which tends to confirm the suggestion that Mme de Rênal is exemplary not for the content of her beliefs, but for the passive manner in which she accepts them. In this she differs crucially not just from Mathilde, but from almost all the other characters in the novel, many of whom draw on the same orthodoxies in order to explain things for which they are glaringly and grotesquely inappropriate.

'Le potin'

These explanations form the last part of the story that *Le Rouge* has to tell about passion. Mme de Rênal's tale may be exemplary, but it is one that almost nobody else in the novel seems prepared to accept and, indeed, one which they apparently cannot even bear to hear. Having failed to exact its tribute from the lovers, society seeks to conceal the fact by concocting versions of its own, and then passing them off as tributes on the lovers' behalf. The majority of these tales are triggered by the scandalous and unexplained behaviour of the lover, exemplified by Julien's shooting of Mme de Rênal in the church; and it is to these tales that the last part of *Le Rouge* is largely devoted. After Julien's imprisonment nothing more happens, effectively, and the final pages are given over to an account of the attempts made by various characters and institutions to interpret and explain the shooting and the events that led up to it.

Although it is written before the shooting, and is also in some senses its major cause, Mme de Rênal's letter constitutes one of the first of these explanatory narratives and can therefore be seen as a consummate example of what Barthes calls 'le potin' (gossip). As we saw in the previous chapter, the lover's discourse and 'le potin' represent two quite incompatible spheres of language. Whereas the lover finds himself unable to use the third-person pronoun with reference to the beloved, and quite powerless to give any descriptive account of him/her ('l'autre est inqualifiable'), 'le potin' is stopped by nothing. The lover's discourse is based on interlocution ('parler *à* un autre'), 'le potin' on delocution ('parler *de* quelqu'un', p. 218, my italics). This distinction is not neutral, since the two are profoundly antagonistic. Delocution tries always to absorb interlocution, and the lover experiences the intrusion of gossip upon his own discourse as a source of pain and anguish. Barthes describes its effects as follows: 'Blessure éprouvée par le sujet amoureux lorsqu'il constate que l'être aimé est pris dans un "potin", et entend parler de lui d'une façon commune' (p. 217). 'Le potin', or what Stendhal calls 'l'opinion publique', is therefore deeply threatening to the lover.

In her letter to the Marquis de La Mole, Mme de Rênal describes Julien exclusively in the terms of such discourse. (In a sense, of course, it is not 'her' letter at all, since it is dictated to her by her new confessor.) Impervious to the inexplicable ('la conduite de la personne au sujet de laquelle vous me demandez toute la vérité *a pu sembler inexplicable*', my italics), the production line of the *doxa* swings into motion and the 'adjectifs immondes' come rolling off it:

Pauvre et avide, c'est à l'aide de l'hypocrisie la plus consommée, et par la séduction d'une femme faible et malheureuse, que cet homme a cherché à se faire un état et à devenir quelque chose ... En conscience, je suis contrainte de penser qu'un de ses moyens pour réussir dans une maison, est de chercher à séduire la femme qui a le principal crédit. Couvert par une apparence de désintéressement et par des phrases de roman, son grand et unique objet est de parvenir à disposer du maître de la maison et de sa fortune.   (p. 431)

The substance of this is little more than a gloss on the two adjectives 'pauvre et avide', in the form of a narrative that explains everything in terms of stereotype (ruthless and ambitious seducer) and motive (greed); and it is written in terms strikingly similar to those used by the prosecuting counsel in the Berthet trial. There remains in it not a trace of the interlocutory, and Mme de Rênal describes her beloved in the most exaggeratedly delocutionary formula: 'la personne au sujet de laquelle vous me demandez toute la vérité'. The letter is an *histoire d'amour* of the most cruelly intelligible kind, as the excessive forces of love that defy the naming powers of language are translated into structures of calculation and deceit, and seem to revert entirely to the forms of the 'parole première' of the novel's original legal and journalistic sources.

The dreadful intelligibility of this letter stands in marked contrast to the silence maintained by Stendhal about the reasons for Julien's violent response to it: his attempt to shoot Mme de Rênal. Some insights into the motives for this silence (and perhaps also into the motives for the murder attempt) may be gleaned from Barthes's remarks, which could be read as having a bearing on the question. If the lover finds it painful enough to hear his beloved caught up in the discourse of 'le potin' as uttered by another, how much greater the torment must be to hear himself described by the beloved herself in these terms. The 'il' which incarnates the values of gossip is endowed with lethal powers: '"il" est méchant: c'est le mot le plus méchant de la langue: pronom de la non-personne, il annule et mortifie son référent; on ne peut l'appliquer sans malaise à qui l'on aime; disant de quelqu'un "il", j'ai toujours en vue une sorte de meurtre par le langage'.[9] Mme de Rênal's letter could be seen as a sort of linguistic murder attempt to which Julien responds with a real one, involving real flesh and real blood. The shooting is the lover's reaction to the violence perpetrated by the *doxa*. Moreover, the shooting is not just a simple reflex response to the pain caused by the letter, since the event itself also constitutes a very powerful challenge to the delocutionary powers of 'le potin': the interlocutory force of the shooting defies the delocutionary powers of either its protagonists or its witnesses, with the result that, psychologically and narratively speaking, it remains inexplicable.

At any rate, Julien himself never offers an explanation, perhaps because any such explanation would lie beyond all rational and intelligible discourse. On his way to Verrières and the church where he shoots Mme de Rênal, Julien stops to write to Mathilde, but finds that he cannot express himself in language: 'il ne put écrire à Mathilde comme il en avait le projet, sa main ne formait sur le papier que des traits illisibles' (p. 432). The illegibility of this letter prefigures that of the crime itself. And indeed, after the shooting, the greater part of Julien's efforts seem devoted to trying to maintain and impose silence around himself and his actions, and to preventing any *histoire d'amour* from being narrated on his behalf. This cannot be out of any desire to save his skin, for through his persistent silence he passes up all chances of acquittal. When he does eventually write to Mathilde from prison, it is only to ask for silence from her: 'Ne parlez jamais de moi, même à mon fils: le silence est la seule façon de m'honorer' (p. 435). Silence is the only means by which he can counter the stereotypes which public discourse will necessarily seek to impose upon him: 'Pour le commun des hommes, je serai un assassin vulgaire' (as Lafargue was for Liprandi). He remains deliberately vague about any motive he may have had. In one of his prison soliloquies he says to himself, 'enfin, j'ai voulu la tuer par ambition *ou* par amour pour Mathilde' (p. 466, my italics), as if it didn't much matter which, if either, of these two rather different motives was the true one; and he fiercely rejects the plausible motive of jealousy suggested to him by his lawyer as a propitious line of defence.

The link between stereotype and self-interest makes it impossible for Julien to supply any motive at all, because whatever story he comes up with will inevitably be recuperated in terms of the *doxa*, and any intelligible interpretation will lend itself in turn to self-interest. It is Julien's refusal to trade or procure his release by recourse to the 'parole première' of public opinion that ensures him a death sentence. His case thereby illustrates far better than that of Altamira the truth of Mathilde's remark that a sentence of death is the only thing in life which cannot be bought; it is his refusal to trade in the currency of intelligibility that ensures the final verdict which is passed upon him. Here he differs quite crucially from his prototypes in Berthet and Lafargue, for he positively and categorically refuses – either in person or through his lawyer – to offer his *histoire d'amour* to the court. Instead, he uses his speech in order to insist on a strictly legal interpretation of his crime: 'Mon crime est atroce, et il fut *prémédité*. J'ai donc mérité la mort' (p. 463). He refrains from adding any further information about his crime, and concentrates – somewhat irrelevantly to any *histoire d'amour* – on the social differences between himself and his judges. The achievement of his speech is primarily a literary and stylistic one: rather than provide the tribute that Berthet and Lafargue offer to their audiences, Julien succeeds in elaborating a discourse that is entirely free of all models. As he himself later remarks about his eloquence, 'J'improvisais, et pour la première fois de ma vie' (p. 467). If one regards improvisation as an alternative to the repetitions of the *doxa* (and in a later chapter I shall be exploring this alternative), one may read it as indicating one way in which writing can bring about an unwriting of the platitudes of intelligibility, while avoiding the temptation to replace them – the temptation to which it is Mathilde's misfortune to succumb.

The other characters (with the exception of Mme de Rênal) are notable for the fact that none of them improvises. Each of them is determined to interpret Julien's action in relation to some preconceived stereotype. Mme de Rênal, who, one would think, would be the person most justified in demanding an explanation from Julien, asks for none. But everyone else seems to regard the absence of any such explanation as a peculiar kind of threat. This is especially true of the religious figures. M. de Frilair finds Julien's apparent lack of intelligible motive especially irritating: 'Ce Julien est un être singulier, son action est inexplicable ... et rien ne doit l'être pour moi' (p. 443). Finding an explanation is not just a matter of intellectual self-respect, since for him it is also an essential part of his strategy for self-advancement. Through Mathilde he hopes to curry favour with Mme de Fervaques, who, in turn, has power to influence the nomination of bishops. Briefly stated, a plausible account of Julien's crime will help him on his way to a episcopal chair. 'Peut-être sera-t-il possible d'en [of Julien] faire un martyr', he muses. 'Dans tous les cas, je saurai le *fin* de cette affaire et trouverai peut-être une occasion de faire peur à cette Mme de Rênal.' Knowledge – or, at least, narrative intelligibility – offers power and the means of using it in the form of intimidation. Eventually M. de Frilair comes up with a version in which jealousy constitutes the motive for Julien's crime. Julien supposedly acted out of jealousy for Mme de Rênal's new religious adviser: 'Pourquoi ... M. Sorel aurait-il choisi l'église, si ce n'est parce que, précisément en cet instant, son rival y célébrait la messe?' (p. 448). As Mathilde rises to this bait that smacks strongly of the tales that were told at the Berthet trial, Stendhal remarks: 'Enfin, l'abbé de Frilair fut sûr de son empire' (p. 449). The intelligible narrative of jealous passion begins to bring in returns for its narrator as it sparks off another tale of jealousy in its listener.

A somewhat more squalid version of this self-interested stereotyping is exemplified by the priest, who is determined to get a confession out of Julien. The aim of this unnamed 'prêtre intrigant' is to 'se faire un nom parmi les jeunes femmes de Besançon, par toutes les confidences qu'il prétendrait en [from Julien] avoir reçues' (p. 474). The priest, who is described as both an intriguer and a hypocrite, installs himself outside the prison in a highly self-dramatising manner, which in itself already predisposes the gaping crowd to certain ideas about Julien. One of the prison warders tells him that, 'On commence à dire ... qu'il faut que vous ayez le cœur bien endurci pour refuser le secours de ce saint homme' (p. 474). The priest thereby adds a flourish to the image of the 'assassin vulgaire' which Julien had already anticipated, and, in so doing, ensures himself the future favours of his female flock.

Mathilde accepts none of these versions, and her self-interest is rather more subtle than that of the two priests. But interpretation there is, and self-interest too. For her, as she puts it to Julien, 'Ce que tu appelles ton crime ... n'est qu'une noble vengeance qui me montre toute la hauteur du cœur qui bat dans cette poitrine' (p. 444). In her book Julien becomes Boniface de La Mole, 'mais plus héroïque' (p. 445). The advantage that she gains from this interpretation is that it promotes her to the role of Marguerite de Navarre, and thus makes her the heroine in a highly public spectacle. Unlike Julien, who preserves his integrity by trying to disengage himself from the opinion-making public, Mathilde actively seeks out recognition from that public: 'il fallait toujours l'idée d'un public et *des autres* à l'âme hautaine de Mathilde' (p. 451). It is the gratification of this approbation that is the reward Mathilde derives from her heroising fable.

Everyone – and no one more than Julien – stands to gain by coming up with a coherent and comprehensible version of his crime. As far as the text itself is concerned, however, it seems that the episode is one of those instances where 'le sujet surpasse le disant', for Stendhal refrains from writing any version at all. The various accounts that the novel represents (such as those of M. de Frilair, the priest and

Mathilde) are shown to be talking around a silence. If Julien succeeds in being 'poetic' as he walks to his death ('Jamais cette tête n'avait été aussi *poétique* qu'au moment où elle allait tomber', p. 487, my italics) it is through preserving his silence and refusing to succumb to the temptation of intelligibility. The novel itself is, of course, subject to the same temptation, and where it succeeds in not betraying that achievement it does so by refusing to endorse or adopt any of the 'prosaic' interpretations of the *doxa* that it nevertheless represents. One of the ways in which Stendhal manages to avoid copying from books – and, more importantly perhaps, to avoid writing a copiable book (and there is no single or simple way) – is by maintaining this kind of silence. Just as Mme de Rênal's passion remains inimitable because she is wrong, so Julien's crime and salvation cannot be imitated because they remain inexplicable. If Stendhal's novel appears to stay at one remove from its subject (love) and never to engage directly with the themes and issues which it values, this is precisely in order to preserve that value.

Le Rouge et le Noir sketches out a number of solutions to the particularly acute form of the problem of the *déjà-dit* in which it has its origins. Having demonstrated through the figure of Mathilde that the Lafargue factor can easily misfire and end up compounding the very cycle of imitation from which it was meant to provide a release, Stendhal goes on to show that other alternatives do nevertheless exist. The most obvious of these is illustrated by Mme de Rênal and her exemplarily held orthodoxies; and there are also the solutions indicated by Julien's behaviour at the end of the novel – improvisation and silence. But although all these do represent genuine alternatives to a repetition of the 'parole première' from which both the novel and the characters are seeking to extricate themselves, it is not immediately obvious who is supposed to benefit from those solutions. Mme de Rênal's solution is a solution for her, but, as I have shown, it is not one that can be repeated by being adopted by anybody else, be it another character in the novel, the reader of the novel, or even its author. Similarly, the solution represented by Julien's silence has its limits; for even if Stendhal's novel does partially emulate the silence that it depicts in Julien, it can only do so to a very restricted degree without ceasing to be a novel at all. Silence does not, in short, offer any extensive solution for the writer. The third possibility, improvisation, might, on the other hand, provide a more applicable option for the novelist; but it is one that cannot be emulated too literally without ceasing to be what it is. An emulated improvisation would not be an improvisation at all, but another imitation. It would seem, then, that the solutions that Stendhal narrates in his tales of the ways in which his characters more or less successfully negotiate the entanglements of the 'parole première' of intelligibility have only marginal relevance to his own literary task.

There does, however, seem to be another solution of a more properly textual kind, which Stendhal's own narration of these first solutions could be seen to be enacting without actually representing it on the diegetic plane. I have already suggested that by making his writing a representation of the inglorious intelligibilities of the *doxa*, Stendhal is developing the beginnings of a response to the problems it poses. The particular form which that representation takes in Stendhal's novel means that the relationship of his writing to the 'parole première' is transformed from one of simple repetition to one of citation. This altered relation to discourse is the solution enacted textually, if not mimetically, by *Le Rouge*; and the discursive extrication that Barthes defines as the task of literature is achieved (though like all such achievements, it is at best precarious) by the slight gap that citation introduces between the novel and the discourses which it represents, and of which it is also necessarily constituted. Their citational status is enhanced by the way in which Stendhal plays one story off against another (Mathilde's story against Mme de Rênal's and those of 'le potin' against all of them), generating a sequence of mutual misprisions and incompatibilities. This creates a situation of dialogic conflict in which the otherness as well as the inevitability of the 'parole première' is brought into focus for the reader. One of the greatest achievements of the novel, therefore, is to have elaborated a series of narratives that offer solutions (ignorance, improvisation and silence) which the reader is prevented from emulating; and to have done so by means of this citational relationship to discourse, which the reader is encouraged to perceive, but which also eludes his or her compulsion to imitate it.

4

THE SPEAKING OF THE QUOTED WORD: AUTHORS, IRONIES AND EPIGRAPHS

J'ai une maladie: je *vois* le langage.

Barthes, Roland Barthes

The authorial voice

In negotiating the *déjà-dit*, Stendhal is forced to take a different path in *Le Rouge* from the one traced by its various characters, and, as I have suggested, one of the more significant paths that he follows is that of citation. Unlike Flaubert, however, Stendhal does not offload all citational uses of language on to others by adopting the silence of authorial impersonality for himself. Nor does he figure his author as an objective recorder of history, placed outside the world he is recording, as Balzac does. Stendhal's author is in the world whereof he speaks, since in the Stendhalian scheme of things it would be hypocritical (as well as impossible) to claim to be outside it.

In Stendhal's view, the only way to use language is to use it in the forms in which it is already spoken. As he says in *Racine et Shakespeare*, 'Il ne faut pas innover dans la langue parce que la langue est une chose de convention' (p. 188). The proper use of language requires the same 'naturel' that is indispensable to authentic forms of passion. The first reason why 'le naturel' is essential to language is that without it speakers become unintelligible: 'Cette chose que voilà s'appelle une *table*; la belle invention si je me mets à l'appeler une *asphocèle*' (*ibid.*). The second is that, without it, language becomes hypocritical. Inventing a new phrase instead of using the perfectly clear and serviceable ones that are already to be found in La Bruyère or Pascal, for example, is the sort of thing that one might expect of a Mme de Staël or a Chateaubriand, a sign of laziness on the part of an author, and a flashy device which offers 'le moyen de faire passer des idées communes ou trop usées' (p. 189). Just as the Wertheran lover discovers novelty by remaining within the lover's code, so the writer, if he has anything worth saying, must remain within the existing linguistic conventions in order to say it. The example of Mathilde as well as that of Don Juan reveals how those who seek originality through an attempted departure from convention at one level are inevitably reclaimed by it at another.

Stendhal therefore acknowledges the necessity of using language as it is already spoken by foregrounding a speaking author in a quite unmistakeable way. This loquacious presence imposes itself upon the reader from the very first line as the author shows him around Verrières, and constantly volunteers his personal opinions about the characters and events portrayed in the narrative. Indeed, the illusion of this presence is so strong that, despite the many contradictions and inconsistencies within this authorial voice, a great many critics have devoted the majority of their efforts to identifying and characterising the personality that lies behind it.

They have come to a variety of conclusions. Georges Blin has found that Stendhal is constantly trying to upstage his characters by imposing his presence on the reader. Victor Brombert sees these authorial intrusions (to use Blin's famous phrase) as a polemical challenge on Stendhal's part to the reigning ideology of his day. Grahame Jones views them as evidence of Stendhal's mixed feelings towards his heroes, whose youthful sublimity inspires him in his older years with both admiration and jealousy. And Jean Starobinski regards all the talk in the novels as a mere front, behind which he finds a vulnerable Stendhal trying to avoid having to confront other people.[1] Whatever the specific interpretation of it, this Stendhalian loquacity seems to be enough to have prompted a search for a human origin, and to have produced a set of characterised personalities with coherent political or psychological axes to grind.

Of course, as Wayne Booth has indicated in his *Rhetoric of Fiction*,[2] even showing is a kind of telling and all texts have an implied author behind them; but there is, all the same, something particularly striking and seductive about the forms that overt telling and direct address can take in fiction. Not only does direct address serve to buttonhole the reader and immediately compel her attention, but it also seems, more than any other narratorial mode, to incite a search for the person behind it. In Stendhal's case, this search has its own peculiar ironies, since 'Stendhal' is only one of the hundred or so pseudonyms to which he had recourse during his life; and, moreover, appended to *Le Rouge*, it no longer even refers to the sharply characterised Prussian officer persona who claimed authorship of *Rome, Naples et Florence*. Stripped of its psychological content, the name attached to *Le Rouge* becomes 'pure signature', as Geneviève

Mouillaud puts it;[3] so that, despite the seductiveness of an apparent presence in the text, one must be alert to the possibility that it has no guaranteed human origin to whom one could attribute its workings and peculiar characteristics.

Another problem in this approach comes from trying to draw the line at which the telling stops. For *Le Rouge* is a novel with many voices and it is not always possible to say with certainty which of them belong to the telling of the author. The text is comprised of a variety of different modes of narration. At the base, so to speak, is a traditional kind of straight 'showing', to which the various forms of telling are often a form of reaction and response. The authorial voice quite frequently falls silent and withdraws completely from the narrative of events, and, as I have already demonstrated, perhaps nowhere more crucially or more significantly than during the shooting episode. The chapter which follows immediately after the shooting itself begins in just such a purely impersonal mode:

Julien resta immobile, il ne voyait plus. Quand il revint un peu à lui, il aperçut tous les fidèles qui s'enfuyaient de l'église; le prêtre avait quitté l'autel. Julien se mit à suivre d'un pas assez lent quelques femmes qui s'en allaient en criant. Une femme qui voulait fuir plus vite que les autres le poussa rudement, il tomba. (p. 433)

Here the sequence of events is given without comment, interpretation or evaluation. Stendhal himself called this kind of straightforward impersonal narrative 'raconter narrativement',[4] and it is evident that, unlike Sterne or Diderot, he did not impose his own voice on his narrative at the expense of the development of that narrative, and his 'telling' is largely confined to the form of discursive response. It is a kind of chatty commentary, appended to an impersonal narrative of events rather than a substitute for it — hence the use of the term 'intrusion' that Blin coined to describe the authorial discourse of Stendhal's fiction. A good example of this kind of authorial intrusion comes at the end of the following extract:

Julien, étonné de n'être pas battu, se hâta de partir. Mais à peine hors de la vue de son terrible père, il ralentit le pas. Il jugea qu'il serait utile à son hypocrisie d'aller faire une station à l'église.

Ce mot vous surprend? (p. 22, my italics)

The author steps back from the narrative, doubly distancing himself from it in order to comment not only on the actions it describes but also on the very words it uses.

The tone of these intrusions can vary enormously; they range from the quirky and partial to the assured and authoritative, and from the trustworthy to the totally unreliable. An instance of the quirky would be the comment made about the plane trees along the Cours de la Fidélité in Verrières:

Je ne trouve, quant à moi, qu'une chose à reprendre au COURS DE LA FIDÉLITÉ: ... ce que je reprocherais au Cours de la Fidélité, c'est la manière barbare dont l'autorité fait tailler et tondre jusqu'au vif ces vigoureux platanes. Au lieu de ressembler par leurs têtes basses, rondes et aplaties, à la plus vulgaire des plantes potagères, ils ne demanderaient pas mieux que d'avoir ces formes magnifiques qu'on leur voit en Angleterre.   (p. 8)

There is nothing here to suggest that Stendhal is feigning the opinions expressed and, indeed, his abhorrence for pruned plane trees is documented in *Henry Brulard*; but it is the modest and considerate 'quant à moi', which suggests that this is a purely personal and possibly idiosyncratic opinion, to which his readers should not necessarily feel themselves bound.

There are not many fully authoritative authorial statements in the text, but there are nevertheless some instances of the type of utterance on which the fiction of Balzac (as the supreme example) is so heavily reliant. These statements are delivered without the usual, characteristically Stendhalian hedges and disclaimers and their apparent trustworthiness derives from their being both apposite to the events of the narrative and in accordance with the broad scheme of values of the Stendhalian universe. The following example would seem to conform to these principles:

Une ou deux fois, durant cette grande scène, Mme de Rênal fut sur le point d'éprouver quelque sympathie pour le malheur fort réel de cet homme, qui pendant douze ans avait été son ami. *Mais les vraies passions sont égoïstes.*
                                                             (p. 128, my italics)

The 'truth' about the selfishness of passion illuminates both Mme de Rênal's behaviour on this specific occasion and also other actions involving true passions. And as if to confirm the truth of this statement, the point is made again at the beginning of part II: 'Toute vraie passion ne songe qu'à elle', writes Stendhal in his account of Julien's emotional pilgrimage to Malmaison (p. 223).

None the less, these general truths are a fairly rare occurrence in Stendhal's fiction and, for every apparently genuine and reliable statement, there are as many (if not more) equally authoritative but quite untrustworthy ones. When Julien is invited to dinner at the Valenods and makes such an impression on the guests with his ability to recite and translate *extempore* from the New Testament, he rises to leave at the end of the evening, and the author comments: 'tout le monde se leva malgré le décorum; *tel est l'empire du génie*' (p. 135, my italics). This remark is presumably not to be taken at face value, first because the Valenod milieu has been fairly thoroughly discredited, so that their admiration must count for very little, and second because Julien's ability to recite by heart is not one of the virtues that the reader is encouraged to admire elsewhere in the novel. 'Tel est l'empire du génie' does not constitute one of the principles of the type that Balzac is constantly deriving from his representation of the characters and society of his novels, and which, as can be seen from the previous example, Stendhal is, on occasion, also capable of producing.

The majority of Stendhal's so-called ironic interventions are of the partial, personal kind. These intrusions are effected by inserting a 'j'avoue que' (or some such phrase), by which Stendhal both dissociates himself from his own narrative and softens the force of the criticism being made. Such is the case with: 'J'avoue que la faiblesse dont Julien fait preuve dans ce monologue me donne une pauvre opinion de lui' (p. 134), an intrusion which also occurs during the Valenod episode. The author's opinions are marginalised in this way, and do not command the belief and assent of the reader – particularly as Julien's feelings on this occasion, far from being a sign of weakness, seem fully justified by the callous way in which Valenod has treated the inmates of the workhouse. In other words, this form of authorial comment opens up a slightly unnerving gap between the asserted values of the author and the implied values of the narrative.

The same sort of effect is produced by Stendhal's adoption of a kind of *style indirect libre* narration where he endorses the character's perspective without any hint as to whether the character in question is right or wrong, should be approved or disapproved of by the reader. In the case of the following example, information from parts of the narrative unknown to Mme de Rênal serves to cast doubt on the value of her 'proof' (Julien has asked her to retrieve the portrait from inside his mattress):

la pauvre femme avait eu la preuve, dans cette journée fatale, que l'homme qu'elle adorait sans se l'avouer aimait ailleurs. (p. 62)

But, in the case of the following, it is virtually impossible to tell whether Julien is right or wrong:

Pour que rien absolument ne manquât à son malheur, il y eut des moments où à force de s'occuper des sentiments qu'elle avait éprouvés une fois pour M. de Caylus, Mathilde en vint à parler de lui comme si elle l'aimait actuellement.

97

Certainement il y avait de l'amour dans son accent, Julien le voyait nettement.
(p. 336, my italics)

Mathilde may be deceiving herself as much as she is deceiving Julien, and Julien may be right in seeing signs that she loves M. de Caylus, but as long as there is no voice of authority to clarify these uncertainties there is no ultimate security of meaning. Stendhal's extensive use of interior monologue is a further device for producing the same effects, since it also creates an impression of loquacity (albeit that of character rather than of author), combined with the possibility of evading authorial endorsement. The second part of *Le Rouge* has a very high proportion of interior monologue, through which a large amount of narrative information is conveyed to the reader, but which, without authorial imprimatur, cannot be regarded as totally reliable.

In Stendhal's fiction, then, there is no sure distinction between the 'shown' voices of *style indirect libre* and interior monologue on the one hand, and the 'telling' voice of the narration on the other, since both are prone to error. The voice that speaks of Julien's 'weakness' is no more reliable than the voice of Mme de Rênal when she thinks she has 'proof' that Julien loves another. In the discursive hierarchy of the narration there is no single level that can be relied upon as a source of truth. This is because in the Stendhalian novel truth is such a vulnerable thing. The example of Mathilde shows that 'truths' are always susceptible to a loss of veracity, and that the truth-value of any statement depends more on the attitude of its speaker than on its actual content. This, at any rate, seems to be the drift of the advice that Stendhal gave in a letter to his sister Pauline: 'Quand un homme te parle, fais-toi avant tout ces questions: 1. Quel intérêt a-t-il à te parler? 2. Quel intérêt a-t-il à te parler dans ce sens? Ne le crois que quand il a intérêt à te dire la vérité' (*Correspondance*, I, p. 129). Motive is all, and the novels take the brotherly lesson a stage further by teaching one to suspect the motives even of those who are telling the truth. In reading Stendhal's novels, the main question is not 'qui parle?', but what are his or her motives for saying it? How seriously does he or she mean it? And the author himself is not exempt from this interrogation.

Bathmologies

These questions affect and potentially undermine nearly every sentence of the Stendhalian novel. In reading, one is never sure how far any utterance is endorsed and how far it is purely citational.

For Stendhal is a past-master of the art that Barthes calls 'bathmology', i.e. the play of the various degrees of involvement or distance from one's own language and utterances.[5] As a writer Stendhal is always at one (or more) removes from his utterances, and seems to make a point of suggesting that he never speaks in his own voice or with full intentionality. Indeed, he shows himself highly suspicious of writers who try too hard to speak in their own voice and endorse their utterances. It was a trait he called 'emphase' and it was the reason why he disliked the works of Racine, Voltaire, Mme de Staël, and most particularly Chateaubriand (whom he nicknamed Castelfugens on account of his tendency towards *emphase*). These would-be innovators in language unwittingly demonstrate that the attempt to charge one's utterances with the full weight of one's own intending presence leads to a kind of linguistic inflation, or what Stendhal called hypocrisy. It is exemplified by the Parisian habit of saying '*coursier* au lieu de *cheval*' (*Henry Brulard*, p. 798), a variant on the hypocritical temptation to use the word 'asphocèle' when speaking of a table. Mme Grandet in *Lucien Leuwen* is the arch-exponent of this *emphase*, having a 'façon de parler toute sentimentale et toute d'émotion', which leads her always to call Paris '*cette ville immense*' and never simply 'Paris' (p. 1332). It is this 'façon de parler' that leads Stendhal to accuse her of hypocrisy and lack of any 'romanesque'. By contrast, the most novelistic character in the novel is Mme de Chasteller, who never says what she thinks or feels, and whose *modus operandi* is largely clandestine and deceitful. She represents the counterpart to the curious Stendhalian equation whereby an endorsed 'sincere' utterance necessarily becomes a hypocritical one, as if the greater the intentional force behind it, the more vacuous the end-product.

But even unemphatic sincerity is open to abuse and falsification, for moments of truth and sincerity can be cancelled at a stroke simply by the introduction of quotation marks. When Julien upsets Mme de Rênal by inadvertently letting slip an admiring remark about Napoleon ('Ah! s'écria-t-il, que Napoléon était bien l'homme envoyé de Dieu pour les jeunes Français! qui le remplacera?', etc., p. 89), he is able to restore his position in her eyes at once by claiming that he was merely quoting:

Il eut assez de présence d'esprit pour arranger sa phrase et faire entendre à la noble dame, assise si près de lui sur le banc de verdure, que les mots qu'il venait de répéter, il les avait entendus pendant son voyage chez son ami le marchand de bois. C'était le raisonnement des impies.

This strategy means that a speaker can always avoid being called to account for anything he might have said. Julien resorts to it again, later in the novel, when he gets carried away in describing his despair to Mathilde. Although Stendhal writes: 'Il lui peignit avec ces couleurs vraies *qu'on n'invente point* l'excès de son désespoir d'alors' (my italics), the colours of truth and the accents of sincerity are conjured away in an instant as Julien comes to his senses and realises that the truth is a very bad strategy in courting Mathilde. He apologises for having '[fait] des phrases pour [lui] plaire', and there is no reason for Mathilde not to believe him when he says: 'Je les ai composées autrefois pour une femme qui m'aimait et m'ennuyait' (p. 410). Whatever Stendhal may say here about the unmistakeable colour of truth, there is in fact no truth in his world that is exempt from bathmological falsification of this kind.

Just as there can be no safeguard for truth, there can be no question, either, of finding the right kind of language for being truthful or sincere. All language is vulnerable to this kind of citational emptying out, as Stendhal himself discovered in the case of the apparently ideal language of mathematics. The appeal of mathematics was originally that it was seemingly resistant to the inflation and hypocrisy of *emphase*, since it precludes the possibility of substituting words like *coursier* for words like *cheval*. But it proves in its way also to be open to the abuses of citation when Brulard discovers that, instead of giving proper explanations for things, the language of mathematics is capable of being parrotted like 'une recette d'apothicaire tombé du ciel pour résoudre les équations' (*Henry Brulard*, p. 861). It turns out that it is possible to utter mathematical truths without either meaning them or even understanding them. The discourse of the 'romanesque' cannot, therefore, consist of writing mathematically, any more than it can consist of writing innovatively or sincerely.

The example of the novels themselves would suggest that the solution lies in a wholehearted adoption of the citational. The voices which Stendhal uses in his fiction are all more or less borrowed, their utterances all more or less placed between quotation marks at varying degrees of distance from any supposed centre of truth or authority. What saves the Stendhalian novel from hypocrisy is its use of hypocrisy as an orchestrated component of its polyphony. It does not have the uniform tone of *emphase*, but is constituted by the discontinuous juxtaposition of a whole variety of different voices and discourses. This results in the 'style hâché' which Stendhal later thought he had perhaps overdone; but in *Henry Brulard* he specifically defends it as a reaction against 'les phrases nombreuses et prétentieuses de MM. Chateaubriand et Salvandy', which he dismisses as 'fatras hypocrites' (p. 745). Although Balzac reproached Stendhal for what he saw as his crude syntax (a charge which Stendhal rejected),[6] the 'hâché' effect of the style is tonal or discursive rather than syntactic; and it derives above all from the disparity between the various voices heard in the text as it constantly shifts register from one to another. It is this unevenness that saves the text from hypocrisy, for the characteristic mark of the hypocrite is uniformity. In *Lucien Leuwen* Stendhal describes 'égalité de caractère' as 'le chef-d'œuvre de cette hypocrisie que l'on appelle aujourd'hui: une éducation parfaite' (p. 1362). It is the Parisians who best exemplify this trait ('qui laisse un fond d'incurable sécheresse dans l'âme qui la pratique'), and Lucien who is the character most prone to 'inégalité'. In *Le Rouge*, even Mme de Rênal's character is only *'en apparence fort égal'*,[7] and Julien, apart from having an obviously uneven temperament (and perhaps nowhere more so than during the shooting episode), seems to incarnate the text's principle of deliberately adopted mask and hypocrisy.

Thanks to the effects of its discordant voices, then, the linguistic texture of Stendhal's novel is anything but smooth: and this impression is heightened by a compositional strategy that refuses to hierarchise the component perspectives of narration in any ascending order of authority, and prefers to juxtapose them. In this Stendhal is quite different from a Balzac whose authorial comments tend to continue and extend the utterances of characters in order to bring out their full implications. But he differs equally from a Flaubert whose whole stylistic effort goes into producing an insidious blurring of voices, a sinuous interweaving of perspectives designed to make the question 'qui parle?' impossible to answer. In Stendhal, it is usually possible to decide who is speaking; what is less easy is to decide whether the speaker really means what s/he says. Each voice comes from a perspective whose limitations are stressed rather than dissolved by the introduction of a second or even a third perspective. A new one always serves to relativise the first, so that the novel's composition as a whole resembles the metaphor that Stendhal uses in the 'Avant-propos' to *Armance*:

Si l'on demandait des nouvelles du jardin des Tuileries aux tourterelles qui soupirent au faîte des grands arbres, elles diraient: C'est une immense plaine de verdure, où l'on jouit de la plus vive clarté. Nous, promeneurs, nous répondrions: C'est une promenade délicieuse et sombre où l'on est à l'abri de la chaleur, et surtout du grand jour désolant en été. (p. 25)

The open, sunny perspective of the doves is limited by and opposed to the shady prospect of the strollers down below; neither can include or accommodate the other, and there is, moreover, no third perspective capable of embracing them both as continuous.

In *Le Rouge* these relativising juxtapositions are used with a variety of different effects. There are the gently comic effects of Julien's and Mme de Rênal's mutual misunderstandings, as illustrated by the following:

> En prononçant la parole *si bien nés* (c'était un de ces mots aristocratiques que Julien avait appris depuis peu), il s'anima d'un profond sentiment d'anti-sympathie.
>
> Aux yeux de cette femme, moi, se disait-il, je ne suis pas bien né.
>
> Mme de Rênal, en l'écoutant, admirait son génie, sa beauté, elle avait le cœur percé de la possibilité de départ qu'il lui faisait entrevoir.   (p. 73)

The narrative commentary seems to undermine Julien's views (and not to explain or interpret them) by introducing Mme de Rênal's totally unrelated view. In this case it is the two perspectives of the characters that are set at odds. On other occasions it is the perspectives of two different milieux that are brought into conflict, sometimes through the agency of character and sometimes through the agency of narrative discourse. In the following example Julien's point of view is used to relativise the provincial outlook represented in the social gatherings of the Rênal household:

> Une action lui semblait-elle admirable, c'était celle-là précisément qui attirait le blâme des gens qui l'environnaient. Sa réplique intérieure était toujours: Quels monstres ou quels sots!

But on this occasion Julien's own debunking perspective is in turn debunked by the further perspective introduced by the narrator: 'Le plaisant, avec tant d'orgueil, c'est que souvent il ne comprenait absolument rien à ce dont on parlait' (p. 40).

The process is endless, because there is no viewpoint which is not potentially subject to further limitations of this kind. This is implicit in a remark made about Julien's state of terror when he arrives at the seminary and waits for Pirard to speak to him. Stendhal, quite characteristically, delegates the commentary to a third party (here a hypothetical 'philosophe'):

> Un philosophe eût dit, *peut-être en se trompant*: c'est la violente impression du laid sur une âme faite pour aimer ce qui est beau.   (p. 161, my italics)

There seems no reason to quarrel with the philosopher's explanation of Julien's terror (Julien is indeed extremely sensitive to the beauty of his mistresses), yet Stendhal deliberately introduces the possibility that this thoughtful philosopher could be wrong, thus putting the reader on her guard against taking any interpretation too seriously.

On occasion even the novel in its entirety, as a potential perspective in its own right, is relativised by being set against other, hypothetical alternatives that it might have adopted or which might be preferred to it. It acknowledges its own limited specificity by emphasising the differences between the course taken by its events or the peculiarity of its characters and events and characters under other circumstances and in other kinds of novelistic discourse:

Si [Mme de Rênal] eût possédé un peu de ce savoir-vivre dont une femme de trente ans jouit depuis longtemps dans les pays plus civilisés, elle eût frémi pour la durée d'un amour qui ne semblait vivre que de surprise et de ravissement d'amour-propre; (pp. 86–7)

or:

A Paris, la position de Julien envers Mme de Rênal eût été bien vite simplifiée; mais à Paris, l'amour est fils des romans. Le jeune précepteur et sa timide maîtresse auraient retrouvé dans trois ou quatre romans, et jusque dans les couplets du Gymnase, l'éclaircissement de leur position. Les romans leur auraient tracé le rôle à jouer, montré le modèle à imiter; et ce modèle, tôt ou tard, et quoique sans nul plaisir, et peut-être en rechignant, la vanité eût forcé Julien à le suivre.

Dans une petite ville de l'Aveyron ou des Pyrénées, le moindre incident eût été rendu décisif par le feu du climat. Sous nos cieux plus sombres, un jeune homme pauvre, et qui n'est qu'ambitieux parce que la délicatesse de son cœur lui fait un besoin de quelques-unes des jouissances que donne l'argent, voit tout les jours une femme de trente ans, sincèrement sage, occupée de ses enfants, et qui ne prend nullement dans les romans des exemples de conduite. Tout va lentement, tout se fait peu à peu dans les provinces, il y a plus de naturel. (pp. 36–7)

Without the provincial setting of Franche-Comté (as opposed to Paris or the Pyrenees), and without the ignorance and inexperience of its heroine, *Le Rouge* would have told a different kind of story and been a different kind of novel, a worldly novel of seduction, whose discourse is drawn into this unworldly narrative on this occasion as if to bring Stendhal's text up against its own limits in a manner that effectively questions the extent of its own authority and hegemony. The same result is, of course, produced for the worldly novel, as the relativising process works in both directions: the limitations of the world view of the worldly novel are shown up by this indication of its inability to acknowledge, let alone understand, the character of

Mme de Rênal and the nature of the situation that has developed between her and Julien.

One can see Stendhal's so-called intrusions as a further instance of this sort of discursive conflict. In the critical literature these ironic authorial utterances of the type 'J'avoue que la faiblesse dont Julien fait preuve me donne une pauvre opinion de lui' have been variously attributed to Stendhal's fundamental timidity (Brombert), or to a masked authorial persona (Abeel),[8] – in any case, to some kind of authorial origin. But it is not the nature of the author which determines the style of these intrusions so much as the social environment in which the character (usually Julien in *Le Rouge*) happens to be in at the given stage of the narrative. They tend to occur most frequently when Julien finds himself up against the more hidebound and opinionated forms of society, notably at the Valenods, in the seminary and in the world of the Parisian salons. The intrusions are a way of ironically citing the opinions of that social world in the text so as to maximise the contrast between the outlook of that world and Julien's own. They are included not because they serve any authorial purpose, but because they provide a different viewpoint to be set against that of the character. The example just quoted comes from the episode describing the dinner at the Valenods, as does the following, which deals with Julien's response to Valenod's order to stop the singing in the workhouse: 'Par bonheur, personne ne remarqua son attendrissement *de mauvais ton*' (p. 133, my italics). It is only in the Valenods' eyes that Julien's sensibility could possibly be said to be bad form, and it is to a large extent by means of these ironic quotings that the views of the Valenods are represented in the text.

These ironies have no moral finality, no corrective intention, since, as I have shown, all truths, moral ones included, are vulnerable to invalidation by quotation. What the intrusions in the different episodes have in common is not, then, a consistent authorial point of view, but simply the fact that they use quotation to draw attention to the values of the world being described and to provide a contrasting point of reference for the views held by the character in question. Their value lies in this contrast and not in their content. The important thing, then, is not to try and reconstruct from these ironies what Stendhal might 'really' have meant, but to recognise in them an instance of his speaking the language of the enemy. For, as Vladimir Jankélévitch points out in his study of irony, the ironist proceeds largely by quotation: 'L'ironiste fait semblant de jouer le jeu de son ennemi, parle son langage, rit bruyamment de ses bons mots, surenchérit en toute occasion sur sa sagesse soufflée, ses ridicules et ses manies.'[9] This would explain why Julien is accused of bad form during the Valenod episode, but of presumption in the seminary:

Toutes les premières démarches de notre héros qui se croyait si prudent furent, comme le choix d'un confesseur, des étourderies. Egaré par toute la présomption d'un homme à imagination, il prenait ses intentions pour des faits, et se croyait un hypocrite consommé.   (p. 168)

(The same charge is made again some twenty pages later.) The language of the seminary is introduced in counterpoint to Julien's perspective so that 'imagination' and 'presumption' refuse to settle into harmony in the sentence given, and continue to jostle and clash in such a way as to keep the two perspectives perpetually at odds. The ironic intrusions during this section oi the novel are mainly written in the language of the seminary, wnich Stendhal invokes as such when he describes the mysterious arrival of 500 francs for Julien as a 'miracle' (p. 192). And indeed, to judge by the placing of Stendhal's approving comment in the margin of the Civita-Vecchia copy of the text at this point – 'Very well le séminaire' – it is quite probable that his achievement in rendering that Jesuitical discourse was what delighted him above all in this episode of the novel, and that this kind of citational irony was one of the major effects he was aiming at.

In the Parisian section the accusation changes again, and Julien is condemned neither for bad form, nor for presumption, but for being ridiculous – the supreme failing in the eyes of Parisian society: 'Nous passons sous silence une foule de petites aventures qui eussent donné des ridicules à Julien, s'il n'eût pas été en quelque sorte au-dessous du ridicule. Une sensibilité folle lui faisait commettre des milliers de gaucheries' (p. 253). Although the charge is soon dropped (Julien does not take long to learn to conceal his 'sensibilité folle' and to avoid 'gaucherie'), the fact that it is framed in terms of 'le ridicule' reveals it to be of Parisian rather than personal, Stendhalian origin. And if Julien is reckoned to be finally beneath ridicule, it is because he is beneath the notice of the aristocratic society that frequents the salon. Once again, the perspective that values 'sensibilité' clashes with one that is concerned only with social style and conformity within the framework of what otherwise appears to be a single authorial utterance. The earlier complaints about bad form (made at the Valenods') and presumption (made at the seminary) are forgotten because they are not relevant to a Parisian scheme of things. This scheme is implicit too in the ironic intrusions concerning Mathilde. She is criticised for lack of prudence in her actions and for lack of delicacy in her speech (p. 294), in short, for being unladylike. This reproach, coupled with the rather indulgent tone in which it is made ('Nous avouerons avec peine, car nous aimons Mathilde …', p. 293), only makes sense in a Parisian milieu which likes its ladies ladylike but has enough snobbery to be prepared to make allowances for the daughter of the Marquis de La Mole.

These languages of the enemy are introduced in the novel under the apparent aegis of the author, but they are always opposed to a differing view (one that takes positive account of imagination or sensibility, for instance) which prevents them from receiving full credence. Where two opposing views are contained within a single sentence (as with 'présomption'/'imagination' and 'ridicule'/'sensibilité folle'), it is clear how the contradiction serves to create a quotation mark effect around the enemy language. Consider two further examples:

Mais l'adresse dont nous lui reprochons l'absence aurait exclu le mouvement sublime de saisir l'épée qui, dans ce moment, le rendait si joli aux yeux de Mlle de La Mole   (p. 334)

and:

[Julien] était mortellement dégoûté de toutes ses bonnes qualités, de toutes les choses qu'il avait aimées avec enthousiasme; et dans cet état d'*imagination renversée*, il entreprenait de juger la vie avec son imagination. Cette erreur est d'un homme supérieur.   (p. 343, Stendhal's italics)

The reproach concerning Julien's lack of style is incompatible with the admiration for his 'mouvement sublime', and so must not be read as entirely serious. Similarly, the acknowledgement of Julien's superiority is incompatible with the charge of error, which has thus to be perceived as an instance of the discourse of another.

The bathmological organisation of the novel means, however, that one is dealing with degrees of quotedness, and not with a simple opposition between true and false statements. In these contradictions one element is only more quoted than the others: on this particular occasion 'erreur' is more citational than 'supérieur', but both voices heard in this sentence are more spoken than speaking. Stendhal's sensitivity to the discourse of the other leads him to produce fiction where things are not simply represented, but also made to speak. The characters and worlds of Stendhal's novels may be seen, but must, above all, be heard. In his essay on Walter Scott and *La Princesse de Clèves*, Stendhal writes: 'il est infiniment moins difficile de décrire d'une façon pittoresque le costume d'un personnage, que de dire ce qu'il sent, et de *le faire parler*' (*Mélanges II: Journalisme*, p. 222, my italics). This remark tellingly points to a major concern of the novel he was working on at the time (*Le Rouge*) and explains incidentally why he dares leave the reader in such a state of ignorance concerning the dresses of its two heroines. Stendhal only fails to indicate that it is not just the characters but whole societies (provincial, religious, Parisian) that are made to speak. The dreary architecture and furniture that deck out the fifteenth-century world of Walter Scott is replaced by a nineteenth-century world that is defined by its speech more than by its material effects and possessions, and whose *doxa* becomes audible through Stendhal's special brand of polyphonic ventriloquism.

It is this ventriloquism that constitutes the pervasive irony of Stendhal's fiction, and not any particular set of opinions or psychological obsessions that he might have had. The best exponent of this kind of irony within the novels themselves is Leuwen *père*, who never expresses himself directly, never says what he means, and indeed never has anything that he means to say. As he remarks to his wife, '[si] ce ministère, qui ne bat plus que d'une aile, vient à tomber, je ne saurai plus que dire, car enfin, je n'ai d'opinion sur rien, et certainement, à mon âge, je n'irai pas étudier pour m'en former une' (*Lucien Leuwen*, p. 1311). Stendhal writes like M. Leuwen speaks, 'comme dans un salon', that is to say, without any intentional seriousness whatsoever.[10] M. Leuwen's famous irony is entirely contentless, and it is this contentlessness that makes it both such an infernal and such a gay phenomenon. In Mme Leuwen's salon the rules that govern behaviour in the de La Mole salon are turned on their head. Whereas in the one 'il n'était convenable de plaisanter de rien' (*Le Rouge*, p. 290), in the 'salon horriblement méchant de madame Leuwen ... tout le monde se moquait de tout le monde, tant pis pour les sots et pour les hypocrites qui n'avaient pas infiniment d'esprit. Les titres de duc, de pair de France, de colonel de la garde nationale, comme l'avait éprouvé M. Grandet, n'y mettaient personne à l'abri de l'ironie la plus gaie' (*Lucien Leuwen*, p. 1175). If there were any axe to grind, the irony would, paradoxically, lose its edge. Its efficacy consists precisely in its lack of seriousness. Du Poirier describes Leuwen as 'un homme de plaisir et d'esprit, dominé par ce penchant infernal, le plus grand ennemi du trône et de l'autel: *l'ironie*' (p. 1038), suggesting thereby that political and ideological opposition is at its most effective when it lacks political and ideological seriousness. Stendhal's irony may well have a political dimension, but if so it is thanks to the absence of overt political purpose, thanks to its gay citationality. The novel is like a kind of salon where, under the régime of the ironic, all languages are treated as enemy languages and stripped of their seriousness in this process of non-purposive quotation. The all-pervading impression of loquacity in the novels derives ultimately from its being the equivalent of a witty conversation in a salon – not from any authorial speaking voice, but from the spoken voices of the worlds and characters it represents.

Epigraphs

In *Le Rouge et le Noir* this citational play with the discourse of the other is carried on not only within the text itself, but also in the epigraphs which accompany it. Each part and each chapter (save for the last four) is introduced with some kind of an epigraph. Their use was current fashion in the literature of the early part of the nineteenth century,[11] but the citational practice that their presence implies must have had a particular appeal for Stendhal. Antoine Compagnon, in his book on quotation, has called the epigraph 'la citation par excellence',[12] and in Stendhal's deployment of them his citational habits are exercised with special and characteristic force.

The epigraph is conventionally used in the serious manner that befits its original function as an inscription on a monument. Its solemn, lapidary quality tends to make of it a particularly authoritative form of quotation. Compagnon distinguishes between quotations that are re-enunciations and those that are denunciations (p.55), and the epigraph generally represents an exemplary form of re-enunciation, where the original statement is fully endorsed and retains its full authority. This is the case with the epigraph to *Anna Karenina*, 'Vengeance is mine. I will repay', which authoritatively orientates and guides the reading and interpretation of the whole text and which itself remains subservient to the authority of the original text quoted (the Bible). Compagnon calls this subservience to the quoted text 'allégation', and he contrasts it to plain 'citation' where the quoted text is enclosed within and wholly dominated by the quoting text.[13] The Bible is, of course, the supreme authoritative text and the one most likely to retain authority in its cited manifestations.

The texts cited by Stendhal in his epigraphs do not include the Bible, nor indeed any of the authoritative texts of his culture. Lacking any inherent authority, they are therefore instances of *citation* as opposed to *allégation*. The question is only whether they are re-enunciations or denunciations. The repertoire of authors invoked by Stendhal in his epigraphs is not particularly venerable. The great majority are contemporary or recent: Byron, Mérimée, Musset, Schiller, Sainte-Beuve, Jean-Paul, and Shakespeare, who may be counted among this number as a new, Romantic discovery. Others were near enough in time to Stendhal for their dates actually or nearly to overlap: Diderot (d. 1784, a year after Stendhal's birth), Beaumarchais (d. 1799), Sterne (d. 1768), Young (d. 1765), Kant (d. 1804), and Mozart (d. 1791). In other words, they all lack the temporal distance that would make them respectable sources of quotation in the 1820s and 1830s. Other epigraphs are attributed to the lowly and ephemeral press (*Le Précurseur*, *The Edinburgh Review* and *Le Globe*), and yet others to various of Stendhal's acquaintances, none of whom had any outstanding distinction: Strombeck, Polidori, Bertolotti and Pellico. More distinguished, but political rather than literary, figures whom Stendhal quotes include Napoleon and Danton, and Stendhal's Grenoblois compatriot Barnave (who was appointed president of the Constituent Assembly during the Revolution and guillotined in 1793). But distinguished though they may be in retrospect, in 1830 their prestige is likely to have been less than minimal among a readership many of whom feared nothing more than a recurrence of the events of 1789. All in all, then, Stendhal's repertory of authors is unlikely to have commanded the respect and assent of the readers of his day.

Added to this, for a reader who shared Stendhal's reading repertoire, the unreliability of the attributions would probably have been extremely disconcerting. Of the seventy-three epigraphs in the novel, only fifteen are correctly attributed. Moreover, of these fifteen, two are inaccurately reproduced.[14] The disjunction between text and author that occurs in the misattributions of the majority of the epigraphs strips them even further of any of the genre's traditional authority, and so makes them doubly citational: these authors are themselves presented as speaking the language of another – although who that other actually is remains in most cases a mystery.

Aside from the problem of authorial authority in the epigraphs, there is also the question of the content of these quotations. By tradition, an epigraph is a weighty affair, concerned with big (abstract and moral) issues which help to organise the themes and interpretation of the text in question. The reference to divine punishment in *Anna Karenina* does precisely this by raising the question of moral responsibility and suggesting a distinction between divine and social justice. The opening epigraph of *Le Rouge* which heads the first volume would seem, on the face of it, to have the range and depth of significance that would conventionally be expected of it: 'La vérité, l'âpre vérité'. Though it is attributed to Danton (and falsely so), it appears to make explicit the veridical implications of the novel's subtitle 'Chronique de 1830'. However, whether or not one is disconcerted by the 'avertissement de l'éditeur' which suggests that this chronicle of 1830 was in fact written in 1827, the precise nature of the truth to be told in the novel is not always clear, and indeed, as I have already argued, truth of any kind in Stendhal's text is an extremely elusive and problematic entity. The epigraph to part II (also fictitious and falsely attributed – in this instance to Sainte-Beuve) seems, in contrast, to deal with a rather trivial topic: 'Elle n'est pas jolie, elle n'a point de rouge.' Nevertheless, given the novel's pre-occupations with vanity, hypocrisy and various forms of mask and disguise, and given too the possible echo of the novel's mysterious title ('point de *rouge*'), it could be invested with more seriousness and read as an indication of the novel's recurrent themes and major concerns. But as a moral guide, it seems a little untrustworthy. Is the reader really being asked to believe in the necessity of masks? And how can it be squared with the apparently contradictory epigraph placed at the head of part I, chapter 14: 'Une jeune fille de seize ans avait un teint de rose, et elle mettait du rouge' (attributed here to Polidori and also fictitious)? This contradiction would seem to suggest that the epigraphs are not, after all, the most reliable moral or interpretative guides to the text.

However, moral guidance was not, apparently, what Stendhal wanted from his epigraphs. A note written in March 1830 says: 'L'épigraphe doit augmenter la sensation, l'émotion du lecteur, si émotion il peut y avoir, et non plus présenter un jugement plus ou moins philosophique sur la situation.'[15] In other words, Stendhal's epigraphs are not designed to compensate for the failure of his authorial persona to provide a reliable interpretative commentary or a moral and philosophical judgement concerning his narrative. Rather, their purpose seems to be primarily diegetic, pointing, like a title, to events and situations to be narrated in the ensuing chapter.[16] In the case of the epigraph to chapter 14 the reference to rouge would seem to point to the unnecessary contorsions Julien puts himself through in his attempt to seduce a woman who in fact prefers his candour to his artifice, and, moreover, had been struck at their first meeting by 'la beauté du teint ... de Julien' (p. 27). The contradictory epigraph at the beginning of part II could, by the same logic, be read as referring to Julien's situation as he enters the world of Parisian society for the first time. By the second chapter of part II it is clear that unless Julien does something about his inelegant provincial ways, he has no hope of making any headway with his social ambitions, and cannot even be of much use to his new employer. The twenty-four new shirts he is given, the promise of dancing lessons to

110

improve his deportment, fail to efface 'les manières gauches de ce jeune abbé' (p. 236), and are only the first stages in his acquisition of the necessary veneer (rouge) that Parisian society requires of its members. It is thus in Parisian eyes and in the Parisian situation that this second epigraph about rouge makes sense in the novel.

The great majority of the epigraphs are diegetically related to the text in this way, and their status is therefore not significantly superior to any of the sentences which constitute that text. There is even, on occasion, a kind of traffic between text and epigraph whereby assertions made in an epigraph are casually repeated in the text and vice versa. This is the case, for example, with the famous epigraph about the mirror: 'Un roman: c'est un miroir qu'on promène le long d'un chemin' (which is fictitious and falsely attributed to Saint-Réal). It appears at the head of chapter 14 of part I, where it has no obvious narrative relevance, but is then repeated in very similar form some 170 pages later as part of an authorial commentary which makes no reference either to its previous appearance in the epigraph or to its supposed origins in Saint-Réal: 'Eh, monsieur, un roman est un miroir qui se promène sur une grande route' (p. 342). The effect of this repetition is not so much to add weight and conviction to the opinions of the author by referring to a cited authority, but, on the contrary, to undermine whatever authority the utterance in its epigraphic form might have had. The same passage in the novel includes a discussion by the author concerning the importance of belonging to a coterie. He sums it up with a formula: 'Malheur à l'homme d'étude qui n'est d'aucune coterie' (p. 341), which is closely echoed in an epigraph that appears fifty pages later at the head of chapter 27: 'Des services! des talents! du mérite! bah! soyez d'une coterie.' This epigraph – perhaps needless to say by now – is quite fictitious and most improbably attributed to Fénelon's Télémaque.

These epigraphic utterances are thus largely re-enunciations of Stendhal's own novelistic discourse. But the effect is neither an unequivocal reaffirmation of it, nor a clear denunciation, but one that hovers between the two, since the form taken by this self-quoting strategy makes it impossible to decide whether the text quotes the epigraph or the epigraph the text. But either way the net result is a high degree of citationality all round – enough, in fact, to produce the most confusing bathmological giddiness. Nevertheless, assuming (for the sake of convenience) that the textual comment about coteries comes first, it is already highly citational in its position there, since it represents an instance of the discourse of the Parisian 'other', which has been introduced as a point of perspectival contrast to Mathilde's night of 'folie'. The epigraph thus quotes the authorial quoting of the Parisian discourse, and is then itself subject to a further degree of quotation through the ironic and highly implausible attribution to Télémaque ...

Stendhal seems, then, to be using his epigraphs as a means of undermining any authority that the authorial voice of the text might otherwise appear to have. Every level of the novel's narrative − be it authorial commentary, character's or milieu's point of view − can be picked out and subjected to this invalidating process of epigraphic citation, casting doubts on both the origins and the seriousness of every statement in the text. The whole strategy seems designed to enable Stendhal to follow Julien's example with Mme de Rênal and Mathilde, and simply opt out of any commitment to utterances for which he might be held responsible: by pleading quotation.

The impression of loquacity that emerges so strongly from Stendhal's fiction has certain implications for an understanding of the nature of his realism. In one sense all the talk is still centred around the silence of a passion that surpasses the saying and which − as the next chapter will show − only readerly reverie can render eloquent. But in another sense, the talk (as citation) becomes itself the major object of representation. It is clear that Stendhal was inclined to see the world not as an inventory of objects, but as an inventory of discourses. Where others, like Balzac, saw things, he heard voices; and, as the extract from the essay on Walter Scott shows, the task of representation consisted for him not in describing or cataloguing the physical world, but in making it speak.

5

THE USES OF READING

La difficulté n'est plus de trouver et de dire la vérité, mais de trouver qui la lise.

Stendhal, *Henry Brulard*

Stendhal's readers

Stendhal's conception of the literary tradition and the cultural context in which fiction is produced is one that gives particular prominence to readers: the expectations of readers are perceived as a conservative force always demanding more of the same from fiction, and so encouraging novelists merely to repeat what has been already said and already written in other novels. The 'Projet d'un article' that Stendhal wrote for *Le Rouge* shows him to be deeply aware of the constraints exerted by the reading tastes of French society in 1830 (or, strictly speaking 1832, since that is when he wrote it). The novel-reading public is sharpy characterised in the article, as are the material and social conditions under which contemporary readers read, and the demands that they expect reading to satisfy. By the way that he writes of these things Stendhal reveals that his overriding aim in *Le Rouge* had been to disengage as far as possible from the expectations and conventions liable to be imposed on him by his public. In particular, he implies that the success of his novel as mimesis is directly correlated with its ability to resist the formulaic representations which readers of fiction have come to expect and to desire. The *doxa* of their expectations threatens his novel both in the writing (he may be tempted to write too much in accordance with his readers' desires) and in the reading (his book may lend itself to being translated back into the terms which it was seeking to avoid); and for this reason (though also for others which will be discussed below) Stendhal's writing in the novel is marked from beginning to end by his awareness of his readers.

This awareness of the reader as other has already been discussed by a number of critics (Starobinski, Brombert, Jones), but these discussions have tended to concentrate on the psychological aspects

113

of Stendhal's sensitivity, and to view his writing as a kind of protective mask designed to defend him against potential attacks from this readership. The pseudonyms explored by Starobinski, and the irony analysed by Brombert and Jones are treated as means of counteracting the vulnerability that is entailed by the self-revelations of writing. This line of critical enquiry, profitable though it has proved to be in the hands of those who have used it (Brombert and Starobinski are among the finest of Stendhal's critics), fits uneasily with the sort of argument being developed in this book. It therefore seems to make more sense to treat this *other* as the agent of a certain perspective on the world and as the wielder of a certain discourse about it, whose effects on Stendhal's own perspective and writing can be just as threatening and potentially devastating as they have been taken to be to his psyche. In this chapter I shall be developing two strands of the argument already outlined in chapter 1 and shall seek to examine in more detail how, on the one hand, Stendhal constructs his writing in *Le Rouge* to anticipate and counter the *doxa* of his readership, and how, on the other, the reader is also shown to be vital to the operation of the novel's mimetic strategies.

Stendhal is placed in something of a double bind by the mimetic demands that he makes on his writing. The reader is essential to Stendhal's 'Chronique de 1830' because only he can vouch for its accuracy; but he is also an obstacle to its realisation because of the effects of his reading habits and fictional tastes. I say 'he' because Stendhal generally addresses the reader in *Le Rouge* on the assumption that he is dealing with a man ('Eh, *monsieur*, un roman est un miroir …' etc.), even though in the 'Projet' he identifies the two main components of the French reading public of 1830 in terms of a largely female readership. However, in his overall analysis of the reading public of 1830 the difference between men and women seems to matter less than the difference between Parisian and provincial. The differences in both geography and education between provincial and Parisian readers had led, in his view, to the production of two quite different types of novel – 'les romans pour les *femmes de chambre*' and 'le roman des salons' ('Projet', p. 714). The 'roman pour les femmes de chambre' has a different format from the Parisian one (twelvemo, as opposed to octavo), has a different publisher (Pigoreau as opposed to Levavasseur or Gosselin), has a far bigger audience ('avant la crise commerciale de 1831, [M. Pigoreau] avait gagné un demi-million à faire pleurer les beaux yeux de province'), and has its own specific conventions as regards both character and style ('le héros est toujours parfait et d'une beauté ravissante, fait *au tour* et avec de grands yeux à *fleur de tête*'). Typical authors of these novels are M. le baron de la Mothe-Langon, 'M.M. Paul de Kock, Victor Ducange, etc.', who are quite unknown in Paris since their many works are profoundly unsuited to Parisian tastes: 'Rien ne semble plus fade, à Paris, que ce héros toujours parfait, que ces femmes malheureuses, innocentes et persécutées, des romans de femmes de chambre.'[1] In contrast, the main aim of the Parisian author is 'le mérite littéraire', and this snobbery is fully matched by the attitudes of his readers.[2] Whereas 'les petites bourgeoises de province ne demandent à l'auteur que des scènes extraordinaires qui les mettent toutes en larmes; *peu importent les moyens* qui les amènent', the ladies of Paris are far more exacting on matters of *vraisemblance* and narrative coherence: 'Les dames de Paris ... qui consomment les romans in-8°, sont sévères en diable pour les événements *extra-ordinaires*. Dès qu'un événement a l'air d'être amené à point nommé pour faire briller le héros, elles jettent le livre et l'auteur est ridicule à leurs yeux' (p. 715, Stendhal's italics). Stendhal mentions Walter Scott and Manzoni as exponents of this classier genre, but he also claims that they are exceptions because they are read as widely in the provinces as in Paris, although for quite different things. The '*exigences opposées*' of the two readerships means that it is 'difficile de faire un roman qui soit lu à la fois dans la chambre des bourgeoises de province et dans les salons de Paris' (p. 715). If Walter Scott succeeds it is because he manages to meet the expectations of both sets of readers without compromising or offending either.

Stendhal implies that it is in writing to bridge the gap between these two audiences that a novelist is most likely to avoid succumbing to the requirements of either group; but he must do so in a way that will not make him the two hundred and first imitator of Walter Scott ('Sir Walter Scott a eu environ deux cents imitateurs en France'). There is no point in avoiding the imitation willed upon him by his readers if it merely means repeating the example of Walter Scott. In any case, he suggests that the temptation is lessened by the fact that he has become weary of Walter Scott. He professes himself 'ennuyé de tout ce moyen âge, de l'*ogive* et de l'habillement du xvᵉ siècle', and claims to have treated the conventions of the Waverley novels with high-handed disdain, boasting that in *Le Rouge* '[il] osa ... laisser le lecteur dans une ignorance complète sur la forme de la robe que portent Mme de Rênal et Mlle de La Mole, ses deux héroïnes, car ce roman en a deux, contre toutes les règles suivies jusqu'ici'. In any case, however, imitation (of Walter Scott) could only be a temporary solution to the problem of the '*exigences opposées*' of his potential readers, since, according to the 'Projet', the works of the two hundred would-be Walter Scotts survive little longer than a year or two and are then completely forgotten.

Being different from Walter Scott (or M. le baron de la Mothe-Langon *et al.*) is not, however, just a matter of perversity: having two heroines because other novelists have had one, or refusing to supply the expected descriptions of their wardrobes. It is not, in other words, a matter of either ignoring or deliberately flouting existing conventions. Instead of closing his eyes to the voracious readers of the provinces ('Il n'est guère de femme de province qui ne lise cinq ou six volumes par mois, beaucoup en lisent quinze ou vingt', p. 713), and to the aesthetically austere ladies of Paris, Stendhal has met them head-on and built their anticipations into the very fabric of his novel. He does this by emphasising the diversity of readers that seemed to make fiction such a difficult undertaking in the first place, rather than by trying to find a new formula that will please the *'exigences opposées'* in the way that Walter Scott did. Indeed, he maximises the heterogeneity of his audience by acknowledging not just the provincial and Parisian readers, but readers whose differences are even more variously characterised. Stendhal alludes at various stages to readers of many kinds: some are men, some are women; some are Parisian, some are provincial; some are desired (the 'happy few'), some despised (the 'âmes glacées');[3] some are liberal, some are not;[4] some live on the second floor and some on the sixth ('Les lecteurs de ce livre doivent habiter le second étage et le sixième');[5] some are contemporary, some are not yet born (in the *Souvenirs d'égotisme* Stendhal places his hopes on being read posthumously: 'J'avoue que le courage d'écrire me manquerait si je n'avais pas l'idée qu'un jour ces feuilles paraîtront imprimées et seront lues par quelque âme que j'aime, par un être tel que Mme Roland ou M. Gros, le géomètre', p. 429.) The exacting demands enshrined in the two dominant fictional traditions as perceived by Stendhal are, therefore, already weakened by his acknowledgement of these other factors in his readership: political factors, class factors, age factors.

The more such factors there are, the less the risk of the hypocrisy that results from imitative compliance with the conventions of any one group. The greatest liberation of all comes from taking account of the posthumous reader about whose expectations and preferences nothing can be known: 'parler à des gens dont on ignore absolument la tournure d'esprit, le genre d'éducation, les préjugés, la religion! Quel encouragement à être *vrai*, et simplement *vrai*, il n'y a que cela qui tienne' (*Henry Brulard*, p. 537, Stendhal's italics). So the tyranny of the contemporary fictional tradition is already undermined by this readerly pluralism, both real and imagined, and far more effectively so than could be achieved by outright opposition to and simple flouting of existing convention.

In adopting this solution Stendhal was building on the capacity for readerly pluralism that he regarded as being in any case the peculiar characteristic of the novel (and this despite his conception of tyranny that particular sub-genres – such as the *roman pour les femmes de chambre* – were capable of exerting over it); and he mentions it as the reason why he abandoned his earlier literary attempts in the theatre for the novel. In his view, the democratisation of theatre audiences since the Revolution was incompatible with what he perceived as the fundamentally monologic basis of comedy; and it is precisely the novel's ability to accommodate a heterogeneous audience that makes it for him the comedy of the nineteenth century.[6] Comedy in the theatre is limited by the choice it has to make between the 'gens grossiers, incapables de comprendre les choses fines' ('Civita-Vecchia', p. 495) and the 'artistes qui ont l'intelligence des *scènes fines*' (p. 496). In writing fiction Stendhal was able to address both the coarse and the refined in his audience, not to mention the liberals and the non-liberals, the Parisians and the provincials, the men and the women, the readers of the present and the readers of the future, etc., etc., etc.

Moreover, Stendhal seems to envisage a number of different types of relationship with his readers, and defensiveness is not his only manner of dealing with the other represented by his reader. The opening remarks of *Lucien Leuwen* are an appeal to a reader whom he addresses as 'lecteur bénévole', and he says that if the reader is not disposed to respond favourably to the words in his text, then the book is not for him. He claims that the novel is written with a strong interlocutory bias, 'comme une lettre à un ami' (as he says of *Henry Brulard*, p. 536), or as a substitute for conversations that can never take place: 'Ce conte [*Lucien Leuwen*] fut écrit en songeant à un petit nombre de lecteurs que je n'ai jamais vus et que je ne verrai point, ce dont bien me fâche: j'eusse trouvé tant de plaisir à passer les soirées avec eux!' (p. 767). Stendhal imagines his readers not just in terms of their multiple characteristics, but also in terms of their multiple relations with the text he is writing: relations of friendship and mutual pleasure, relations of suspicion and hostility (as in the political suspicions that he envisages *Lucien Leuwen* provoking), as well as relations of non-comprehension or offence.

This diversity of both character and reading style amongst his anticipated audience is, as I have already suggested, an important part of his strategy for avoiding the hypocrisy that sabotages both mimesis and originality. It prevents any one group from calling the fictional tune, and makes it easier for Stendhal to write a novel that is neither a *roman pour les femmes de chambre*, nor a piece of Parisian snobbery, nor yet an imitation of Walter Scott. His preoccupation with his readers, in both its negative and positive forms, is inseparable from his mimetic project: the chronicle of 1830 cannot be written without the readers of 1830; and yet the truthfulness of that chronicle (the 'âpre vérité' promised in the epigraph) cannot be guaranteed without finding other ways of reading in order to counter the hypocritical imitations which are the form that reading tends to take amongst the audience of 1830.

Parisian readings

The Parisian reader plays a central role in the construction of Stendhal's portrait of the society of 1830. It is through him that a topical mimetic reading is established, and it is to a large extent by means of the appeal to the Parisian reader's experience that the veracity of the novel's social portrait is authenticated. For it is only the contemporary reader who can judge whether *Le Rouge* is indeed a chronicle of 1830, and whether it lives up to the claims for truth attributed to Danton in the novel's first epigraph. The Parisian reader is presumed to know, like Stendhal, that France has changed beyond recognition in the first thirty years of the century, and that the image of French society and *mœurs* portrayed in the tales of Marmontel and the novels of Mme de Genlis are quite out of date ('Projet', p. 713). He is assumed, by implication, to have been a guest at 'les bals de cet hiver' (p. 341), and more explicitly to be acquainted with the tedium of the salons: 'Tout l'ennui de cette vie sans intérêt que menait Julien est sans doute partagé par le lecteur' (p. 396). HIs are the standards that are invoked by the author as guidelines for interpretation, and at the outset of the novel author and reader are clearly defined as belonging to the same Parisian world.

It is by this means that Stendhal is able to bring the two main components of his envisaged readership (the provincial and the Parisian) into dialogue. Instead of pandering to both sets of tastes by alternating their preferences (which is how Walter Scott manages to succeed with both camps), Stendhal brings them into confrontation. The Parisian reader is set down in the provinces in the guise of a 'voyageur parisien', a kind of tourist whose concerns and interpretations differ on almost every score from those of the provincials around him. He is *surprised* by M. de Rênal's nail factory, *shocked* by his air of self-satisfaction, *struck* by Sorel's sawmill (pp. 4–5) – a series of small collisions which reveal the disparity in experience and presuppositions that exists between the provincial and the Parisian. Even the Parisian's view of the view, to which he turns in order to forget the asphyxiating provincial obsession with money, differs from that of the provincial; for where the Parisian reader dallies with the author, 'songeant aux bals de Paris abandonnés la veille' (p. 7), and admiring the natural beauty of the landscape, the provincial is shrewdly calculating the revenue that the tourist trade is likely to bring. These misinterpretations and surprises have to be set aright for a Parisian audience over and over again, in a manner that ends up by relativising the assumptions and conventions of both groups in question, and thus undermining any authority that each might otherwise have had as a model for imitation.

The Parisian needs to have provincial sayings pointed out to him ('Mme de Rênal ... avait été la beauté du pays, *comme on dit dans ces montagnes*' (p. 13, my italics). He needs to be told about local practices with which he is apparently unfamiliar – how they stuff their mattresses, for example. And his ignorance of social and cultural values in the provinces appears to be total: left to himself he would be incapable of deciphering the harsh economic truths that lie behind the picturesque surface of his surroundings: '*Rapporter du revenu* est la raison qui décide de tout dans cette petite ville qui vous semblait si jolie' (p. 8). He even needs the character of the novel's provincial heroine explained to him: 'Mme de Rênal était une de ces femmes de province que l'on peut très bien prendre pour des sottes pendant les quinze premiers jours qu'on les voit. Elle n'avait aucune expérience de la vie, et ne se souciait pas de parler' (p. 35). These two factors make her appear stupid to Parisian eyes, since experience of life[7] and the ability to hold one's own in company are the *sine qua non* of Parisian success, as Julien's encounter with the salons of the Faubourg Saint-Germain will in due course illustrate. The Parisian reader is shown to be liable to misjudge a character who is not only exemplary but also a product of the times in which he himself lives: writing about her in his 'Projet d'un article', Stendhal claims that 'cette femme [était] impossible dans les mœurs égrillardes qui envahirent la France à la mort du superbe Louis XIV en 1715 et qui ont regné jusqu'à la mort funeste de son arrière-petit-fils Louis XVI en 1793' (p. 720), a remark which suggests that he is likely to have taken as much pride in the mimetic accuracy of her portrait as he claims to have done in his depiction of 'l'amour parisien'.

Through this juxtaposition of provincial and Parisian readings of the provinces Stendhal creates a dialogic effect which, as it is developed, leads to a questioning of the Parisian interpretative system that is established at the opening of the novel. The Parisian reader, whose presence originally seemed designed to provide a recognisable frame of reference for other readers, gradually becomes the object of a second reading. There is, in other words, a slight shift in the diegetic status of this reader (although he remains at all times a characterised rather than an implied reader)[8] and he begins to lose his interpretative authority as his values are progressively turned against him by the text, receding further and further from its central concerns. This process is already begun in the portrait of Mme de Rênal and is continued in such characteristically ironic remarks as:

Il ne faut pas trop mal augurer de Julien; il inventait correctement les paroles d'une hypocrisie cauteleuse et prudente. Ce n'est pas mal à son âge. Quant au ton et aux gestes, il vivait avec des campagnards; il avait été privé de la vue des grands modèles. Par la suite, à peine lui eut-il été donné d'approcher de ces messieurs, qu'il fut admirable pour les gestes comme pour les paroles.

(p. 44)

This forces the reader to endorse and acknowledge values (hypocrisy) which his vanity would normally make him prefer to deny. In this case he cannot, since the remark is made with such incontrovertible aplomb by an author with whom the reader has become so inextricably identified (as a worldly Parisian).

This kind of remark continues to put the Parisian reader in an increasingly awkward position until authorial values eventually become more distinctly dissociated from Parisian ones. A much quoted instance is the comment made about Julien's entry into the café at Besançon:

Quelle pitié notre provincial ne va-t-il pas inspirer aux jeunes lycéens de Paris qui, à quinze ans, savent déjà entrer dans un café d'un air si distingué? Mais ces enfants, si bien stylés à quinze ans, à dix-huit tournent *au commun*.

(p. 155, Stendhal's italics)

The Parisian is invited to share his younger brother's patronising scorn for Julien's inexperience, but is then roundly punished for having done so by being called common. On this occasion, provincial qualities are unequivocally preferred to Parisian ones.

The Parisian's role in the interpretation of the text virtually ceases to function in this explicit way beyond the end of part I. In part II it is the turn of the provincial (largely in the figure of Julien) to make what he can of the Parisian world. In this reversal of roles the Parisian is still the loser, for by presenting Paris through the eyes of Julien, Stendhal creates an effect similar to that of Montesquieu's *Lettres persanes*: Parisian customs are rendered ridiculously arbitrary by Julien's introduction to them. The split between Julien's view and that of the Parisian reader is made explicit at the beginning of what chapter 2 calls Julien's 'Entrée dans le Monde':

Les salons que ces messieurs [Julien and l'abbé Pirard] traversèrent au premier étage, avant d'arriver au cabinet du marquis, vous eussent semblé, ô mon lecteur, aussi tristes que magnifiques. On vous les donnerait tels qu'ils sont, que vous refuseriez de les habiter; c'est la patrie du bâillement et du raisonnement triste. Ils redoublèrent l'enchantement de Julien. Comment peut-on être malheureux, pensait-il, quand on habite un séjour aussi splendide! (p. 229)

Here, unlike the provincial world of part I, the Parisian's experience of the world is directly relevant to the world described (Paris). It is a world which he recognises and understands.[9] But as Julien gains in experience and loses his initial naivety, he seems to move further and further away from, and not closer to, this Parisian view of things. He learns to speak the 'langue étrangère' of the salons,[10] takes fencing lessons, dancing lessons, and, in short, becomes a dandy. But it is not these accomplishments that endear him to Mathilde or which make him the hero of Stendhal's novel. A split between provincial and Parisian readings thus gives way here to a split between actions and characters which are repeatedly defined as 'singulier' on the one hand, and Parisian *convenances* on the other.

The world 'singulier' is used to describe Julien in all the different milieux in which he finds himself, but in Paris this singularity poses a serious threat to the Parisian reader's interpretative capacity. Significantly, it is the Parisians who find Julien 'fort singulier' in the de La Mole salon (p. 241); for singularity in Stendhal is generally synonymous with a failure or an inability to comply with the reigning *convenances*, and in this case those *convenances* are the Parisian reader's main point of reference for interpretation. Mathilde too (for all that she herself is also baffled by Julien) shares this quality, and it is her singularity that is shown to pose the greatest challenge to the decorum of Parisian readings. Croisenois notes that 'Mathilde a de la singularité', and adds, 'c'est un inconvénient' (p. 274). The author mentions that 'ce personnage fait exception aux mœurs du siècle', although he does so in order once more to turn the novel's values

121

against Parisian ones when he goes on unflatteringly to accuse Mathilde's compatriots of chicken-heartedness: 'Ce n'est pas en général le manque de prudence que l'on peut reprocher aux élèves du noble couvent du Sacré-Cœur' (p. 294). The crisis in the Parisian reading provoked by these instances of 'singularité' comes to a head during Mathilde's night of 'folie'.

Here the author creates further bewilderment by invoking the Parisian reader once more, only to confront his values with a character (Mathilde) who refuses to conform to them: 'Ce personnage est tout à fait d'imagination, et même imaginé bien en dehors des habitudes sociales qui parmi tous les siècles assureront un rang si distingué à la civilisation du xixᵉ siècle' (p. 341). The reader figure is described as one of the 'âmes glacées' who are likely to take offence at this portrait, and the author goes on elaborately to dissociate them (the Parisian 'âmes glacées') from the supposedly un-nineteenth-century behaviour of Mathilde:

Cette page nuira de plus d'une façon au malheureux auteur. Les âmes glacées l'accuseront d'indécence. Il ne fait point l'injure aux jeunes personnes qui brillent dans les salons de Paris de supposer qu'une seule d'entre elles soit susceptible des mouvements de folie qui dégradent le caractère de Mathilde.

This move seems at first to be designed to save the Parisian reader's face, but it does just the reverse, for in the next breath the author says that in fact Mathilde is after all a part of the real world that he is portraying:

Eh, monsieur, un roman est un miroir qui se promène sur une grande route. Tantôt il reflète à vos yeux l'azur des cieux, tantôt la fange des bourbiers de la route. Et l'homme qui porte le miroir dans sa hotte sera par vous accusé d'être immoral! Son miroir montre la fange, et vous accusez le miroir! Accusez bien plutôt le grand chemin où est le bourbier, et plus encore l'inspecteur des routes qui laisse l'eau croupir et le bourbier se former. (p. 342)

The Parisian's reading fails not only in its response to what lies outside his world (singularity), but − and this is a much more serious charge − in its response to certain aspects of his own. The Parisian's touchiness on matters of decency seems to blind him to a part of the reality for which he has hitherto acted as the key and the guarantor. Readerly *convenances* are demonstrated to be part of a representation which they are incapable of recognising. The world to which the Parisian reader belongs produces a kind of astigmatism in its inhabitants which prevents them from seeing it for what it is. But without the Parisian reader to authenticate the portrait of the society of 1829–30, how is this portrait to be read by its non-Parisian readers?

The uses of reading

Before answering this question, more must be said about Mathilde's topicality. Some (real) contemporary readers seem to have had no difficulty in recognising the reality of the portrait of Mathilde. Count Alexis de Saint-Priest wrote a dialogue in which one of the speakers claims to recognise the type and says:

Voulez-vous une peinture fidèle du grand monde: lisez *Rouge et Noir*; faites connaissance avec mademoiselle Mathilde, le type des demoiselles du faubourg Saint-Germain. Voilà de la vérité! voilà de l'exactitude! C'est là dans toute la force du terme un auteur bien informé et un livre de bonne foi![11]

This view certainly tallies with Stendhal's claim in the 'Projet' that his depiction of Parisian love constitutes a major realist achievement in his novel. So that the assertion in the text that Mathilde is 'imaginée bien en dehors des habitudes sociales' of the time would appear to be a dig at the Parisian reader's ticklishness on matters of taste, and to suggest once again that these 'habitudes sociales' prevent him from recognising the social realities of which they are a part. Like the pistol shot of politics, she may 'mortally offend' half the readership, even if she does not bore the other half (p. 361). The good taste which Parisian social habits are designed to maintain is thus incompatible with the mirror principle; for just as the exclusion of politics from the novel would ruin the portrait of France in 1830, so too would the exclusion of Mathilde and her 'amour de tête'. The harsh truths of the day, whose depiction is the novel's avowed aim, prove to be too much for the reader of the day.

There seems, therefore, to be no reader capable of recognising the truth of Stendhal's portrait. Mimesis becomes tangled in a paradox whereby the reader is asked to recognise his own world, and at the same time is shown that this world provides an inadequate framework for that recognition. The nature of the society being represented prevents the representation of it from being fully perceived within it. This problem raises again the question of how this partially un-recognisable representation of 1830 is to be read. The novel itself contains suggestive accounts of different uses of reading which may have some bearing on the problem. There are many readers in *Le Rouge*, and reading takes many different forms. Broadly, though, reading falls into two categories: private, or clandestine reading, and socially useful reading. It is this socially useful reading that is associated with the Parisian, and leads one to suspect that Stendhal's Parisian reader would not in any case be reading referentially (i.e. for a portrait of a particular material and social reality), but strategically, as a means to further his own advancement within that social reality.

Reading for success

Reading as an activity is itself made necessary by the society described in the text being read. Books are needed to provide an antidote to the boredom that is the product of the social changes that have taken place since 1789 ('Projet', p. 713), and which it is the novel's purpose to document. Reading compensates for the absence of social gatherings and conversations that made life in eighteenth-century France such a pleasure, and which, according to Stendhal, still existed in the Italy of his day (witness the remarks to this effect made in *De l'Amour*). Nineteenth-century French society, however, not content with simply making reading necessary, goes so far as to adapt it to its own particular purposes: reading is made the passport to social acceptability, even social success, and there is censorship not only in what is read, but also in how it is read.

René seems to be the set text for entry into the de La Mole salon. Familiarity with Chateaubriand's novel saves its young readers from ridicule, and provides them with the necessary model to imitate. Julien fails to read quite the right texts (despite the fact that he reads more than anyone else in the novel),[12] and, with the exception of the 'volume dépareillé' of *La Nouvelle Héloïse* that he finds while he is at Vergy, makes the (socially) crucial omission of fiction. Nevertheless, his initiation into society in the de La Mole household is effected by means of a testing of his reading. His time at the seminary has already taught him the social uses of reading: reading the wrong texts for the exam gets him ranked 198th instead of first, although his knowledge of the same texts on the occasion of his meeting with the archbishop delights the old man, who rewards him with a fine edition of Tacitus. These two events, then, prepare Julien for the first social hurdle encountered over the dinner table in the Faubourg Saint-Germain − a discussion of Horace. Here his response shows him in a good light for a provincial, but a poor one for a Parisian, which is to say that what he reads passes muster, but how he reads it doesn't. Mercilessly quizzed by the academician across the table,

Julien répondit en inventant ses idées, et perdit assez sa timidité pour montrer, non pas de l'esprit, chose impossible à qui ne sait pas la langue dont on se sert à Paris, mais il eut des idées nouvelles quoique présentées sans grâce ni à-propos et l'on vit qu'il savait parfaitement le latin. (p. 235)

Julien fails to conform to Parisian norms because he invents his ideas, rather than repeating the orthodoxy of the academy, and because he doesn't speak 'la langue dont on se sert à Paris', a language which, to judge by other cases, is best learned parrot-fashion. Croisenois and

Norbert are probably some of the best practitioners of this language
– Croisenois because he is such an elegant copy of René, and Norbert
because he makes no bones about wrapping up his reading in a series
of 'idées toutes faites'. (The abbé Pirard knows enough of Paris to
warn Julien in advance that he is likely to be asked to teach Norbert
'quelques phrases toutes faites, sur Cicéron et Virgile', p. 225.) In any
case Norbert regularly comes to the library to mug up topics for the
evening's conversation: 'Norbert ... venait étudier un journal, pour
pouvoir parler politique le soir' (p. 237), in other words to rehearse
the catechism that newspapers are, not just for the liberals, but for
the ultras too. Society seems, then, to determine the form that reading
should take and the uses to which it should be put: imitation and
repetition. Under these circumstances, *Le Rouge et le Noir* itself seems
particularly unsuitable for a Parisian reading. It constantly offends
standards of decent amusement (e.g. Mathilde's night of 'folie'),
renders its culminating action inimitable, and, as the last section of
this chapter will show, invites another kind of reading which more
or less precludes any repeatable 'phrase toute faite'.

The second form of reading that the text represents is clandestine
reading, which is offered as an alternative to social reading. Mathilde
and Julien are the main secretive readers in the text. Their self-imposed
secrecy is partly the result of censorship, for both read politically
unacceptable texts: Julien reads Napoleon at night in the Rênal
household, his lamp hidden in an upturned vase; and Mathilde, whose
clandestine reading is mainly political, comes by her texts through
theft.[13] She steals books from her father's library, and indeed theft
seems to add a particular spice to reading in her case and to give the
reading of all stolen books a politically subversive character. For
example, the private collection of 'nouveautés un peu piquantes'
which Julien is responsible for buying on the Marquis's behalf, is
regularly purloined:

[Julien] eut bientôt la certitude que pour peu que ces livres nouveaux fussent
hostiles aux intérêts du trône et de l'autel, ils ne tardaient pas à disparaître.
(p. 304)

Nevertheless, neither Mathilde's nor Julien's motives are genuinely
radical alternatives to Parisian reading since, for both of them, reading
offers models which happen to be socially unacceptable: Napoleon
for Julien, Marguerite de Navarre for Mathilde. This type of reading
is subversive to the extent that its texts are censored, its heroes
unorthodox, and its mode is clandestine. But it shares with Parisian
habits the aim of imitation, and thus belongs ultimately to that camp.

Performative readings

The alternatives to the problematic referential reading of *Le Rouge* are not, however, limited to these socially more or less acceptable repetitions and imitations. There is, for example, a rather different experience of reading indicated by Saint-Giraud on the mail-coach that takes Julien to Paris, when, in describing his 'politics' to his friend Falcoz, he says: 'un bon livre est un événement pour moi' (p. 219). This mode of reading (which he does not elaborate on) contrasts significantly with the socially utilitarian and imitative readings which are far more frequently evoked in the novel, and it is the one used ultimately to clinch the novel's mimetic purpose. In *Henry Brulard* reading is represented almost exclusively as event, and as very similar to Mathilde's sixteenth-century ideal of love: 'il n'était point l'amusement de la vie, il la changeait'.[14] Brulard's reading is a series of decisive events which have a permanent effect on his life and personality. The discovery of *Don Quixote* was 'peut-être la plus grand époque de [s]a vie' (*Brulard*, p. 618); Ariosto 'forma [s]on caractère' (p. 619); and without Horace and Euripides he would have succumbed to the tyranny of Raillane and become 'un excellent jésuite ... ou un soldat crapuleux, coureur de filles et de cabarets' (p. 627). The intervention of books in his life is of unsurpassed importance for two reasons: first, because these books become the grid through which he constructs and interprets his experience (this factor is, of course, not without its dangers); and second, because the reading of them constitutes a kind of experience which is second only to love itself. (I shall be discussing Brulard's reading in more detail in the next chapter.)

Le Rouge itself does not offer its ('real') reader any model of a performative reading to follow, not least perhaps because to do so would be to introduce imitation into this reading process and so undermine its essential status as event. Instead, it elicits such a reading through its repeated use of the *imprévu* and through comedy. *Rêverie* and *hilarité*, the two main reader responses that these strategies instigate, are the two inseparable experiential forms that a performative reading of *Le Rouge* would take.

As the novel moves towards its finish, the incidence of what it calls *folie* and *l'imprévu* significantly increases. The shooting episode as a whole is *imprévu*, and is composed of largely inexplicable elements. An index of the extent of the inexplicable in this episode can be gauged from the number of explanatory notes to chapters 35 (the shooting) and 36 (Julien's imprisonment) in Castex's edition, most of them consisting of explanations to fill out the abrupt and elliptical utterances of the narrative. For instance, the brusque 'Adieu' with which Julien parts from Mathilde is felt to require expansion and clarification. So is the following sentence: 'Julien sauta à bas du fiacre, et courut à sa chaise de poste', where the lack of clear motive needs, apparently, to be compensated for. The reason why Julien is unable to form the words of a letter to Mathilde gives rise to further editorial intervention and a discussion of divergent scholarly responses: according to Martineau, Julien is in the grip of 'un tremblement nerveux qui l'empêche d'écrire', whereas Castex suggests that the problem may be due to the poor suspension of the poste-chaise in which Julien is travelling (p. 637). In either case it is clear that this is an instance of what Wolfgang Iser would call a blank or a gap that needs to be filled by the reader.[15] The number of blanks at this point is extremely high, and the question is: what sort of procedure should be used to fill them?

On this Stendhal's text is not nearly so directive as Iser's model would suggest, and the reader is confronted with a thoroughgoing indeterminacy concerning the appropriate level of reading. Castex, in accordance with the principles of good scholarship, has gone for a material and historical reading of the particular blank under discussion: stage-coaches of 1830 offered a far smoother ride than the faster poste-chaises. Martineau's reading at this point is based on the conventions of psychological realism: it assumes that the hero's feelings and emotional responses are the main object of the text. Neither reading, however, explains why the blank should be there in the first place, and, in a sense, the alacrity with which both editors rush to fill the gap gives them a certain resemblance to Mme de La Mole and the other *grandes dames* who are so offended by Julien's unconventional behaviour on his arrival in the salon: '*L'imprévu* produit par la sensibilité [in this case Julien's] est l'horreur des grandes dames; c'est l'antipode des convenances' (p. 254). The *imprévu* of Julien's actions at the climax of the novel is, precisely, a flouting of reading *convenances*, be they scholarly, psychological, or whatever.

Even Stendhal seems to have bridled somewhat at the degree of *imprévu* in his text — at least on the level of style. He complains of it in *Henry Brulard* (p. 225), and it is a recurrent theme in his notes in the Civita-Vecchia copy of the text: the style, he says, is 'trop abrupt, trop heurté', and he advises himself to 'Ajouter des mots ... pour aider l'imagination à se figurer' (p. 493). But it does seem that it is the impoverished imagination of the *âmes glacées* that he has in mind, and there are two marginalia in chapter 17 of part I which would support this view: 'Pas assez développé. Qu'est-ce que cette bataille? diront *les gens sans esprit*'; and 'Quelle rapidité! Pour *les demi-sots*, n'est-ce pas de la sécheresse?' (p. 495, my italics). The *âmes sensibles* can presumably cope with the *imprévu* and the reason for this may well be their mode of reading, which is not dependent on *convenances*. Certainly no convention-bound reading can deal with the increase of *folie* that occurs towards the end of the novel. As Shoshana Felman remarks, *folie* tends to appear with gathering frequency towards the end of each of the novels, and *Le Rouge et le Noir* is no exception.[16] And, as she also points out, the mark of the *fou* is his lack of a common language with others (including, in this instance, the reader), and his inability to make his 'parole solitaire' understood (*La 'Folie'*, p. 162). *Folie* and its cognate *singularité* are terms which are associated first with Mathilde, and then, more extensively, with Julien,[17] and this characteristic suggests that the conventional assumptions which form the basis of most readings may not be adequate to their task in this last part of the novel.

If the *âmes sensibles* succeed in making sense of the final pages of the novel, this is because their reading is not grounded in a particular kind of language, or any particular set of conventions which they will be seeking to translate the fictional text back into. Their reading must necessarily be conducted in a state of hilarity and reverie, and they will be profoundly moved by it. In Stendhal's world, these three things (hilarity, reverie and *attendrissement*) tend to go together, and laughter is an essential prerequisite for being moved. In *Henry Brulard* he claims that his love of *opera buffa* is due to the fact that only in this genre can he be moved to tears: 'Je ne puis être touché jusqu'à l'attendrissement qu'*après un passage comique*' (p. 912, Stendhal's italics).

There are many kinds of laughter in Stendhal, but this particular and vital form depends on a freedom from both convention and a narrow referentiality.[18] Of all Stendhal's heroes, Lucien Leuwen is probably the most prone to laughter, and this tendency can be correlated with the particularly hidebound nature of the society in which he moves. Nancy is obsessed with its *convenances*, and Lucien's first outburst of laughter is provoked by his encounter with the utterly proper and utterly self-important prefect, M. Fléron. The effect of the man's appearance is enough to produce an uncontrollable explosion of laughter in Lucien, which is echoed time and again in the novel. *Le Rouge* represents a similarly sober world where laughter is proscribed by the *convenances*. It is explicitly forbidden in the de La Mole salon, where 'il n'était convenable de plaisanter de rien'

(p. 290). But precisely because of the hold of these rules, there is statistically more laughter in this part of the novel than in any of the others.[19] Julien himself has two notable moments of this *rire fou*: once in Verrières after his Jesuitical conversation with Maugiron, the sub-prefect ('A peine M. de Maugiron sorti, Julien se mit à rire comme un fou', p. 131); and once in Paris when Mme de Fervaques enquires about the references to London and Richmond in Julien's latest letter to her. No one is more hidebound than her, nothing more conventional than the letters that Julien writes to her, so that his response is inevitably to 'céder au rire fou' (p. 395). The element of *folie* in these outbursts is what makes them genuine moments of hilarity, and not instances of *le rire affecté*, which is the social conformist's response to all that he regards as 'ridicule'.[20]

The only other moment of this sort of hilarity occurs on the visit of the singer Geronimo to the Rênal household. As a singer and an Italian, he is the antithesis of all that provincial France stands for. The exaggeratedly foreign accent in which he tells his comic tale has the children in fits of laughter, and the comic aria he sings reduces everyone to tears through laughing (pp. 145–6). The prime feature of this laughter is its essential gaiety, its total lack of malice and self-interest. The effectiveness of laughter as an antidote to *convenances* lies in this gaiety and the element of *folie* that it implies. It is the laughter of the *opera buffa* and the only possible prelude to *attendrissement*.

Stendhal devotes a number of pages to comedy and its attendant *rire fou* in his essay on 'Le rire' in *Racine et Shakespeare*. Borrowing from Hobbes, he defines laughter as '*cette convulsion physique ... produite par la vue imprévue de notre supériorité sur autrui*' (p. 63), and he lays considerable stress on the importance of the *imprévu* in this process: 'cette supériorité est une chose si futile et si facilement anéantie par la moindre réflexion, qu'il faut que la vue nous en soit présentée d'une manière imprévue' (p. 64). The *imprévu* takes comedy out of any context of convention or conformity, which preclude genuine laughter. Falstaff is the epitome of the *rire fou* because of his capacity for the gaiety whose chief quality is its unpredictability (p. 65). Molière, in contrast, is associated with a false laughter, *le rire affecté*, whose motive is revenge. His comedy is therefore essentially not comedy at all, but satire, a product of the society in which he wrote and whose religion was imitation (p. 67). Imitation is incompatible with *le rire gai*, and for Stendhal laughter is a reprieve from the obligation to imitate: 'si j'entre au théâtre, je veux qu'on me fasse rire, et je ne songe à imiter personne' (p. 70). Equally, hilarity has to be

129

dissociated from the referential mode of satire, which is always directed at specific targets in social reality. If the *happy few* who read *Lucien Leuwen* are to participate in Lucien's outbursts of laughter, it must be at the expense of any narrow reference to contemporary France:

Cette chose si amusante, la satire personnelle, ne convient donc point, par malheur, à la narration d'une histoire. Le lecteur est tout occupé à comparer mon portrait à l'original grotesque, ou même odieux, de lui bien connu.

(*Lucien Leuwen*, p. 1067)

In other words, both modes associated with a Parisian reading of Stendhal (mimetic and imitative) are unequivocally excluded from the hilarious performative reading that is elicited from the *happy few*.

Le Rouge should, therefore, be seen as a Stendhalian kind of *opera buffa*, in which any hilarity it provoked would be accompanied by *attendrissement*. Stendhal certainly alternates moments of comedy with moments of more emotive appeal, and perhaps nowhere more strikingly so than in the representations of love. Each affair is initiated by a hugely comic *quid pro quo* as each partner misinterprets the motives of the other. And yet, at the same time, love is clearly a matter to be taken seriously and wholeheartedly responded to. This response depends on the reader's ability to recreate an equivalent emotional experience on his or her own behalf. As the first of the 'Projets de préface' to *De l'Amour* makes clear, reading about love is entirely dependent on the reader's own experience of love: 'Il faut, pour suivre avec intérêt un examen philosophique [or, in the case of *Le Rouge*, a novelistic portrayal] de ce sentiment, autre chose que de l'esprit chez le lecteur; il est de toute nécessité qu'il ait vu l'amour' (*De l'Amour*, p. 325). The reading of a text is, in Stendhal's view, only possible if the experiences that it represents are re-evoked and reconstituted *within* the reader. He or she cannot be merely a passive spectator of the representation on the page.

This emphasis on experiential reduplication gives the question of referentiality a rather different slant. Representational accuracy in the text itself has no necessary link with the readerly experience which, for Stendhal, is the only basis for guaranteeing the truth of the text. The novelist shares with the dramatic poet and the painter the difficulty of having to depict passions which are essentially invisible. As Stendhal writes in the *Histoire de la peinture*, 'On ne peut les trouver que dans son propre cœur', since no description can ever convey the reality of something of which one has no experience oneself (II, pp. 33). Passion is communicated only if it has been genuinely felt by both author and reader. It is mediated through a painting or a novel, in which it is never directly represented, but to which the reader must respond. Equally, however, the author may not deceive by dreaming up passions and experiences he has never had because, 'une anecdote est-elle vraie, elle excite la sympathie la plus tendre; est-elle inventée, elle n'est que plate' (*Histoire de la peinture*, II, p. 245).

This irrelevance of representational content to the response it evokes is illustrated by an anecdote that Stendhal includes in *De l'Amour* (and also in the *Lettres sur Haydn*). The happiest moment in the life of his English friend Mortimer had been the welcome given him by his beloved Jenny on his return home from a trip abroad. The significance of the moment for Mortimer was that it had proved to him that Jenny loved him, and he had held on to the memory of it long after he had lost Jenny through her infidelity. But recounting the episode to Stendhal, he was unable to remember a single detail which might substantiate this proof, and all that remained of it in his memory was the recollection of Jenny's dress being caught on the thorns of an acacia bush. The memory of the acacia had become the trigger for the entire emotional content of the experience; and ever after the sight of an acacia would make him tremble under the emotional effects of an event whose representational content had been completely erased (*De l'Amour*, p. 95). All that a performative reading requires of a representation is the equivalent of Mortimer's acacia, a detail to trigger the affective response which is the ultimate goal of Stendhal's texts.

According to Stendhal, no representation can ever be fully realistic, because it is never taken or mistaken for reality.[21] It we admire a landscape by Claude Lorrain, 'ce n'est pas que nous supposions les arbres que nous voyons capables de nous donner de l'ombre, ou que nous songions à puiser de l'eau à ces fontaines si limpides'. The effect of the painting depends, rather, on the pleasure it elicits, in which case, 'nous *figurons vivement* le plaisir que nous aurions à nous promener auprès de ces fraîches fontaines et à l'ombre de ces beaux arbres' (*Racine et Shakespeare*, p. 159). The illusion of reality is not in the text but in the reader, and it is the product of the text's power to move him or her (since Mme Roland is, so to speak, the incarnation of the *âme sensible* or the happy reader in question, the re-introduction of the feminine pronoun here is timely). An *âme glacée* will remain unaffected by the most poignant depictions of love and persist in seeing in them only folly. The painters of the *beau idéal* (Raphael and Correggio), as Stendhal calls them, are in themselves neither more nor less realistic in this sense than the *peintres miroirs*, such as Gaspard Poussin and the Dutch school. In both cases,

On se sent tout à coup plongé dans une rêverie profonde, comme à la vue des bois et de *leur vaste silence*. On songe avec profondeur à ses plus chères illusions; on les trouve moins improbables; bientôt on en jouit comme de réalités. On parle à ce qu'on aime, on ose l'interroger, on écoute ses réponses. Voilà les sentiments que me donne une promenade solitaire dans une véritable forêt.   (p. 179)

Performative readings become the only relevant index of life-likeness, however improbable or *invraisemblable* the issues in question. And this is the main reason why the novel is conceived as a bow, a device which provides the technical means for bringing forth mimetic sounds from the reader's soul.

It is therefore the readers whom Stendhal never met, those who were ten or twelve years old when he wrote *Souvenirs d'égotisme*, those of 1880, those of 1935, perhaps – who knows? – even those of the 1980s and nineties, who Stendhal thought would have the best chance of achieving such a reading. They are less likely to be distracted by the irrelevance of contemporary reference, and are assumed to be less bound by *convenances*, less likely to be in search of a model to imitate. It is only in the light of a performative reading that the text's truthfulness may be properly assessed. Stendhal gains the place he hoped for alongside the 'immortal *Tom Jones*' by resisting the temptation to conform to the *convenances* of his day, and by not writing like the Jesuit that he could so easily otherwise have become.

The performative reading of Stendhal's fiction may be the decisive form that reading has to take when it comes to gauging the novel's authenticity, but it cannot be treated as the only form. No novelist can afford to ignore the socially and generically consecrated readings that await his novel – in Stendhal's case, avid provincial readings and elitist Parisian readings – for fear that they may commandeer all other possible readings in the text. Readerly monologism is as undesirable as any other kind of monologism, hence the need to pluralise anticipated responses to the text (as Stendhal does in *Le Rouge*): undercutting the Parisians by including provincial reading voices in the text, and showing that even in Paris it is not just the slaves to the affectation of rhetoric who constitute the novel's readership, but the inhabitants of the second and the sixth floors too. A novel that devoted all its efforts to producing in its readers the aphasic tremblings of Stendhal's friend Mortimer might find itself a victim of the same helpless inarticulateness. Mimesis of the highest order can be validated only by a performative reading, but it rests on mimesis of a humbler but equally necessary kind, and one to which readers are equally essential. The *histoire de mœurs* requires a reader to corroborate its accuracy; and the misreadings to which even the most mimetically accurate text is susceptible are ascribed in *Le Rouge* to a social context of reading which is anticipated by and in the novel in a manner that also contributes significantly to its realism. The mimesis achieved by *Le Rouge* depends on its being situated both in relation to the responses of the *happy few* and to the real historical context in which it was actually received and so variously read.

Part Four
VIE DE HENRY BRULARD

6

THE READER AND THE LIFE

C'est [au lecteur] d'assembler ces éléments et de déterminer l'être qu'ils composent.

Rousseau, *Les Confessions*

The reader of autobiography

The centrality of reading to the workings of Stendhal's writing extends beyond the domain of the novel to include that of autobiography; and just as the mirror held up to reality in *Le Rouge* requires the reader to make it operate like a bow, so the reader is integral to the autobiographical project of the *Vie de Henry Brulard*. The lessons learned from the novel are adapted and applied to the writing of the life. In some ways this connection is made more obvious by the fact that recent critical approaches to autobiography have given enormous emphasis to the reader (more than is generally accorded to the reader of fiction); but in general this critical preoccupation with reading in autobiography has been used primarily to legitimate the generic distinctiveness of autobiography. Indeed, it would seem that if there wasn't a reader to say so, autobiography (as a genre if not as a practice) would not exist. As Philippe Lejeune puts it, 'le genre autobiographique est un genre contractuel', dependent upon a pact or 'contrat de lecture'.[1] The function of the reader of autobiography has, however, been almost exclusively limited to the staking out of the generic terrain, and there has been relatively little critical concern with any other aspect of the reader and the reading of autobiography.[2]

This is all the more surprising in view of the fact that much contemporary critical and linguistic theory regards subjectivity (of which autobiography is supposedly one of the most direct expressions) as necessarily entailing intersubjectivity. Emile Benveniste, for example, not only treats subjectivity as a matter of linguistic rather than empirical fact ('Est "ego" qui *dit* "ego"'), but he claims in addition that *je* only ever exists in relation to a *tu*: 'Je n'emploie *je* qu'en m'adressant à quelqu'un, qui sera dans mon allocution un *tu*.'

And furthermore, the actual constitution of the self of the *je* depends on a relationship of interlocution with an other: 'C'est cette condition de dialogue qui est constitutive de la *personne*.'[3] The logical consequences of this kind of claim in the domain of autobiography would seem to indicate that one ought not to be looking at the autobiographical *je* in complete isolation from its dialogical counterpart, and that the reader might have a role to play in autobiography which goes beyond that of a contractual agreement to make generic distinctions between autobiography and other related (or unrelated) genres. However, this is a distinction which the discussion in this chapter will override (or rather evade by dismissing it as a separate issue) in order to explore the way in which self-representation in the autobiographical *Vie de Henry Brulard* proves to be as dependent upon its readers and upon the experience of reading as it is in the mimesis of the novels. The demands of veracity are just as great for self-narration as in fictional representations; and in *Brulard* that veracity proves to be as vulnerable to the platitudes of the *doxa* as it was in *Le Rouge*; and readers represent the same combination of threat and solution to the aims of autobiographical writing as they do in the fictional texts.

Benveniste's argument suggests that the centrality of reading is not peculiar to Stendhal, but that interlocution is essential to the very constitution of the *self*. Similarly, the rhetoric of confession traditionally associated with autobiography implies that the *sincerity* or authenticity of the autobiographical account depends on having the right relation with its addressee. The reader could therefore be seen as having a role in relation to both these factors − self and sincerity: liable to be called as a passive witness to the representation of a particular self and the sincerity of its author's intentions; or else to be invited to take a more active role, be it in the construction of the autobiographical persona or in the deciphering of a partially concealed authenticity.[4] Indeed, one could argue that all autobiographical texts need to go beyond the 'autobiographical pact' that makes a generically specific reading possible, and to position their readers so as to make sincerity and self-revelation possible. It is not just the genre which requires a reader, but the autobiographical project itself.

In the case of *Henry Brulard*, Stendhal's reader is genuinely and seminally involved from the outset in the project of self-discovery that the writing of his autobiography is designed to accomplish. Prior to the writing Stendhal claims to know nothing of the sort of person that he is and has been: 'Qu'ai-je donc été? Je ne le saurais' (p. 532). His first instinct is not to resort to introspection in order to discover the answers to his questions, but simply to ask a friend. The problem, however, is to find a friend who can be relied upon to provide a sufficiently shrewd and well-informed answer: 'A quel ami, quelque éclairé qu'il soit, puis-je le demander?' The decision to write an autobiography follows from Stendhal's realisation that none of his friends knows enough about him to be able to tell him what kind of a person he has been. So it is the writing of the life itself that will supposedly bring the self-knowledge that Stendhal feels a man of fifty ought to have: 'Je devrais écrire ma vie', he says to himself; 'je saurai peut-être enfin, quand cela sera fini dans deux ou trois ans, ce que j'ai été, gai ou triste, homme d'esprit ou sot, homme de courage ou peureux, et enfin au total heureux ou malheureux' (p. 533). But his friends are not forgotten, since he ends the sentence by proposing to read his memoirs to his closest friend in Civita-Vecchia, where he was living at the time: 'je pourrai faire lire ce manuscrit à Di Fiore'.

More crucially, though, from the very outset the writing is conceived through and through in relation to an addressee. For Stendhal, the kind of sincerity on which self-knowledge depends can only be achieved by imagining self-narration as a form of address. As he settles down to his project Stendhal writes: 'j'ai fait allumer du feu et j'écris ceci, sans mentir j'espère, sans me faire illusion, avec plaisir *comme une lettre à un ami*' (p. 536, my emphasis). The friend or friends (for usually he mentions several) that Stendhal envisages as recipients of his autobiographical letter are, however, imaginary ones. He assumes that his reader–friends will be reading him some way ahead in the future − presumably posthumously − in 1880, 1900, or even in 1935. The friend to whom the autobiographical text is addressed is therefore by definition unknown: 'Quelles seront les idées de cet ami en 1880?' he asks. 'Combien différentes des nôtres!' But this is precisely what makes it possible for Stendhal to write with sincerity: 'parler à des gens dont on ignore absolument la tournure d'esprit, le genre d'éducation, les préjugés, la religion! Quel encouragement à être *vrai*, et simplement *vrai*, il n'y a que cela qui tienne' (p. 537, Stendhal's italics). The sincerity of Stendhal's text can only be guaranteed by a posthumous reader–friend, a condition which is bound to make the reader–friend's verdict on Stendhal's personality come too late to be of much use to him during the life which he feels would benefit from that knowledge.

The emphasis seems then to have shifted slightly; whereas initially sincerity was merely the pretext for self-knowledge, when the project actually gets under way self-knowledge appears more as a posthumous by-product of the pleasurable experience of writing with sincerity, which becomes the work's chief *raison d'être*. In both cases, though, the role of the reader–friend is an integral and essential part of the enterprise; in being conceived by analogy with a letter-writer, Stendhal's *je* is wholly dependent on the *tu* to whom it addresses itself, and the self-narration of his autobiography is consequently and self-confessedly dialogical in construction. *Brulard*'s reader is therefore passively necessary as both a catalyst and a guarantee for Stendhal's sincerity (passive because it is enough for him or her simply to be there – or be imagined); and is actively required to make the kind of evaluation about Stendhal's personality that he himself was unable to undertake.

Stendhal seems in general to assume good will (or the benevolence he ascribes to his reader in the preface to *Lucien Leuwen*) on the part of his autobiographical reader. This means that his autobiographical writing reveals altogether much less anxiety about the demands of the public than does his fictional writing. It may partly be a question of genre, since autobiography was less well established and institution-alised than the novel in the early nineteenth century; although, between them, the existing example of Rousseau's *Confessions* and the rumoured existence of Chateaubriand's *Mémoires* provide powerful instances of Parisian stereotype and hypocritical *emphase*: Jean-Jacques had already furnished the model for Julien's sensibilities in *Le Rouge*, and, presumably, the need to counter the potential temptations of a style *à la* 'Castelfugens' was no less pressing in the autobiography than it had been in the earlier novels. It is perhaps the posthumousness of the envisaged reader of Stendhal's autobio-graphical text which is the chief factor enabling him to dispose of the problem that haunts the fictional texts through their contemporary readership. Nevertheless, the reader of the *Vie de Henry Brulard* shares with the reader of the novels the dual task of helping to corroborate a represented object (in this case the 'physiognomy' of the autobiographical subject), and of validating the text as mimesis through her or his performative response to it.

Verdicts

However, in spite of his original intentions, Stendhal proves to be deeply pessimistic about the possibility of arriving at the kind of self-knowledge which the questions 'Qu'ai-je été? que suis-je?' (p. 532) appear to be in search of. And furthermore – indeed rather more importantly – he seems equally doubtful about the value that any verdict which presumed to offer an answer to these questions might have, for he suggests that such a verdict would in the end destroy the truth that they appear to be in pursuit of. I shall therefore be seeking to show how the reader comes to be involved in the process of deferral or suspension of the self-knowledge that the autobiography proposes as its initial goal.

First, Stendhal repeatedly indicates that in purely mechanical terms self-knowledge is an impossible feat. At the most basic level the human subject cannot turn his gaze upon himself: 'quel œil peut se voir soi-même?' (p. 535) — which is the reason why he originally thinks of asking his friends to tell him what they see. But even if self-scrutiny were materially possible, human memory tends to destroy a significant amount of the evidence that the autobiographer is trying to retrieve. Stendhal compares himself on a number of occasions to a fresco, parts of which have disappeared: 'A côté des images les plus claires je trouve des *manques* dans ce souvenir, c'est comme une fresque dont de grands morceaux seraient tombés' (p. 644, Stendhal's italics). And to complicate matters even more, these gaps are largely caused by the most central and intimate part of his being, namely his emotions: 'Je n'ai aucune mémoire des époques ou des moments où j'ai senti trop vivement' (p. 628). The lived manifestations of the most vital and characteristic part of his self (the way he feels and the manner in which he pursues 'la chasse du bonheur') have been obliterated in his memory by their sheer intensity. By the same token, if he is inclined to think of himself as a brave man, this is perhaps only because he happens to have retained particularly vivid memories of the circumstances of the duels in which he has been involved. Memory is a blank on some of the most important moments in Stendhal's existence, and is no doubt highly selective in its recall of the others, with the result that complete self-portraiture is bound to remain a purely chimerical project.

Nevertheless, Stendhal does toy briefly with the fantasy that on the question of his talent at least he might one day find an arbiter in the shape of the spirit of Montesquieu: 'S'il y a un autre monde, je ne manquerai pas d'aller voir Montesquieu, s'il me dit: "Mon pauvre ami, vous n'avez pas eu de talent du tout", j'en serai fâché mais nullement surpris' (p. 535). In the meantime, though, the only verdicts he is likely to receive will come from much lesser mortals, his friends in the world of the living.

These verdicts will unfortunately be worthless, for none of Stendhal's friends has ever known anything about the most important thing in his life — love: 'A quel ami ai-je jamais dit un mot de mes chagrins d'amour?' (p. 532). But in any case Stendhal is apt to be highly sceptical about the various judgements — good as well as bad – that have been made about him during the course of his life. Most critics have commented on the fact that he spent his childhood being called a 'monstre' and 'une âme atroce' by his Aunt Séraphie.[5] In the autobiography he deals with the charge by pointing out that these are the accusations of a woman suffering from 'toute l'aigreur d'une fille dévote qui n'a pas pu se marier' (p. 551).[6]

What has been less widely discussed is Stendhal's uneasy response to his image in the eyes of his contemporaries, people with whom he had a rather less fraught relationship than with the 'diable femelle' who was his aunt. Indeed, Stendhal begins his autobiography not by taking on the 'monstre' accusation, but by considering his social reputation as 'un homme de beaucoup d'esprit et fort insensible, roué même' (p. 532), 'l'homme le plus gai et le plus insensible' (p. 541). To this worldly and insouciant portrait may be added the glamour of having twice seen himself described in print as 'brillant' (p. 543). Unlike his reputation at home with his family in Grenoble, the mirror held up by Stendhal's social contemporaries is highly flattering and, on his own admission, not entirely unfounded. So, given that one of the questions his autobiography is supposed to answer is whether he is or has been 'un homme d'esprit ou un sot', it is surprising that the apparently unanimous testimony of his friends and acquaintances is dismissed by him as irrelevant to the autobiographical aims of the text. The first reason is that their judgement is made on very partial evidence: since Stendhal has never spoken to anyone about his love-life, none of his friends and acquaintances can have known that his conversational skill was (according to Stendhal) developed only in 1826 as a sort of compensation for the 'despair' that he felt after the combined catastrophes of the death of Mathilde Dembowski and the ending of his affair with Clémentine Curial. The significance of the worldly judgement about Stendhal's social brilliance is obviously going to be affected by knowledge of its private emotional context (which incidentally also gives the lie to the presumably hurtful claims about Stendhal's insensitivity).

The second reason for scepticism about the portrait of his reputation is that, like Séraphie's 'monstre' accusation, it perhaps reflects more on the people who make it than on the person it purports to describe. Being thought brilliant is all very well, Stendhal says, but it's the sort of quality that is liable to bring out the worst in one's friends, so that the compliment may be tinged with not a little spite and envy. (He adds that many of his friends would gladly have paid good money to have a glass of dirty water thrown over him whenever he had even the smallest good fortune such as a new set of clothes, let alone the accolade of a reputation for brilliance, see p. 545.) Moreover, in Stendhal's view, many of the people responsible for his reputation were 'des êtres trop communs pour juger du brillant; par exemple, comment un comte d'Argout peut-il juger du *brillant*? Un homme, dont le bonheur est de lire deux ou trois volumes de romans in-12 pour femmes de chambre par jour!' (p. 543, Stendhal's italics). The implication of this is that the judgement, flattering though it is, and true as it might be, nevertheless places him within the *doxa* of bourgeois Parisian culture (the one that thrived on the banalities of the *roman pour femmes de chambre*), in other words the chief thing which it has been Stendhal's lifelong mission to avoid being contaminated by. To describe himself in its terms, therefore, would be to destroy the very qualities that might distinguish him from it.

The fact is that all judgements, true as well as false, are liable to be made in the name of the *doxa*. In this sense, the problem is not so much one of untruth or falsity as of the discourse in which even truths may be uttered. On this issue (as on many others) Stendhal has an uncanny resemblance to Barthes.[7] We find Barthes too addressing the question of his reputation at an early stage in his autobiography, but the culprit he names is not the limited evidence on which it might have been based, or a cultural proclivity towards vulgarity, but, more precisely, a fact of language, the adjective:

L'Adjectif: Il [i.e. Barthes himself] supporte mal toute *image* de lui-même, souffre d'être nommé. Il considère que la perfection d'un rapport humain tient à cette vacance de l'image: abolir entre soi, de l'un à l'autre, les *adjectifs*; un rapport qui s'adjective est du côté de l'image, du côté de la domination, de la mort.   (*Roland Barthes*, p. 47)

For Barthes, reputations or self-images are sustained by the adjective, and are thus fatally imbricated with the *doxa* (Aristotle's term is given new currency by Barthes and is discussed at some length in *Roland Barthes*). And as he says in *Le Plaisir du texte*, adjectives are 'ces portes du langage par où l'idéologie et l'imaginaire pénètrent à grands flots'.[8] In Barthes's view, adjectives can never succeed in describing or revealing a person; all they do is affirm the supremacy of the *doxa*. They dominate and ultimately destroy the subject in a process whose dependence on the priority of that subject is merely illusory. In the autobiography Barthes goes on to suggest that the way to get round the tyranny of the *doxa* is to refuse the adjective and adopt the genuinely dialectical form of what he calls the 'entretien amoureux', a discourse which operates without adjectives and outside the *doxa*. This idea is developed in the *Fragments d'un discours amoureux*, where it is suggested that it is only thus that the uniqueness of the beloved can be preserved in the lover's eyes; as we have already seen from the earlier discussion of Barthes's *Fragments*, the lover cannot name his beloved in adjectival terms, and this is precisely the mark of his status as lover. The situation in which Barthes sees the lover's discourse taking place is remarkably similar to that of the auto-biographical project as seen by both him and Stendhal, since the success of that project depends for both of them on avoiding the 'adjectivisation' of the autobiographical subject; their strategic responses to the threat of what Barthes calls the *doxa* and Stendhal vulgarity are thus broadly very similar.

Returning now to *Henry Brulard* in the light of this comparison with Barthes, one can see as a first element in Stendhal's strategy the way in which from time to time he lets himself anticipate the kind of adjectival verdict that a negatively imagined reader, more typical of his own day than of the utopian 1880s, might plausibly feel tempted to make. The occasions where this happens are usually the narration of moments when Brulard's reactions to a situation were as intense as they were unconventional, and with which he still, decades after the event, completely identifies. The most striking instances of this are those where Brulard rejoices at the death of someone he hated: the execution of Louis XVI, the guillotining in Grenoble of two generals during the Terror, and the death of his Aunt Séraphie. In recording his delight on these occasions he anticipates the adjectival response typical of the prevailing *doxa* of his day: 'Si les Parisiens sont aussi niais en 1880 qu'en 1835, cette façon de prendre la mort de la sœur de ma mère me fera passer pour *barbare, cruel, atroce*' (p. 736, my italics). Stendhal's counter to this adjectival *niaiserie* on the part of his hypothetical anti-reader is not a better or truer set of adjectives, but the empty demonstrative 'tel', which, significantly, is the only adjectival entry in Barthes's dictionary of the lover's discourse:

TEL. Appelé sans cesse à définir l'objet aimé, et souffrant des incertitudes de cette définition, le sujet amoureux rêve d'une sagesse qui lui ferait prendre l'autre *tel qu'il est, exonéré de tout adjectif.*

(*Fragments*, p. 261, my italics)

As autobiographical narrator, Stendhal behaves rather like Barthes's lover towards his past self when he writes: 'Le lecteur pensera peut-être que je suis cruel mais *tel* j'étais à dix ans *tel* je suis à cinquante-deux' (p. 634, my italics), or 'Quoi qu'il en soit *telle* est la vérité' (p. 736, my italics again). By unwriting the adjectives that he attributes to his Parisian anti-reader, and by replacing them with the contentless demonstrative *tel*, Stendhal is negatively indicating the sort of response that the undefined reader of 1880 might, by inference, ideally be inclined to make.

This is why the posthumous reader of 1880 or 1935 is so important to Stendhal, for he or she is conceived as the antithesis of – or at least as a total stranger to – the *doxa* of his own particular historical context; and Stendhal imagines them living in a world completely different from his own, sharing none of its prejudices, education or religion. Not only does the otherness of these readers make sincerity possible, but for Stendhal it also makes them highly desirable, and he explicitly compares them to people he has loved or imagined loving in his own lifetime. He is thrilled to think that, as he puts it, 'je cours la chance d'être lu en 1900 par les âmes que j'aime, les Mme Roland, les Mélanie Guilbert, les [*un blanc*]' (p. 536). In a near-identical passage in *Souvenirs d'égotisme* he dreams of being read by 'un être tel que Mme Roland ou M. Gros, le géomètre' (*Souvenirs*, p. 429). Mélanie was a former mistress, Mme Roland a Girondin leader who was executed in 1794 and was the author of a volume of memoirs which she wrote in prison while awaiting her death; she remained a lifelong feminine ideal for Stendhal. Gros taught Stendhal mathematics in Grenoble and Stendhal retained an equally deep and long-lasting admiration for both his political ideals and his intellectual honesty. It is Stendhal's desire for this kind of reader, that is to say, for an inherently desirable kind of reader (and not one of the *âmes froides et vulgaires* whom he occasionally envisages as potential readers of his text), that makes his autobiography a viable project, and that also gives particular pertinence to Barthes's concept of the *entretien amoureux*.

And yet for Stendhal it is precisely the unknown quantity that this future reader represents which makes him or her so desirable – hence perhaps the blank after Mélanie's name in the text. So desirable because the pay-off for writing for an unknown posthumous audience is that they will reciprocally guarantee an equivalent unknownness in the autobiographical *je* who is addressing himself to them. Being outside Stendhal's social and cultural world, they can be counted on not to make the sort of judgements which the *doxa* of that society tends to promote. Paradoxically, therefore, the key to the success of the Stendhalian autobiography becomes the avoidance of the sort of judgement that it seemed initially to be in search of. If Stendhal admits towards the end of the book that he has been unable to discover what sort of a person he was, whether he was 'bon, méchant, spirituel, sot' (p. 804), this inability should not be read as an indication that he has failed in the task he set himself, but that the original project was wrongly conceived. The text's quest for self-knowledge no longer takes the form of a search for self-definition, but is guided by Stendhal's desire for a reader whom he cannot name or characterise and who, by the same token, cannot name or characterise him.

'L'entretien amoureux'

Nevertheless, very little is actually said in the text about the positive and constructive role that this reader plays in the formation of that text. When Stendhal pauses to think about the reader's probable response to what he has written, he is usually rather pessimistic. He repeatedly refers to the boredom that he thinks his confessions will induce. Why on earth, he wonders, should any reader be interested in him and his memories: 'Que lui fait tout cet ouvrage?' (p. 600), 'Qui lira 400 pages de mouvements du cœur?' (p. 953). And the qualities he most frequently mentions as the only ones that will make reading possible are forgiveness, patience and courage – not a very appealing proposition for a text which claims to be written 'comme une lettre à un ami'. Stendhal's ideal reader–friend is barely inscribed in the text which she (she because the reader of the autobiography is more often imagined as female than as male) has nevertheless made possible by being its addressee. The reasons for this silence are not hard to find, given the importance of adjectival reticence concerning the auto-biographical subject. Reticence about both subject and reader will help to keep shut the floodgates through which the *doxa* threatens to come flooding in, and destroy the unique *tel* quality that makes each desirable to the other (and which, of course, is also an effect of that desire).

The relatively scanty evidence about the ideal reader of 1880 may therefore be regarded as an indication that the autobiographical text is for Stendhal, as it is for Barthes, an *entretien amoureux* between subject and reader, and that the reader is conceived primarily as a partner in this *entretien*. The justification for this assumption is first and foremost Stendhal's hope of being read in 1900 'par les âmes *que j'aime*, les Mme Roland, les Mélanie Guilbert, [etc. etc.]'. His claim to love these readers, and the presence of the name of a former mistress among them, does immediately suggest a 'rapport amoureux' of the most obvious kind. And it has in fact been suggested that the ideal reader whom Stendhal has in mind for his autobiography is his mother (who died when he was only seven and whom he adored with an uninhibited oedipal passion),[9] in which case Mme Roland could be seen as an image of this maternal reader and so complete a fairly conventional and really rather banal scenario of desire.

But Stendhal is doing something more than attempting to relive or recreate the pleasures or the lost loves of his past; the figure of the beloved is largely a pretext for the recourse to the lover's discourse, whose value is primarily linguistic rather than amorous in that it offers a means of evading the deadly trap of vulgarity and banality (a response into which one can, as we have just seen, all too easily lapse). If one adds Gros's name to the list of desired readers (it appears alongside that of Mme Roland in the *Souvenirs* passage quoted above), then one might begin to look more closely at certain features of the *discours amoureux* that Gros's presence helps to draw attention to. First is the fact that both Mme Roland and Gros are not just souls whom Stendhal adored, but authors in their own right and speakers of a certain kind of discourse. Mme Roland was, as mentioned already, the author of a set of memoirs, which Stendhal read with great passion and enthusiasm, and which must have had particular value for him, because the prison cell and the death sentence which provided the context for the writing of her memoirs are always the ultimate guarantee of authenticity and absence of hypocrisy in the Stendhalian universe. The courageous way in which Mme Roland faced her death placed her, in Stendhal's eyes, firmly outside the hypocritical conventions of the era of nineteenth-century bourgeois monarchy. The lack of hypocrisy and the un-Parisian nobility of spirit that Stendhal saw in Mme Roland and her *Mémoires* must have seemed to him to set standards which his own writing should seek to match, and to which it might also be regarded as a response. In writing *for* a reader like Mme Roland, Stendhal was simultaneously writing *as* her reader.

The same discursive purity is associated with the mathematician Gros. Mathematics for the young Brulard represented the antithesis of the bourgeois hypocrisy that he so loathed in Grenoble: 'Mon enthousiasme pour les mathématiques avait peut-être eu pour base principale mon horreur pour l'hypocrisie ... Suivant moi, l'hypocrisie était impossible en mathématiques' (p. 853). His subsequent doubts about the purity of mathematical discourse are assuaged by the lessons he took with Gros, and he describes studying maths with this 'grand homme' as 'un plaisir vif, analogue à celui de lire un roman entraînant' (p. 862), a remark which suggests a plausible and extremely significant similarity between Gros's mathematical discourse and the literary text of Mme Roland's *Mémoires*. In both cases Stendhal presents himself as the reader of a text 'exonerated' from hypocrisy (the way that

Barthes's beloved is exonerated from adjectives), and to which, as I say, his own text may be conceived as a response (with the same exonerating effect).

It is important to stress that what matters in all this is the quality of the discourse that the relationship of the *entretien* produces, and Stendhal makes it quite clear that he doesn't expect any love in return for his own passionate adoration for these ideal readers. Indeed, he imagines Mme Roland being bored and losing interest in a book like his that doesn't have any descriptions in the style of Walter Scott. And he is fairly sure that Gros disliked him as much as he (Stendhal) adored and respected him (Gros). In fact, he says, all his 'passions d'admiration' have provoked antipathy from their objects ('J'ai déplu à M. de Tracy et à Mme Pasta pour les admirer avec trop d'enthousiasme', p. 863); and presumably, had he had the occasion to meet her, Mme Roland would have been no exception to this unfortunate rule. For this reason, then, Stendhal can hardly be said to be writing in order to win love from the recipients of his autobiographical text.

What is more, in Stendhal's experience, the presence of the passionately beloved has always had a destructive effect on the very self that the autobiographical project is initially in pursuit of. In the presence of the few 'hommes énergiques' that he knew and admired in his youth (one of them being 'l'incomparable Gros'), as later in the presence of 'les êtres que j'ai trop aimés, [j'étais] muet, immobile, stupide, peu aimable et quelquefois offensant à force de dévouement et d'*absence du moi*. Mon amour-propre, mon intérêt, *mon moi* avaient disparu en présence de la personne aimée, j'étais transformé en elle' (p. 547, my italics). Stendhal's passions are not only offensive and emotionally counterproductive, but also make him other than the *moi* that he is. For all these reasons, then, it would be mistaken to see the ideal, desired readers of Stendhal's autobiographical text primarily as desired persons. They share the quality of 'le *naturel* ou l'absence d'hypocrisie' that Stendhal now sees that he has always valued in his friends (p. 805, Stendhal's italics), not a quality that defines them as particular individuals so much as the (non-)quality that makes possible the *entretien* of both friendship and love.

Forming character

In the light of all this it seems that reading and writing are for Stendhal analogous to, or even particular forms of, the *entretien amoureux*, and there is powerful confirmation of this view in the accounts that

Stendhal gives of his own reading experiences in the *Vie de Henry Brulard*. What these passages imply is that the autobiographical project is completed for Stendhal by constituting the self *as* a reader as well as *for* a reader. Most of what Stendhal says about reading refers to his own childhood experiences, and he doesn't say anything about Mme Roland's *Mémoires* in the text itself, since he didn't read them until 1805, when he was twenty-two, in other words after the period covered by *Brulard*. Although the texts of his ideal reader – authors are not among those that feature in the autobiographical account, the autobiography may still be regarded as a response to those texts (as also perhaps to the other texts that he does talk about).

What Stendhal says about his reading has to be set in the context of his ideas about self and personality. He has a rather un-Romantic lack of solemnity in his view of the self, which he regards as a kind of blank which eventually takes on a certain shape as a result of a series of purely fortuitous events. He is acutely aware of how easily he could have become other than what he is: a Jesuit (p. 627), a 'coquin' (p. 605), rich (p. 605), 'méchant' (p. 624), 'un soldat crapuleux coureur de filles et de cabarets' (p. 627), etc., etc. A number of these accidental happenings are meetings with people whose influence was decisive – the one with Gros, for example: 'le hasard voulut que je visse un grand homme et que je ne devinsse pas un coquin' (p. 859). But the most frequently cited and perhaps also the most decisive encounters were not with people but with books. Stendhal repeatedly refers to the importance that certain books have had for him and regularly draws up lists and rankings of these books, with Shakespeare, Cervantes and Ariosto placed at the head (and Rousseau almost invariably placed 'en second rang', pp. 911–12).

These books did not just form Stendhal's taste, nor simply determine his vocation as a writer (which they did only incidentally); nor yet did they merely provide him with the few moments of pleasure that he had in his lonely and miserable childhood; they actually made him the person that he has become: 'L'Arioste forma mon caractère' (p. 619); his discovery of *Don Quixote* was 'peut-être la plus grande époque de ma vie' (p. 618); the experience of reading his uncle's collection of novels was 'décisive pour mon caractère' (p. 699); reading Shakespeare was like a rebirth (p. 779); *La Nouvelle Héloïse* saved him from being 'un *scélérat noir* ou un coquin gracieux et insinuant' and instead made him 'profondément honnête homme' (p. 716, Stendhal's italics); and, finally, the six months he spent in Paris alone in a fifth-floor garret at the age of sixteen reading La Bruyère, Montaigne and Rousseau was a period which he also claims 'forma [s]on caractère'

(p. 538). Reading for Stendhal was thus literally a character-building experience. This wasn't so much because of anything he learned from books in any positive sense, but because reading for him was always one of the highest forms of pleasure and one of the intensest kinds of emotional experience. He was 'mad' about *Hamlet* (p. 538), he became 'amoureux fou de Bradamante' while reading Ariosto (p. 619), and read Richardson's *Charles Grandison* 'en fondant en larmes de tendresse' (p. 821). The pleasures of reading Montesquieu or Walter Scott (always undertaken 'avec délices') are the only acceptable substitute for love itself (p. 544); his favourite authors give him a 'plaisir profond ... allant jusqu'au *bonheur*' (p. 911, Stendhal's italics), and the passion with which he read his uncle's collection of novels proves to be as inexpressible as any other. Even by eighteenth-century standards, the emotional intensity of Stendhal's reading seems unusual and extreme.

Both reading and love offer an escape from contemporary 'hypocrisie', and most of Stendhal's preferred reading consisted of books even farther removed from his own culture than the projected reader of 1880 would be. His top three writers (Cervantes, Shakespeare and Ariosto) date from the sixteenth century, and even with those books that are closer to him in time, Stendhal is careful to distinguish between the banality of the *romans pour les femmes de chambre*, or the hypocrisy that he sees in writers such as Racine and Chateaubriand on the one hand, and the texts that give him pleasure on the other. The text of pleasure transports him out of the mediocrity and the hypocrisy of the surrounding *doxa*, and the texts of unpleasure (the hypocritical Racine, the Jesuitical Marmontel, Virgil, Voltaire, etc.) don't. (There were plenty of books that Stendhal positively hated: the opposite of pleasure in reading is rarely indifference.) So that although it was pleasure in the text of pleasure (and the comparison with Barthes inevitably makes itself felt again) that formed Stendhal's character, it did so in a way that made any judgemental, adjectival definition of that character quite impossible to undertake, and it exists simply as a *tel* in the autobiographical text. Stendhal's *moi* is a reader of texts of pleasure, constructed as an interlocutor in the non-ideological, *doxa*-free *entretien amoureux*, and only becomes available in the autobiographical text through a continuation of the same *entretien* with its own readers.

Grammatical attitudes

Indeed, as Benveniste reminds us, it is the essence of dialogue to make the roles of *je* and *tu* alternate, and for him the self in language is only constituted through this alternation: '[la] condition de dialogue ... est constitutive de la *personne*, car elle implique en réciprocité que je deviens *tu* dans l'allocution de celui qui à son tour se désigne par *je*' (p. 260). If the dialogue or *entretien* in which Stendhal is engaged is genuinely reciprocal, then Stendhal must be seen as both reader and subject, the reader of other authors and subject of the text which they in turn read. And, of course, the same must necessarily apply to them: Mme Roland and M. Gros are equal interlocutors who are both subjects of their own discourse (of which Stendhal is a reader) and also readers of Stendhal's autobiographical text. The *je—tu* axis is a two-way one, or, as Barthes puts it in *Le Plaisir du texte*, 'le texte périme les attitudes grammaticales':

> Sur la scène du texte, pas de rampe: il n'y a pas derrière le texte quelqu'un d'actif (l'écrivain) et devant lui quelqu'un de passif (le lecteur); il n'y a pas un sujet et un objet.

And he goes on to quote Angelus Silesius's claim that 'L'œil par où je vois Dieu est le même œil par où il me voit' (p. 29), a phrase in which one might perhaps read a solution to the problem raised by Stendhal's question: 'quel œil peut se voir soi-même?' Since the autobiographical self is also a reader, and the reader an autobiographical author in her own right – since both, in other words, are indistinguishably both – it no longer seems possible to speak with any clarity or certainty about what the role of the reader of Stendhal's autobiography might be. Though the confusion itself is perhaps testimony enough of the centrality of reading to the autobiographical text.

But the reading role occupied by Mme Roland must by now seem too impossibly ideal for the more ordinary reader of autobiography (and in the end we are all ordinary readers of autobiography), so a conclusion ought perhaps to outline the sort of path a reading of the *Vie de Henry Brulard* might realistically begin to follow. First, it does seem that Stendhal's reader of the 1980s should abandon the search for any definable Stendhalian physiognomy or *moi*, and recognise that the autobiographical subject has been undone in one sense by the text that constitutes him in another sense. He has been dissolved and absorbed, as Barthes says, like a spider into 'les sécrétions constructives de sa toile' (*Plaisir*, p. 101), leaving only the textual effect of the haunting presence of an author lost within the text. The reader may then testify to the fact that she has been manipulated by the text into experiencing its author as an object of desire, and possibly even admit that she ends up wanting to say what Louis Marin is brave enough to state outright at the beginning of his essay on *Brulard*: 'Beyle is for me, not only a writer, but also an intimate friend.'[10] This enviably lame admission would at least have the virtue of being a sign that the reader had made the first gesture of response to the text's aim and offered his own small contribution to keeping closed the profoundly anti-autobiographical floodgates of the *doxa*.

The *Vie de Henry Brulard* provides documentary evidence of the importance that reading had for Stendhal, both as part of the biographical content of his book and as an inevitable complement to the writing of it. To this extent the detour via the autobiographical texts taken in this chapter provides further justification for my own critical preoccupation with the issue in the discussion of the novels. But the discussion of *Brulard* also confirms the nature of the reading practice that Stendhal's writing — both fictional and autobiographical — requires. Reading may have a generically distinctive role to play in autobiography, and the reader of the life is not required to perform in quite the same way as the reader of the novels. But what is nevertheless common to both Stendhal's fiction and his autobiography is the way he relies on his reader to save his writing — to exonerate it, as I have said — from the *doxa*. In both cases this is achieved largely by the shifting of the discursive axis from reference to conation (to use Jakobson's terms again) in a move which Marin's comments are ample testimony to, and whose value lies in the way in which it creates a resistance to the monologism of adjectivisation, of public opinion, of the *vraisemblable*.

Part Five
LA CHARTREUSE DE PARME

7

THE REPRESENTATION OF POLITICS AND THE POLITICS OF REPRESENTATION

La politique corrompt toujours la beauté; c'est que la politique veut agir sur le plus grand nombre.
Stendhal, *Journal*

Le discours politique n'est pas le seul à se répéter, et à se généraliser, à se fatiguer.
Barthes, *Roland Barthes*

Politics and/in literature

The pistol shot of politics that rings out in each of Stendhal's novels is regularly described in them as a gross impropriety which detracts from the harmonies of the novel's central imaginative concerns, but which the demands of accurate representation unfortunately make a necessary component of the fiction. The mirror principle imposes its exacting requirements, and the reluctant novelist must comply. In *Armance* it is a precise and dutiful historian who finds himself professionally obliged to record a conversation between Octave and Armance which happens to touch on political issues:

Ce n'est pas sans danger que nous aurons été *historiens fidèles*. La politique venant couper un récit aussi simple, peut faire l'effet d'un coup de pistolet au milieu d'un concert. (*Armance*, p. 105, my italics)

In *Le Rouge* the apology appears as a parenthetical comment in the account of the royalist conspiracy which Julien is brought in to memorise. Here the author emphatically opposes politics to the passionate and energetic interests of the imagination, and it is his publisher who reprimands him sharply with a reminder of his obligations to the mirror principle:

– La politique, reprend l'auteur, est une pierre attachée au cou de la littérature, et qui, en moins de six mois, la submerge. La politique au milieu des intérêts d'imagination, c'est un coup de pistolet au milieu d'un concert. Ce bruit est déchirant sans être énergique. Il ne s'accorde avec le son d'aucun instrument. Cette politique va offenser mortellement une moitié des lecteurs, et ennuyer

155

l'autre qui l'a trouvée bien autrement spéciale et énergique dans le journal du matin ...

   – Si vos personnages ne parlent pas politique, reprend l'éditeur, ce ne sont plus des Français de 1830, et *votre livre n'est plus un miroir*, comme vous en avez la prétention ...   (*Le Rouge*, pp. 360–1, my italics)

For the author the mention of politics is graceless, boring and possibly offensive, and in *La Chartreuse* this condemnation is compounded with the accusation of squalor.[1] In the passage that introduces Bruno's report to Gina of the political consequences of Prince Ernest's death Stendhal writes:

La politique dans une œuvre littéraire, c'est un coup de pistolet au milieu d'un concert, *quelque chose de grossier* et auquel pourtant il n'est pas possible de refuser son attention.

   Nous allons parler de *fort vilaines choses*, et que, pour plus d'une raison, nous voudrions taire; mais nous sommes forcés d'en venir à des événements qui sont de notre domaine, puisqu'ils ont pour théâtre le cœur des personnages.   (*La Chartreuse*, p. 435, my italics)

Stendhal is claiming in these remarks that politics are an integral part of both historical and social reality (the reality of France in 1827 and 1830 for *Armance* and *Le Rouge*, and the reality of the hearts and minds of the protagonists of *La Chartreuse*). However squalid, offensive and boring, politics must be included in a novel which makes any claim for itself as a mirror held up to reality. In other words, the validity of the novel as representation depends on the inclusion of politics in its narrative.

   But if mimesis requires the inclusion of politics in literature, that inclusion makes space for reading responses that are liable to undermine or distort that mimesis. For, says Stendhal, to introduce politics into literature is to introduce the 'odious'; and with the odious comes 'la haine impuissante', whose effects are first to destroy the 'plaisirs délicats qui sont l'objet des efforts du poète' (*Racine et Shakespeare*, p. 115), and second to trigger in the reader a political animus that is bound to be directed against the author. The mechanism of this latter effect is described by Stendhal in the second preface to *Lucien Leuwen*, where he complains of the way that his representations of political realities are regularly used against him by his readers, who cannot resist the assumption that someone who depicts republicans in his novels must necessarily be 'un républicain enthousiaste de Robespierre et de Couthon', even if it means accusing him ten pages later of passionately wanting 'le retour de la branche aînée et le règne de Louis XIX' on account of his fictional portrayal of people who do have desires of this political kind. Despite Stendhal's plaintive question in the 'Avant-propos' to *Armance*, 'De quel parti est un miroir?', when it comes to politics, the mirror is always assumed to be partisan. Mimetic fidelity to reality demands that politics form a part of the mirror's reflections, but their inclusion renders mimesis deeply vulnerable to distortion through the enraged presumptions of its readers.

For all Stendhal's suggestion that politics can theoretically be bracketed out of a literature in which they figure as a sort of after-thought imposed by the requirements of mimesis, politics permeate all aspects of the social and cultural reality of Stendhal's novels. As Auerbach remarks, 'contemporary social conditions are woven into the action [of *Le Rouge*] in a manner more detailed and more real than had been exhibited in any earlier novel' (*Mimesis*, p. 403). Politics are not just an isolated area of social reality, but colour every part of social existence.

In the case of Stendhal, this colour does not derive so much from his particular political convictions as from his understanding of the political mechanism that inspires his reader's distorting responses to representations of political reality. In the preface to *Lucien Leuwen*, Stendhal insists that his own politics are irrelevant to the political reality he is portraying, but describes himself − for the record, as it were − as 'un partisan modéré de la Charte de 1830'. Elsewhere he presents this political stance as a kind of reasonable and moderate support for the inevitable:

tout homme éclairé voit avec assez de netteté que la France finira par obtenir une constitution raisonnable et un véritable gouvernement avec les deux Chambres, et que l'époque de l'établissement d'un système juste et constitutionnel sous la direction d'un ministère de *centre gauche* n'est reculé que de quelques années.

(*Lettres de Paris. 1825*, pp. 79−80, Stendhal's italics)

He doesn't expect full justice from the judicial system until around 1840, and thinks that 'positive liberty' is unlikely to come about until 1860; but he has no doubt that this is the course that things will eventually take. (The failure of 1830 put back this programme for a while, but did not substantially alter the ultimate outcome in Stendhal's eyes.) By presenting his politics as moderate support for the inevitable, Stendhal is seeking to suggest that the politics in his novels are not designed either to promote or to oppose any particular political programme.[2]

Politics belong in Stendhal's novels because they are part of a social reality which constitutes both the object of the novels' representation and the context in which they will be read. And if one shifts the perspective a little, one can see that politics are also essential to his novels' relation to that reality: in certain forms, politics provide the kind of energy needed to counteract the etiolation and imitativeness which at the same time constitute one of the other forms that politics can take in that political reality. There are politics in the *doxa*, and there are politics in the explosive energies that resist the *doxa*.

In the same letter where Stendhal describes his political views, he also announces the imminent entry of these political energies into contemporary literature when he writes, 'La Révolution va produire son effet sur la littérature' (p. 80). Politics, he says, are about to put an end to the literature of the Ancien Régime which has survived anachronistically into the nineteenth century, since writers whose talents have been exercised exclusively in the political sphere are beginning to turn to literature: 'La littérature est sur le point de changer complètement et de revivre sous nos yeux grâce aux hommes qui, comme M. de Ségur, ne sont écrivains que parce qu'ils ont perdu leurs fonctions politiques.' This M. de Ségur is a former general and the author of the reputedly highly successful *Histoire de Napoléon et de la Grande Armée pendant l'année 1812*. The other works that Stendhal mentions as instances of this literary revolution are Daru's *Histoire de Venise*, Barante's *Histoire des ducs de Bourgogne*, Fain's *Cabinet de l'Empereur* (these authors are all men of action turned writer), and Mignet's two-volume *Histoire de la Révolution française* which Stendhal judges to be 'supérieur à tout ce qui a paru depuis cinquante ans' (p. 81). The obscurity of these titles might tend to cast doubt on the view that Stendhal is putting forward if it didn't also tally with his belief that the arts can be at their most sublime when they become a channel for obstructed political energies. In the *Vie de Rossini* Stendhal explains the quality and significance of music in Italy as an indirect effect of political tyranny:

Sous un climat brûlant, sous une tyrannie sans pitié, où parler est si dangereux, le désespoir ou le bonheur s'expriment plus naturellement par un chant plaintif que par une lettre. On ne parle que de musique; on n'ose avoir une opinion et la discuter avec feu et franchise que sur la musique.   (I, p. 144)

Under political tyrannies political energies are diverted into song, producing music of a force unknown under the more liberal conditions of French government, and culminating in Italian opera, whose superiority to its French equivalent is a constant refrain of Stendhal's writing (and forms the underlying theme of the Rossini book). The energy that Stendhal admired in the crimes of Berthet and Lafargue was the only form that political energy could take amongst people of their class; and it is because of this diversion that these crimes of passion acquired the political significance which Julien stresses in relation to his own action during his trial in *Le Rouge*.

On the whole, however, politics in the France of the 1820s and thirties tend predominantly to reveal another face — the face of banality and repetition. They are rarely manifest in the guise of the violent energies associated with the Revolution. Far more often politics are reduced to being mere political opinion; and since opinions in Stendhal's world tend to be concocted for the benefit of the public, political opinion is merely one manifestation of public opinion, the *opinion publique* which controls the enervating *convenances* of modern-day Paris. The involvement of newspapers in the political sphere means that, in the France of the Restoration and the July Monarchy, politics are expressed as parroted opinion and platitude; so that liberals are not only — or rather, not even necessarily — people who want to see the liberties promised by the Revolution realised in institutional form (in accordance with the outline contained in the *Lettres de Paris*), but the people who repeat the *doxa* contained in *Le Constitutionnel*. Politics in this form, far from providing the impetus for a revolution in literature and putting an end to 'toutes les vieilles absurdités littéraires ... dans une Saint-Barthélemy générale' (*Lettres de Paris. 1825*, p. 80), are profoundly inimical both to revolution and to literature, and promote a conformity of opinion and style which Stendhal's own fiction continually strives to resist.

Literature therefore has everything to gain from politics as a revolutionary force, and everything to lose from politics as a practice of the *doxa*. This paradox goes some way to explaining the ambivalence of Stendhal's remarks about the place of politics in literature. It is an ambivalence which may be further clarified by borrowing a distinction that Barthes has made between *le politique* (the political) and *la politique* (politics).[3] This distinction lends support to the idea that in Stendhal politics as the political (*le politique*) are an integral dimension of contemporary social reality, and also an aspect of the literature that seeks to represent it; whereas politics as rhetoric and platitude (*la politique*) would deny the reality of literature's representations by translating those representations into a set of authorial opinions, and so sap the energies of a literature that refuses to comply with the *convenances* of its own repetitive discourse.

This is why politics are at once odious and vital for Stendhal's fiction: odious as opinion, vital as the channel for the energies which oppose the *doxa* of opinion. The ambiguity is inherent in the pistol-shot metaphor through which Stendhal expresses his view of the relation between literature and politics: on the one hand, there is the positive violence of the shooting (an extreme version of the *imprévu* discussed in chapter 5); and, on the other, there is the implication that politics destroy the musical harmonies of the literary arts. Politics in the positive sense are an essential ingredient in Stendhal's writing, imbuing his novels with a force which politics in the negative sense simultaneously seek to undermine. This tension runs right through the novels, and can be seen not only in their representations of events with an overt political content, but in the way that the novels position themselves in relation to the political *doxa* which threatens to destroy both their energies and the mimesis to which they are committed.

Political quixotry

La Chartreuse de Parme is saturated with politics and the political from beginning to end: the canon's nephew warns the narrator at the outset that this is a tale likely to incur him political opprobrium; the novel proper opens with Napoleon's liberation of Milan from Austrian tyranny, and closes with Mosca's restoration of justice and stability in the state of Parma; it describes events of self-evident political significance, like the battle of Waterloo, the assassination of a prince, the republican revolt and its suppression; and it portrays in the minutest detail the political mechanisms of the Italian court at Parma. But just as, at a conceptual level, politics is a word with at least two different senses, *La Chartreuse* depicts it as an activity with a variety (at least the three that are discussed in this chapter) of different applications and styles.[4] The novel does not just portray events that have a political and historical dimension; it depicts characters who illustrate a variety of ways of being political, and demonstrates through them that politics exist in more than one variety of styles.

First are the characters whose politics are a matter of conviction and belief (primarily Fabrice, Clélia and Gina). Paradoxically, it is precisely these characters who are often thought of as being excluded from the political scope of the novel, since it is through them that the 'intérêts de l'imagination' are sustained in the manner that the author of *Le Rouge* contrasts so starkly with the world of politics. But to take one's cue from his remark is to ignore the fact that it is the most special and energetic characters (in *La Chartreuse* at least) who are the ones with the strongest political convictions. Fabrice's involvement with politics extends well beyond the role he is forced to play as victim of the political intriguing at the Parmesan court. He is a fervent monarchist and shares with the Prince of Parma himself the belief that Louis XIV represents the ultimate ideal in government. As he explains to the Prince:

je tiens ... que tout ce qui a été fait depuis la mort de Louis XIV, en 1715, est à la fois un crime et une sottise.   (p. 144)

He believes passionately that, 'les mots *liberté, justice, bonheur du plus grand nombre*, sont infâmes et criminels', and that republicanism is nothing less than heresy.

It is true that Fabrice's arch-royalist political faith (and 'faith' is the word that Stendhal uses to describe his politics) is, for all its ideological fervour, not without its ideological contradictions. The believer in a Louis XIV monarchism is a former volunteer in Napoleon's army, and still reads 'avec délices les journaux français, et faisait même des imprudences pour s'en procurer' (p. 146). Nor is the man in whom the word 'liberté' inspires such horror perturbed by the fact that his passion for Clélia is involving him with 'une petite sectaire de libéralisme' (p. 338) – in other words, just the kind of heretic he abhors. *La Chartreuse* is certainly unpolitical in the sense that Stendhal appears not to be concerned by his hero's ideological incoherence, and not interested in bringing him round to a better, more consistent or more enlightened position. And he even passes up the chance of making any dramatic capital out of the ideological differences between Fabrice and Clélia, differences which neither of them seems even to notice, let alone to worry about.

It is more likely that Fabrice's ideological confusion is a mere side effect of the nature and quality of his ideological belief, regardless of its content. What Stendhal would have his readers notice is that it is possible to have this kind of faith and passion (which he otherwise claims to be incompatible with politics) within the political sphere itself; and, moreover, that this quality of conviction should be appreciated as a contrast to the cynical and self-interested motives that determine political behaviour at the court.

This difference points to the existence of a second political style, which is exemplified by the Prince's response to Fabrice's credo in which he (the Prince) is too suspicious to be able to see the testimony of an ideological ally; indeed, he is so ensnared by anxiety and suspicion that he convinces himself that Fabrice is merely repeating the lessons of his republican aunt in order to serve the interests of her political advancement. This blindness and unease is typical of the kind of politics that does, without doubt, fall outside the domain of imagination and energy, and does therefore represent a kind of politics for which apologies would be appropriate.

There is, however, a third political way in which quixotry and suspicion are more evenly balanced – Mosca's. In one sense Mosca could be regarded as the central political figure in *La Chartreuse*, and as the novel's most successful politician. His political activity is motivated neither by ideological conviction nor by the motives of personal self-advancement, but is inseparable at every stage from the passion that Stendhal's comments in *Le Rouge* define as the antithesis of the political. Politics for him are the necessary consequence of his passion for Gina, and of hers for Fabrice. He stays in Parma for Gina's sake, initially because it is only by remaining minister at the court that his income will be high enough to keep them both happy and amused; and subsequently because Fabrice's fate (which is Gina's sole preoccupation) becomes inextricably bound up with Parma and its political institutions. Mosca has nothing to prove by way of political ideology, no programme to implement, and his political ambitions are restricted to maintaining a harmonious order at the court of Prince Ernest and to keeping Parma's prisons empty. Politics to him are a game like whist or chess in which, before Gina's arrival, he is determined simply to be the best player. As he explains to her:

je m'habille comme un personnage de comédie pour gagner un grand état de maison et quelques milliers de francs. Une fois entré dans cette sorte de jeu d'échecs, choqué des insolences de mes supérieurs, j'ai voulu occuper une des premières places; j'y suis arrivé.[5]

That he is Parma's most skilful political player is demonstrated by the summary of his political achievements with which the novel ends:

Les prisons de Parme étaient vides, le comte immensément riche, Ernest V adoré de ses sujets qui comparaient son gouvernement à celui des grands-ducs de Toscane.

Mosca shares with François Leuwen and Stendhal's author–narrator the ironist's lack of purpose and belief. However, this lack of political purpose proves to be necessary not just for political stability in government, but also for the protection of the energies of passion. Ideological agnosticism is as essential to good politics as good politics are to passion. And in the characters of Fabrice and Mosca one can see that, far from interrupting narratives, weighing down the imaginative flights of literature, or destroying the energetic harmonies of the novel, politics are crucially involved in all, including the most sacred and sublime, aspects of the novel. As Harry Levin has written, 'The shooting is on the program; the pistol is in the score; the Stendhalian performance would be incomplete without it.'[6]

The sublime is dependent on the political for its very survival, and this is true even of the instances of sublimity in the sphere of politics themselves; for too quixotic a view of politics leads inevitably to political disaster. Fabrice and Clélia, when they think about politics at all (and, for all his royalist fervour, Fabrice 'ne songeait pas deux fois par mois à tous ces grands principes', p. 146), take an extremely idealistic view, to the point where their political beliefs become positively counterproductive. On the whole, political sense proves to be incompatible with political ideals. For instance, Clélia's high-minded republicanism induces in her an antipathy towards the court, which constitutes Parma's only political arena. So that if she were to take her politics at all seriously at a practical level, she would find that her ideals had removed her from the only institutional sphere in which politics can effectively be practised in Parma.

The fate of Ferrante Palla's republican uprising bears this paradox out even more forcefully. With eyes which 'respiraient le feu d'une âme ardente' (p. 388), and which were 'remplis d'une exaltation si tendre', he has all the hallmarks of a political Don Quixote − 'toujours rempli d'imaginations romanesques et touchantes ... toujours nourrissant dans son âme quelque contemplation héroïque et hasardée' (De l'Amour, p. 243). His passionate hatred of the prince, whom he regards as a tyrant ('J'exècre le prince, qui est un tyran', p. 389), is an instance of his 'imaginations romanesques et touchantes', and his assassination of that 'tyrant' nothing less than 'héroïque et hasardé'. Its consequences are, however, chaotic and, without the intervention of Mosca, would have been disastrously counter-productive. Mosca describes the scenario that would have ensued as follows:

Les troupes fraternisaient avec le peuple, il y avait trois jours de massacre et d'incendie (car il faut cent ans à ce pays pour que la république n'y soit pas une absurdité), puis quinze jours de pillage, jusqu'à ce que deux ou trois régiments fournis par l'étranger fussent venus mettre le holà.   (p. 444)

Republican passions would inevitably have ended in the repression and real tyranny of Austrian rule (as indeed happened in 1831 after the republican uprising in Modena). Exaltation, even of the most politically laudable kind, is liable to make for very bad politics, and to open the way to a régime in which it has a far smaller chance of survival than it does under the orderly but agnostic reign of Mosca's ministry. Quixotry is as likely to lead to as much chaos and repression as the régime of the 'vils Sancho Pança' (Rassi, Fabio Conti and Zurla) who take over the government of Parma on Mosca's departure, and reduce it in no time to a state of highly dangerous disorder. It is Mosca who tells Fabrice that, 'De tout temps les vils Sancho Pança l'emporteront à la longue sur les sublimes don Quichotte' (p. 189); but, in fact, political order and political success (in other words, the kind of administration that Mosca is described as having established at the end of the novel) depend as much on Mosca's ability to control and restrain the sublime Don Quixotes of this world as on his capacity to outmanoeuvre its Sancho Panzas.

There is also an element of politically counterproductive quixotry in most of Gina's dealings at the court. Her exaltation, it is true, is not strictly political, and is inspired by more private passions. However, this makes little difference to her political behaviour, since the most politically exalted characters in the novel (Fabrice, Clélia and Ferrante Palla) are also the novel's most exalted lovers; and when it comes to his motives for poisoning the Prince, Ferrante Palla's republican idealism is almost indistinguishable from his passionate adoration of Gina. Gina's power at the court comes from her ability to charm, and in particular from her ability to charm away the boredom which goes with the mediocrity and conformism that constitute the courtier's lot. She breathes a kind of quixotic gaiety into life in Parma, which can be captivating, but also catastrophic. The Princess, whom Gina brings back to life with her friendship and unorthodox frankness, is extremely suspicious of the very energy which has nevertheless rescued her (the Princess) from a sad decline into old age and from her conviction that she is the unhappiest person in Parma. It is her distaste for the energy of Gina's passion that leaves her unmoved when Gina comes to ask for her help in saving Fabrice from poison:

La princesse, qui avait une répugnance marquée pour l'énergie, qui lui semblait vulgaire, la crut folle, et ne parut pas du tout disposée à tenter en sa faveur quelque démarche insolite. La duchesse, hors d'elle-même, pleurait à chaudes larmes, elle ne savait que répéter à chaque instant:

— Mais, madame, dans un quart d'heure Fabrice sera mort par le poison! (p. 474)

The princess's failure to respond to this plea demonstrates very poignantly that energy is not a politically productive virtue.

When she enlists the help of Prince Ranuce-Ernest, Gina almost ruins the chances of success that she has by allowing her emotions of the moment to insult his dignity and self-image through her reference to poison. In her desperation to save Fabrice, she blurts out, 'on empoisonne Fabrice dans votre citadelle! Sauvez-le!', with the result that the Prince loses all sympathy for Gina's passion and Fabrice's plight. It is a gross political blunder to suggest that poison is used in Parma, and the Prince is appalled and offended to think that

on administre du poison dans mes états, et cela sans me le dire! Rassi veut donc me déshonorer aux yeux de l'Europe! Et Dieu sait ce que je lirai le mois prochain dans les journaux de Paris! (p. 477)

Gina's sublime disdain for vulgar political strategy and her passionate spontaneity could easily have led to the death of another sublime character — as she realises to her anguish:

Si je n'eusse pas parlé de poison, se dit-elle, il m'accordait la liberté de Fabrice. O cher Fabrice! ajouta-t-elle, il est donc écrit que c'est moi qui dois te percer le cœur par mes sottises!

In the event, however, she wins the Prince's co-operation by acquiescing to a deal whereby the Prince offers to save Fabrice in return for her granting him 'tout ce que [s]on amour peut désirer de plus heureux', as he puts it with all the tact that his base designs can muster (p. 479). The political errors of her quixotry have to be paid for by complying with the calculating opportunism of a Sancho Panza. (It is horribly ironic, of course, that Clélia has already saved Fabrice, so that the Duchess's agony and humiliation are quite unnecessary.) This scene is in many ways a more urgent and desperate replay of the one with Prince Ernest IV, where it is Gina's spontaneous and unpolitical expression of her scorn for the Prince that leads to Mosca's compensatory omission of the key phrase 'procédure injuste' and subsequently to Fabrice's arrest. Its political lessons are exactly the same: namely, that it takes good political strategy and not the sublimities of passion both to save the lives of passionate heroes (i.e. Fabrice), and to restrain the Sancho Panzas who are scheming to poison (i.e. Fabio Conti) and seduce (i.e. the Prince).

So, although Stendhal claims that the 'intérêts de l'imagination' are disrupted and deflected by the inclusion of politics in the novel, as far as the action itself is concerned, those interests are shown to depend crucially on politics for their survival and continuation. What is more, they frequently appear to be more severely threatened by their own unthinking energies than by any political intervention from the outside.

Politics thus have a complex role to play in Stendhal's mimetic project. As *doxa*, politics reveal the deadly potential that all platitude has; but, equally, politics as an instance of the *imprévu* that relates them to the violence of Lafargue's crime of passion, politics as ideal, can be equally negative because self-destructive. Moreover, the irrational harmonies of political idealism would seem in any case to lie beyond the reach of intelligible discourse (the discourse on which the novel has ultimately to rely), just as the predictable platitudes of the political *doxa* threaten the novel's own discursive harmony through the sickening over-intelligibility of their interpretation of the world. The solution – if one may speak of solutions in a situation of this kind – can be neither the promotion of pure ideals, nor the promulgation of any particular political programme. The novel represents politics by showing how each (ideal and *doxa*) seeks to undermine the other: ideal to explode platitude and platitude to recuperate ideal. It is Mosca who succeeds in holding the balance between these two forces and so allows the novel's own representation to take place.

'Frapper les imaginations'

Stendhal is not therefore using his heroes in *La Chartreuse* either to propound or to challenge any particular political programme. The republicanism of Ferrante Palla and Clélia (which one would expect Stendhal's own political sympathies to endorse) is counterweighted by Fabrice's monarchist ideals, by Mosca's agnosticism, and by the disastrous consequences of the attempt to put that republicanism into action. Instead, the novel's revolutionary energies are indiscriminately confused with other passions. The interests of the imagination include the political; they also depend on politics (though a politics of a rather different style) for their survival, and for protection against themselves. If there is political violence in the novel it is almost always associated with these passions; for the pistol shots that ring out in the harmonies of Stendhal's fiction tend to be fired exclusively by the quixotic characters, and all the murders that take place in *La Chartreuse* are committed by the very characters who sustain the novel's imaginative interests: Giletti is murdered by Fabrice, Prince Ernest IV by Ferrante Palla and at Gina's request, and sixty-odd republicans are shot down on the orders of Mosca. Although the politics of the Prince and his court may be vile, they are rarely, if ever, violent.

Political power in Parma is wielded not so much through direct action as through an ability to control representations; for, ultimately,

Stendhalian politics are less concerned with actions than with their representation.[7] Prince Ernest IV, whom Ferrante Palla execrates as a tyrant, has actually only ever had two men put to death (and, even then, not at his own instigation, but Rassi's). His power rests on his ability to 'frapper les imaginations', as he puts it himself (p. 126), rather than on a capacity to strike with any physical force. Furthermore, the two liberals whom he has executed meet their punishment not for any actions they have committed, or even intended to commit; they die for having represented him, or, rather, having misrepresented him, as a tyrant. In the words of the account that Mosca gives to Gina:

Il paraît que ces imprudents se réunissaient à jour fixe pour dire du mal du prince et adresser au ciel des vœux ardents, afin que la peste pût venir à Parme, et les délivrer du tyran. Le mot *tyran* a été prouvé.

(pp. 120–1, Stendhal's italics)

Power and the political contestation of power are seen to lie in words rather than deeds. It is for this reason, then, that the verbal representation of things becomes the central political issue of the novel. Political power goes to those who are the most skilful manipulators of representations, or, as is more frequently the case, of *mis*representations. In this way the theme of politics allows Stendhal to explore some of the implications and problems of the very principle that brings politics into the novel in the first place: the accurate representation of reality. In Stendhal's fiction politics do not just constitute a part of the representation of reality, but, far more importantly, play a large and powerful role in raising questions about the very form of that representation.

The account of the change of political rule which opens the novel with the arrival of Napoleon in Milan already defines political power in terms of a conflict of representations: the Austrian defence against Napoleon seems to consist largely of a widely disseminated misrepresentation of the French:

huit jours encore avant l'arrivée des Français, les Milanais ne voyaient en eux qu'un ramassis de brigands, habitués à fuir toujours devant les troupes de sa majesté impériale et royale: c'était du moins ce que leur répétait trois fois la semaine un petit journal grand comme la main, imprimé sur du papier sale. (p. 5)

Similarly, the defeat of the Austrians seems to be brought about by Gros's satirical caricature of the Austrian governor of Milan, the Archduke Ferdinand. Hearing of the exploits of the Archduke in the café des Servi, Gros takes the ice-cream menu, printed on 'une feuille de vilain papier jaune':

Sur le revers de la feuille il dessina le gros archiduc; un soldat français lui donnait un coup de baïonnette dans le ventre, et, au lieu de sang, il en sortait une quantité de blé incroyable. La chose nommée plaisanterie ou caricature n'était pas connue en ce pays de despotisme cauteleux. Le dessin laissé par Gros sur la table du café des *Servi* parut un miracle descendu du ciel; il fut gravé dans la nuit, et le lendemain on en vendit vingt mille exemplaires.
(p. 7)

The twenty thousand copies that are sold the next day are infinitely more powerful and infinitely more effective than any physical action that the bootless and hatless French army could possibly have undertaken. In other words, the French liberation of Milan is achieved by a contest between a genial French military painter ('un jeune peintre en miniature, un peu fou, nommé Gros, célèbre depuis, et qui était venu avec l'armée', p. 7), and a reactionary newspaper. The 'folie' and the comic gaiety of Gros's caricature make it seem inevitable in Stendhalian terms that the French should win this non-violent combat of representations. But there is nevertheless an element of vileness in the allusions to the representational process itself: the reactionary newspaper is printed on dirty paper ('imprimé sur du papier *sale*') and the ice-cream menu on which Gros draws the Archduke is also contaminated with the same negative connotations, being 'une feuille de *vilain* papier jaune'. There is already a hint here that there may be something slightly squalid about the whole business of representation itself.

This suggestion emerges again, in connection first with the Austrian Empire, and then with the court of Parma. Austria appears to rule largely on the basis of false accounts: the return to what Stendhal calls the 'idées anciennes' in the *tredici mesi* that follow the 'deux années de folie et de bonheur' is marked by the publication of the 'news' that 'Napoléon avait été pendu par les Mamelucks en Egypte, comme il le méritait à tant de titres' (p. 13). And the good standing that the Marquis del Dongo has with the Austrian administration derives largely from the totally fictitious intelligence that he regularly supplies them with. His tactic is constantly to misrepresent to the Austrians the number of French soliders in the regiments seen moving on the roads:

il avait soin de diminuer d'un grand quart le nombre des soldats présents. Ces lettres, d'ailleurs ridicules, avaient le mérite d'en démentir d'autres plus véridiques, et elles plaisaient.   (pp. 17–18)

As far as a régime like the Austrian Empire is concerned, falsehood seems to have greater political appeal than truth.

More significantly, however, it is the false version of events that Fabrice's brother Ascanio gives to the Austrians about his trip to Waterloo that first puts Fabrice on the wrong side of the law, and sets the pattern for his subsequent career. Ascanio denounces Fabrice to the Milanese police 'comme étant allé porter à Napoléon des propositions arrêtées par une vaste conspiration organisée dans le ci-devant royaume d'Italie' (p. 84). This account is quite at odds with the admittedly scanty and peculiar motives that are given by Stendhal for Fabrice's departure for Waterloo: Fabrice tells Gina that he wants to go because Napoleon 'avait tant d'amitié pour ton mari' (p. 30); and the totally irrational reasons that clinch this rather arbitrary-sounding decision are, first, the fact that he sees an eagle just when he hears the news of Napoleon's return from Elba and, second, the fact that he finds 'his' chestnut tree in leaf. These superstitious and private motives do not lend themselves very easily to a political inter-pretation, but this is nevertheless the one that Ascanio constructs, with the result that his politically effective, coherent and plausible version is set at variance with the true, if rather incoherent and politically irrelevant account given by the text. The politically motivated interpre-tation that Ascanio puts on Fabrice's quixotic impulses places Fabrice at the mercy of the Milanese authorities, turning him into a pawn in a political game – as we see from the manoeuvres that Gina is obliged to undertake on his behalf. This event illustrates once more the fact that power (which is Ascanio's here) is a function of representation; but, in addition, it shows that conflicts of representation do not take place only between different political groups, each with similar sorts of interest. Political power consists as much as anything in the wresting of the unsayable from the silence of the sublime, and in giving it a representational form.

Political plots

The particular form that these political representations tend to take is a narrative one. Whereas Fabrice's and Stendhal's version of the Waterloo venture is decidedly lacunary, Ascanio's deposition trans-forms these enigmatic lacunae into narrative intelligibility, particularly through his reference to 'une vaste conspiration'. The refusal to confront the inexplicable is invariably the mark of the narrative constructions put on things by the representations of most of Parma's politicians. This is particularly true of Mme Raversi and Rassi. Raversi is narrative personified, being repeatedly described by the text as a successful 'intrigante': 'une intrigante, capable de tout, et même de réussir' (p. 112), '[une] intrigante consommée' (p. 124). She proceeds both by hatching intrigues on her own account, and – more characteristically and more significantly – by reading intrigue in the actions of others. Her political power lies largely in her ability to narrativise and so misrepresent a number of situations and events which Stendhal's own text refrains from recounting, save in the most oblique and roundabout terms.

The central event of this kind is the murder of Giletti. This violent and quite unpremeditated episode lies at the heart of all Parma's politics, and their function is to reduce its shocking arbitrariness to the dimensions of self-interested intelligibility. It is Raversi's account of the murder that first turns it into a political issue:

Grâce aux nombreux amis de la marquise Raversi, le prince ainsi que toute la ville de Parme croyait que Fabrice s'était fait aider par vingt ou trente paysans pour assommer un mauvais comédien qui avait l'insolence de lui disputer la petite Marietta. (p. 223)

From this Stendhal derives the very principle which lies behind all the political dealings in and around the court of Parma: 'Dans les cours despotiques, le premier intrigant adroit dispose de la *vérité*, comme la mode en dispose à Paris' (Stendhal's italics). The political goal that Raversi is aiming at through her representation of Giletti's murder is nothing less than 'la chute du ministère ultra et de son chef le comte Mosca'. Whatever Stendhal or the modern reader might think about the murder, the contemporary Italian would, under other circumstances, have seen it as a trivial and insignificant matter. Public opinion seems to regard it as a 'vétille' (p. 407), Gina dismisses it as 'un petit assassinat comme on en compte cent par an dans ces heureux états' (p. 301), and even Fabio Conti describes it as 'une bagatelle' (p. 281). To an Italian way of thinking the murder of an actor who earned only thirty-two francs a month by a man of Fabrice's birth is not in itself a serious matter. Only the misrepresentations of politics manage to make it significant enough to become the episode on which the entire action of the novel comes to hinge:

Puisque pour une pareille vétille, un coup d'epée maladroit donné à un comédien, un homme de la naissance de Fabrice n'était pas mis en liberté au bout de neuf mois de prison et avec la protection du premier ministre, *c'est qu'il y avait de la politique dans son affaire.* (p. 407, my italics)

A further aspect of the politicising of this episode concerns the representations that Raversi's liberals put on the extremely delicate and extremely passionate situation of the triangle involving Mosca, Gina and Fabrice. The precarious balance of the peculiar situation is preserved because each of them refrains from naming or describing it too explicitly. Reticence is the key to the survival and the dignity of all the emotions involved. Mosca maintains his position and his passion by not naming his jealousy:

> une fois que j'ai prononcé le mot fatal *jalousie*, mon rôle est tracé à tout jamais. Au contraire, ne disant rien aujourd'hui, je puis parler demain, je reste maître de tout. (p. 153)

He lives in dread of the consequences that the naming of passions could bring:

> le hasard peut amener un mot qui donnera un nom à ce qu'ils [Gina and Fabrice] sentent l'un pour l'autre et après, en un instant, toutes les conséquences. (p. 155)

Despite Mosca's assumptions about the lack of awareness on Gina's and Fabrice's part, Fabrice does have some insight into the situation; and he too has the wit to realise that silence is essential to it: 'Fabrice ne pouvait se résoudre a gâter un bonheur si délicieux par *un mot indiscret*' (p. 157, my italics), and to see that too much explicitness would turn the whole thing into something unspeakably vulgar:

> La position où le hasard me place n'est pas tenable, se disait-il. Je suis bien sûr qu'elle [Gina] ne parlera jamais, *elle aurait horreur d'un mot trop significatif comme d'un inceste* [my italics]. Mais si un soir, après une journée imprudente et folle, elle vient à faire l'examen de sa conscience, si elle croit que j'ai pu deviner le goût qu'elle semble prendre pour moi, quel rôle jouerai-je à ses yeux? exactement le *casto Giuseppe* (proverbe italien, allusion au rôle ridicule de Joseph avec la femme de l'eunuque Putiphar). (pp. 156–7)

The too-meaningful word would, of course, be incest itself. But the horror it would inspire would not be so much because of its being a taboo, but more because it would be so appallingly familiar, so terribly 'prosaïque'. The sublime energies of passion would suddenly find themselves *en plein roman pour femmes de chambre* and simply disappear in the squalid atmosphere of the *déjà-lu* and the *doxa*. Fortunately, though, Gina is able to conceal the truth about her feelings from herself, and her self-deception, combined with the reticence of Mosca and Fabrice, saves the situation from the disaster of vulgarity that too precise a representation would inevitably bring.

Raversi has no such scruples, and the liberals thrive on their public representations of this delicate triangular passion:

> dans le parti libéral dirigé par la marquise Raversi et le général Conti, on affectait de ne pas douter de la tendre liaison qui devait exister entre Fabrice

171

et la duchesse. Le comte Mosca, qu'on abhorrait, était pour sa duperie l'objet d'éternelles plaisanteries. (p. 280)

Not only is this representation squalid in its stereotyped intelligibility, but it is specifically wrong in casting the Count as dupe. Mosca is actually the most clear-sighted of the three, a fact which only those who know the value of silence can appreciate. In all this Raversi exemplifies perfectly (if perfectly vilely) the principle whereby 'le premier intrigant adroit dispose de la vérité'. This political principle has a corollary in that Raversi's narrative skills could also be an index of her political power, for she is able to pass off her version of events as 'the truth' even when they entail a number of *invraisemblances*. For instance, if disposing of the life of a small-time actor is a mere 'bagatelle', it seems unlikely that Fabrice would have called upon the services of 'twenty or thirty' peasants in order to do away with him.[8] In any case, Raversi's representational skills are not those that Stendhal's own representation seeks to emulate; and the power that enables her to exercise them so effectively is not something that he envies, so that she is allowed to have her say in the novel, rather than being challenged with an alternative and more accurate scenario. The novel contents itself with the reticent hint that reticence is preferable to representation as a means of bringing one closer to the truth. The success of this 'intrigante' should be ascribed less to any scheming as such than to her ability to represent things in a way that 'strikes the imaginations' of the right people in the right way. It is by this means that representation itself is put under suspicion in the novel, revealing it as an activity that is likely to have political motives on the part of those who undertake it (Raversi), and to threaten political reper-cussion for the sublime victims who figure in it (Fabrice, Gina, Mosca). In other words, the very process which justifies the presence of politics in the text in the first place – the mirroring of reality – ends up by being thoroughly compromised by the object it is charged with reflecting – politics.

The association of (mis)representation with narrative is strongly evident too in the political dealings of perhaps the most pathetic of *La Chartreuse*'s politicians, Rassi. The basis of his power lies in his ability consistently to represent events as conspiracies. His hold over the Prince before the Mosca era is such that he is even able to make the Prince go against his own better judgement and human instinct in having two men put to death in the most horrible way. He achieves this simply by representing calumny as conspiracy: 'Le mot *tyran* a été prouvé. Rassi appela cela conspirer' (p. 121). Anything can be turned into a conspiracy — even thirty foolhardy citizens meeting to read *Le Constitutionnel* — and it is through these narratives that Rassi's credit with the Prince is assured. As soon as his credit begins to drop, 'il se hâte de découvrir quelque nouvelle conspiration des plus noires et des plus chimériques' (p. 105), and power is his again.

During Mosca's reign Rassi's conspiracy theories go into decline and he resorts to the most transparent and preposterous inventions: he describes Fabrice, who has never for a moment questioned the Christian principles of his Jesuit upbringing, as being *'d'une impiété notoire'* (p. 272, Stendhal's italics); and, even more ludicrously, has Fabrice publicly accused after his escape from the tower, *'de s'être dérobé à la clémence d'un prince magnanime'* (p. 423, Stendhal's italics again). Stendhal's use of italics for these versions of reality shows just how absurd they are. But when Rassi's political fortunes are on the ascendant again, plausibility and conspiracy re-emerge as the key elements in his political manoeuvrings. As minister for justice, he develops an inordinate interest in how Ernest IV met his death, an issue which had not previously been of particular political or even private concern. He does so, not because he believes that a crime has taken place and that a criminal should be brought to justice, but because by 'proving' that there had been a plot to poison the late Prince, he hopes to gain a hold over the new one. His version, whereby the Prince died at the hand of Jacobin conspirators, would be politically far more effective than the truth, which, as it happens, he is nowhere near guessing. If Gina devotes so much energy and ingenuity to getting the Prince and his mother to burn the files containing Rassi's 'evidence', it is less because she is afraid of being found out than because she knows that, if it gains hold, the Jacobin conspiracy theory will deprive her of her present commanding position at court, and allow Rassi in instead. As she explains to the Prince himself:

Le feu prince a-t-il été empoisonné? c'est ce qui est fort douteux; a-t-il été empoisonné par les jacobins? c'est ce que Rassi voudrait bien prouver, car alors il devient pour votre altesse un instrument nécessaire à tout jamais.

(pp. 456–7)

She clinches her case by pointing out that the Prince's current reputation is infinitely preferable and more secure than the one that he would have if Rassi's version of political reality were given official sanction:

Vos sujets disent généralement, ce qui est de toute vérité, que votre altesse a de la bonté dans le caractère; tant qu'elle n'aura pas fait pendre quelque

173

libéral, elle jouira de cette réputation, et bien certainement personne ne songera à lui preparer du poison.   (p. 457)

It is both more flattering to the Prince's vanity and a far more effective security policy to preserve an image of bountiful majesty than to accept Rassi's report and be obliged to implement its judicial consequences. The question of whether the report might or might not have some basis in truth is irrelevant to the requirements of political expediency.

In the end Rassi's tactics do not prevail, but not just because they make for bad policies. They fail because, as I shall show, his own image is vulnerable to the representations put on it by others. But what his tactics do demonstrate, along with the example of Raversi, is that the stuff of politics is the stuff of fiction. Narrative constructions of reality and representations of the real constitute the basic forms of both activities; the kinds of skill that succeed in the one sphere seem to correspond to the ones that bring success in the other. If Rassi fails to achieve lasting political power, this is largely because he is actually a rather bad novelist. His fictions are patently implausible, and his plots of a crudely sensational cloak-and-dagger brand. Raversi's relative political success makes her the equivalent of the best-selling novelist of the *doxa*, who cannot conceive of existence except in terms of the stereotypes which the average reader and courtier are only too eager to accept. In these fictions the representation of a triangular affair inevitably makes the older man the dupe of the lustful machinations of the worldly woman and the ambitious young man. Only Mosca, the cleverest politician that Italy has known for centuries,[9] has the least inkling of the sort of principles that might make Stendhal the best novelist in France's new post-Revolutionary world.

Political polyphonies

Mosca's politics are based on the principle, first, that representations are not definitive but strategic; and, second, that success consists not in imposing a single version of reality (which is what both Raversi and Rassi try to do), but in maintaining a plurality of representations and in recognising the limitations of the validity of all of them. Mosca's policies work by juggling and containing the fictions of others rather than by constructing any of his own to put in their place. His standing with the Prince is achieved by endorsing the Prince's own self-image, in contrast to the strategy adopted by Rassi, whose position had been based entirely on his ability to frighten the Prince with conspiratorial versions of events. When Mosca searches the palace for Jacobins under beds and in double-bass cases, he does so more in order to preserve a certain image of the court than to protect the Prince from physical violence, because in the long run a proper concern with the images of things brings greater security than a pre-occupation with purely physical safety. Not only is the Prince made to feel that this sordid inspection does not conflict with the fiction of his being a latter-day Louis XIV, but, in addition, Mosca actually manages to persuade him that it is an essential precaution against misrepresentation: 'songez aux sonnets satiriques dont les jacobins nous accableraient si nous vous laissions tuer ... Ce n'est pas seulement votre vie que nous défendons, c'est notre honneur' (p. 106). The misrepresentations of political satire are more to be feared than assassination itself.

In the confrontation between Gina and the Prince over the warrant for Fabrice's arrest, Mosca's political instinct is to save the Louis XIV image from the threats posed by the alternative version that Gina unwittingly and impulsively puts over; the Prince realises that Gina has it in her power to burden him with 'la réputation d'un tyran ridicule qui se lève la nuit pour regarder sous son lit' (p. 263). As far as Mosca is concerned, the omission of the words 'procédure injuste' from the document declaring the Prince's belief in Fabrice's innocence has nothing to do with Fabrice or his arrest; it is above all a device for cancelling the representation of the Prince as a 'tyran ridicule'. Mosca's intervention in the episode leaves the Prince's version of reality intact as he manages to persuade him that 'l'histoire anecdotique de Louis XIV n'avait pas de page plus belle que celle qu'il [the Prince] venait de fournir à ses historiens futurs' (p. 267). Mosca's political skills here consist in his ability to pastiche the style of other fictions and produce Saint-Simonian versions of the Prince's court at Parma; although, as he recognises later, the omission of the key words proves to have been a very serious error where Fabrice is concerned. (There is a price to be paid for this diplomacy, and I shall be returning to this question below.) Even so, Gina and many other critics of Mosca's actions fail to appreciate what the political consequences of the damage to the Prince's reputation and vanity might have been without Mosca's reparative statesmanship.

Mosca's handling of Ferrante Palla's uprising is also based largely on his ability to control the representations involved. The confrontation between government and insurgents takes place, significantly, around and in front of the statue of Prince Ernest IV, which becomes the focus for the struggle for power: the republicans are out to tear it down, and Mosca draws up the palace troops to defend it. The fact that the Prince is depicted in the statue wearing Roman dress serves to emphasise that this image is indeed a fiction; but such is the importance of fictions that Mosca — for the first time in his ministry — is actually prepared to have people killed in order to keep it intact. Mosca spills blood in order to preserve a certain image of the state of Parma, not in order to assert his own political authority. The whole episode is ultimately resolved less by brute force than by the amount of attention that Mosca devotes to the control of the representations at stake, including those of the uprising itself. Barbone, who was actually lynched by the crowd, is officially reported in Parma's press as having died as the result of an accident; the sixty dead republicans are said to be travelling abroad, and their families are bribed and threatened to persuade them to corroborate this report; and, finally, a man from Mosca's ministry is dispatched to vet the versions of the uprising that are likely to appear in the newspapers of Milan, Turin and even as far afield as Paris. In all this there is never any question of Mosca's own personal or political convictions. He neither believes the late Prince's version of himself, nor is he committed to proposing any alternative. A subtle but telling hint of Mosca's political agnosticism is discreetly indicated by the text in the form of the chip that remains in the Prince's statue as the only indication that the revolt ever took place. It seems to suggest that while Mosca was prepared to defend the image of the Prince, that defence was not so wholehearted as to leave it quite intact, and the chipped toga remains as a quiet reminder of the value of Mosca's disinterested pluralism.

The power of this pluralism can also take the form of an exclusion of possible fictions, and this is the basis of Mosca's hold over Rassi. Rassi would dearly love to be able to rewrite his public image, which over the years has become synonymous with all that is vile and squalid:

le petit peuple donnait le nom de *Rassi* aux chiens enragés; depuis peu des soldats s'étaient battus en duel parce qu'un de leurs camarades les avait appelés *Rassi*. Enfin il ne se passait pas de semaine sans que ce malheureux nom ne vînt s'enchâsser dans quelque sonnet atroce. Son fils, jeune et innocent écolier de seize ans, était chassé des cafés, sur son nom. (p. 313)

By promising him a title, Mosca has it in his gift to annul this version of the man, and to allow him to construct another around the name Baron Riva, an identity that offers the courtier the hope of one day becoming 'le chef libéral et adoré de toute l'Italie'. But without

Mosca's consent this fiction has no chance whatsoever of imposing itself on reality, and in the event Rassi is forced to go on living with the reputation that his real name had won for itself.

Mosca's politics consist of the kind of ironic polyphony that characterises Stendhal's own authorial practice. He juggles and manipulates the representations of others, leaving them slightly chipped (like the statue) or tarnished (like Rassi's reputation) as a mark of his own distance from them and of his refusal to endorse any of them as adequate versions of either the truth or reality. Whether the Prince is 'really' a *tyran ridicule* or a *roi soleil* is neither here nor there for Mosca; it is just that, having considered the two alternatives, it makes better political sense to support the latter view. Political harmony of the kind that Mosca achieves at the end of the novel rests on the principle of representational polyphony, whose effectiveness depends precisely on the acknowledgement of the limits of all representations. And if political representations cannot definitively represent even political realities (as we see from the impossibility of deciding which is the better epithet for the Prince), how can they begin to give an adequate account of things that so surpass the saying that not even the novelist dares speak of them?

Mosca's experience of love is an education – that is also a political education – in both reticence and pluralism. He learns to see the sense of keeping silent rather than use words like 'jalousie'; he suffers from the crystallising lover's propensity to see things in several different lights at once, and realises that a definitive representation of any reality is ruled out not so much by lack as by excess:

Comment rapporter tous les raisonnements, toutes les façons de voir ce qui lui arrivait, qui, durant trois mortelles heures, mirent à la torture cet homme passionné?

Unable to fix on a single version, a definitive 'façon de voir', Mosca makes prudence the better part of passion, and concludes:

Puisque je suis aveuglé par l'excessive douleur, suivons cette règle, approuvée de tous les gens sages, qu'on appelle *prudence*. (p. 152, Stendhal's italics)

The sublime defies representation by the very plurality of representations that it conjures up in the passionate soul, and it is this that distinguishes it from most of Parma's political representations of reality. Raversi's versions of reality may be wrong in content, but they are more fundamentally erroneous for being so emphatically monocular. By contrast, Mosca's political skill derives precisely from his encounter with passion, which teaches him not only that the sublime is best left unsaid, but also that monocular visions both limit and distort the experiences that they purport to describe. The verbal prudence that determines his response as an 'homme passionné' to his moments of emotional crisis also characterises the principles of his political behaviour. Reticence in the form of an uncommitted representational polyphony is the factor that raises Mosca's politics from vileness to wisdom (Mosca is repeatedly described as 'sage' in the novel), and allies this political wisdom to the polyphonic ironies that constitute Stendhal's own authorial practice as a novelist.

Yet the analogy is not quite complete. Nor could it be; because if Stendhal's novel is to be truly polyphonic it cannot limit itself to merely duplicating Mosca's political strategies. It must include other political styles – both the revolutionary style of the more energetic characters and the narrative *vraisemblances* of the politicians of Parma – alongside Mosca's. Mosca's politics operate by manoeuvring the political constructions of one set of characters, and by containing and preserving the energies of another; if they avoid the base calculations of the first, they nevertheless have little of the impetus of the second. In a sense, they are flawed by their very wisdom, as the episode of the omitted phrase demonstrates: Mosca's concern to preserve the stability of the political institutions of Parma (the court) through his endorsements of the Prince's self-image has potentially fatal consequences for Fabrice, and therefore indirectly for Gina too. Mosca's polyphony isn't a model that can be imitated, and Stendhal represents him with the same kind of flaw that Mosca's own politics succeed in leaving upon the image of the Prince.

Equally, however, Mosca's tarnished status is not just a comment on his political style, because the error he makes over the omitted phrase is an error that circumstances force upon him: to have offended the Prince by including a reference to the 'procédure injuste' might have been more energetic, but it would have constituted just as great an error in its way, since offended royal pride might have produced other negative consequences for the characters in question. Political agnosticism and representational polyphony do not guarantee immunity against political consequences and the representations that others will put upon agnosticism.

It is only with these considerations in mind that it is legitimate to extrapolate on to Stendhal's fictional style: for Stendhal's own polyphonic practices, and his own agnostic pose cannot exempt him from the consequences of the situation in which he finds himself. The fears expressed in the prefaces to *Lucien Leuwen* and *La Chartreuse* are fully justified: he must recognise that his novel will excite impotent hatreds; he certainly runs the risk of being branded an 'assassin' or its equivalent; he will quite probably be accused of being both an ultra and a Jacobin; and the public is more than likely to want to smash the mirror in which political realities are being reflected.

La Chartreuse may be called a political novel, not because it proposes any political solutions (which it does not), nor because it records a particular political reality (which of course it does); it can be called a political novel primarily because it proposes a certain view of politics as an activity and as an outlook – or rather, as a variety of different activities and outlooks (the quixotic, the base and the polyphonic). Stendhal's thinking about politics in his fiction seems to have emerged and grown out of the sorts of issue that dominated his thinking about love and truth. But, although in one sense political themes merely allow Stendhal to develop a number of variations on recurrent personal and literary preoccupations, in another sense Stendhal offers some extremely sophisticated and modern insights into the basis of political power and the nature of the political outlook. His implication that the acquisition of political power does not depend so much on having the right ideological or even practical solution for a given state of affairs as on the ability to manipulate image and representation anticipates a characteristically twentieth-century view of politics, which one would normally ascribe to the post-war growth of the role of the media in political campaigns and debate. Stendhal, however, saw that the very things that made writing problematic for the novelist – namely the spread of literacy and the development of conformity through the printed word – could also have far-reaching political consequences.

Equally, though, by defining politics in these terms, and by giving them such a large role in his fiction, Stendhal is able to use political themes in order to explore some of the fundamental issues of his own practice as a novelist – in particular his commitment to mimesis. Indeed, it is by emphasising representation as both a political and a novelistic practice that Stendhal is able to define it as a problem for the novelist in the first place. The aestheticisation of politics (to use Walter Benjamin's phrase) in his fiction enables him to point simultaneously to the political implications of the aesthetic.[10] In representing politics in his text, Stendhal politicises representation by showing that it is liable either to have political motives, or else to have political repercussions in the constructions that may subsequently be put on it. The faithful historian of *Armance* and the mirror tucked into the author's saddle-bag in *Le Rouge* cannot record political reality with impunity, since the object reflected in the mirror will reveal that mirrors are always political — which is to say that they are always implicated in the circumstances which are contained in their own reflections. In the end, therefore, the achievement of this political novel is to show that when politics invade the mirror which supposedly reflects them, the mirror itself is liable to become entangled in the political contents of its own reflections.

8

A HERO WITHOUT QUALITIES

L'auteur pense que, excepté pour la passion du héros, un roman doit être un miroir.

Stendhal, *Lucien Leuwen*

Character degree zero

Fabrice is unlike Stendhal's other heroes, and indeed unlike the heroes of most realist fiction in that he has no errors to correct, no ideals to revise. He needs no *Bildung*, no education, sentimental or social, since he is born perfect and dies exemplary. Whereas Julien spends most of his short life energetically pursuing false ambitions and in a state of delusion about the path that will lead to happiness, Fabrice never has to be put right. This perfection makes him a most unusual fictional hero, and *La Chartreuse* a most unusual novel. But what makes both hero and novel decidedly peculiar is the fact that, although Fabrice is undeniably perfect, it is almost impossible to say what that perfection consists of. In short, he seems to constitute something of an anomaly in the nineteenth-century novel: a hero without qualities, undeniably a hero, but lacking in the characterfulness that is normally thought of as essential to the genre.

In the last chapter I tried to show that the most valuable and important aspects of the novel – its central characters and situations – eluded the grasp of the majority of the politically ambitious (as opposed to politically inspired) characters in the book, and that their vain ambitions involved them in a constant misrepresentation of the characters and motives of Mosca, Gina and Fabrice. But the reader, who has nothing to gain from such vilifications, is nevertheless liable to find that Fabrice consistently and most perplexingly continues to elude her grasp.

This elusiveness of Stendhal's characters tends to make them curiously unmemorable, a quality rarely remarked upon by critics (who have a professional interest in not forgetting characters), but one that is noted by Zola in his essay on Stendhal, where he asks,

181

'D'où vient-il que les personnages de Stendhal ne s'imposent pas davantage à la mémoire?' (p. 102). He complains that 'Julien Sorel ne laisse aucune idée nette' (p. 103), and attributes this lack of characterological clarity to Stendhal's disproportionate stress on the cerebral and the psychological to the exclusion of the physical and social dimensions of personality. Zola had his own naturalist axe to grind, but he does seem to be drawing attention here to an aspect of Stendhal's characters which most critics are too efficient to recognise; they tend to compensate for any gaps or uncertainties in character-isation by filling them in and fleshing them out through their own interpretative activity. But if one allows the picture to stand uninter-preted for a moment, one cannot help being struck in *La Chartreuse* by the lack of any 'idée nette' in the character of Fabrice in particular, a lack which seems to me to be even greater than in the case of Julien Sorel which Zola cites in his essay.

Fabrice never quite emerges into focus, and seems somehow to have been placed in the equivalent of a representational blind spot in the overall panorama of the novel. Stendhal himself hints at a rather different explanation from Zola's when he makes the strange claim in the preface to *Lucien Leuwen* that 'excepté pour la passion du héros, un roman doit être un miroir'. As Lucien himself is so thoroughly mistaken about so many things, the exclusion of his passion from the novel is barely noticeable in its fulsome chronicle of his errors and delusions. But confronted with Fabrice's perfection, the mirror of *La Chartreuse* reveals the full extent of the absence of its hero's passion in its reflection.

The reason for Stendhal's strange claim in *Lucien Leuwen* and for the elusive representation of his hero in *La Chartreuse* is perhaps best sought in his fear of being misread, and of being used as a source of models to imitate in the manner which betrays the very ideals of authenticity that, in Stendhal's view, the best novels try to sustain. In this way the ideal *Nouvelle Héloïse* is perverted by the Parisian girls who make every tear a pretext for seeing themselves as a latter-day Julie d'Etange; and so one might perhaps explain the failures and delusions of many of his characters as one means of preventing this kind of Parisian response to his novels. As I argued in chapter 3, Stendhal makes it impossible for even the vainest or most Parisian of his readers to copy Julien or Mme de Rênal. Similarly, neither Octave nor Lucien can be said to propose an imitable ideal: if death is the solution to Octave's situation, then the reader's knowledge that it wasn't necessary is unlikely to make him want to repeat this Wertheran solution.[1] And the happy ending that reunites Lucien with Mme de Chasteller was simply never written, so that the reader has no chance of ever learning, let alone repeating the trick that brings about this conclusion. With Fabrice, on the other hand, Stendhal places at the centre of the novel a character who would seem to have nothing to learn about where the path to happiness lies. But in spite of this, Fabrice fails to function as an (imitable) ideal. In reading *La Chartreuse*, one doesn't for a moment want to *be like* Fabrice in the way that one can understand wanting to be like Rousseau's Julie. Indeed, it would be rather hard to say what *being like* Fabrice would consist of, precisely because of his lack of definable qualities to emulate.

Fabrice's place as the hero of the novel is assured, then, on two counts: first, because he is perfect, and second, because that perfection is both undefinable and (therefore) inimitable. Nevertheless, his position as hero makes *La Chartreuse* a most disconcerting kind of novel, since Fabrice's characterlessness creates a thoroughgoing indeterminacy concerning the nature of the story that it tells. The title seems to anticipate a narrative about Fabrice's adventures by directing attention to their final outcome in the charterhouse. Furthermore, the tale on which the novel is based, the 'Origine des grandeurs de la famille Farnese', and the fragment that Stendhal based on it ('La Jeunesse d'Alexandre Farnese')[2] place Fabrice's prototype, Alexandre, firmly at the centre of the stage. On the other hand, the 'Avertissement' to *La Chartreuse* unequivocally announces 'l'histoire de la duchesse Sanseverina', and leads the reader to expect an account of *her* adventures at the court of Parma. Fabrice isn't even mentioned.

This indeterminacy is revealingly discussed by Balzac, who regards it as a flaw in his otherwise enthusiastic account of the novel, 'Etudes sur M. Beyle'. He seems to have been particularly disturbed by the novel's ambivalence about its narrative centre, and he accuses Stendhal of confusion and of having betrayed the principle of unity by not making it clear whether he is writing the life of Fabrice, or a tale about the court of Parma with Gina as heroine. Balzac's own reading certainly makes Gina the central pivot of events, and his 'analysis' (actually more of a summary) barely mentions Fabrice. He regards the opening episode in Milan, the character of Blanès and the ending as superfluous to this intrigue, which he describes as 'la grande comédie de la Cour' (p. 1209), and which he suggests should really end when Fabrice becomes archbishop and Gina and Mosca return to the court as man and wife. The reason why he opts for this reading is that, in his view, the character of Fabrice is not powerful enough to serve as the centre of gravity in the novel. Balzac finds Fabrice being constantly upstaged by the other characters, and for him to be the central figure in the story

Fabrice aurait dû ne pas se trouver primé par des figures aussi typiques, aussi poëtiques que le sont les Princes, la Sanseverina, Mosca, Palla Ferrante [*sic*].

(p. 1210)

For the novel to become the story of Fabrice, Fabrice would have to become a different kind of character:

l'auteur eût été obligé de lui donner une grande pensée, de le douer d'un sentiment qui le rendît supérieur aux gens de génie qui l'entouraient et qui lui manque.

Thus reconstructed, Fabrice would become a recognisable *type*, who could give this version of the novel the title it should, in Balzac's view, properly have had: '*FABRICE, ou l'Italien au dix-neuvième siècle*'. In this novel, Fabrice's defining characteristic would have been 'le Sentiment', and the text could then have been read around a thematic opposition between Fabrice's 'Sentiment' and Mosca's 'Talent'. Or, as Balzac also puts it, it would have shown that: '*Sentir* est le rival de *Comprendre*, comme *Agir* est l'antagonisme de *Penser*.' But it is precisely because Fabrice is perfect that this version of the novel does not exist. We cannot read him as the incarnation of *Sentiment*, or indeed of any other nameable quality, because it is precisely by *not* being a type, and by *not* being the incarnation or model of any quality whatsoever that Fabrice remains exempt from the potential corruption of imitation. Unlike Werther and René, who provided a model for countless early nineteenth-century readers (including the young members of the de La Mole salon in *Le Rouge*), Fabrice has no features or qualities that could provide his readers with a role.

His inimitable perfection is Stendhal's solution to the problem of authenticity in realist fiction, but it is a solution which produces a quite different kind of novel from the ones that are usually associated with the genre. The heroes of Balzac's fiction, for example, are both a part of the represented world and a key to its interpretation. They are distinctly less than perfect, but at the same time are perfectly intelligible as the incarnations of this or that quality: paternal devotion in Goriot, ageing virginity in Bette, avarice in Grandet. As Nathalie Sarraute says, in Balzac's novel,

l'avarice *était* le père Grandet, elle en constituait toute la substance, elle l'emplissait jusqu'aux bords et elle recevait de lui, à son tour, sa forme et sa vigueur.[3]

It is the characterfulness of characters in realist fiction that provides it with what Leo Bersani calls its 'ordered significances', and which in turn create a certain set of expectations and impose a certain kind of reading on the novel in the realist era – a reading for which Stendhal's novels are particularly ill-suited.[4]

This reading is particularly unproductive in the case of Fabrice. Character-based readings of realist fiction have two principal underlying presuppositions: first, that character will provide the main material for interpretation, and second, that the development of character (its *Bildung*) will provide the core of the narrative's preoccupation. A novel like Jane Austen's *Pride and Prejudice* illustrates these principles very well, for not only does the interpretation of character constitute the main interest of the narrative, but in addition, the very outcome of the plot depends on the characters' own perspicacity concerning character. Elizabeth Bennett has to see through Darcy's pride, a perception that is only made possible by the development of her own character. So that seeing beyond the appearance of pride depends on her maturing out of prejudice. Here, it is not just that character provides the basis for the novel's intelligibility as a structure of thematic oppositions, but also that self-knowledge and perspicacity as to character are internalised and thematised as an integral concern at the level of the plot itself. When one turns to Stendhal, however, his fiction fails notably to correspond to this format: not only is it hard to say what Fabrice's character consists of, but he and the novel's heroine, Clélia, are strikingly impercipient about both themselves and each other, and continue in this state of blindness even after they have fallen in love, thus breaking a cardinal rule of Jane Austen's fiction, namely that love and marriage depend entirely on the mutual understanding of the partners involved.

'Adorable'

Now that I have outlined the nature of the problems involved in understanding Fabrice's function in *La Chartreuse*, it is time to look more closely at the ways in which Stendhal *does* write about him in the novel, and to try and see more clearly how that writing furthers the strategies at work in his fiction. I shall begin by looking at the various procedures of characterisation that Stendhal employs for Fabrice. Fabrice is treated right from the very start as the novel's hero; this position is not something that he has either to earn or to prove by some test of character. As Gilbert Durand has shown, Fabrice is a hero, not so much for any intrinsic heroic qualities that he may have, but because he is blessed with all the archetypal hallmarks of heroism which transcend the dimension of individual characteristics. The circumstances of his birth are exceptional, his future is predicted by oracles, and he is given a variety of 'doubles', both positive and negative (helpers and enemies), who all serve to focus attention on him as the central character, regardless of the content of his particular personality.[5] Durand goes on to demonstrate that the action is archetypally constructed so as to confront Fabrice with a series of tests or obstacles to be overcome and from which he will emerge doubly confirmed as hero. In other words, Fabrice's status as the novel's hero is established not in terms of any individual personal qualities, but by purely formal archetypal markers.

The rare remarks that the author actually makes about Fabrice's character tend also to be more or less contentless in that he seems more concerned to establish Fabrice's otherness or 'singularité' than to describe any qualities that might make him singular in the first place. There cannot be much above six or seven specifically authorial characterisations of Fabrice in the course of the five hundred or so pages that make up the novel. The drift of these rather nonchalant and unemphatic remarks portrays Fabrice as a 'personnage passionné' (e.g. p. 32), who has no interest in the imitation of others, for example:

il n'y avait pas encore de place pour l'*imitation des autres* dans cette âme naïve et ferme (p. 100, Stendhal's italics)

and:

Il avait l'âme trop haute pour chercher à imiter les autres jeunes gens.
(p. 140)

In Stendhalian terms, passion and the lack of concern to imitate go together, for, as *De l'Amour* repeatedly demonstrates, imitated passion ceases to be *amour-passion* and becomes *amour de vanité* instead. True passion can have no model, and it is this absence of any model to guide Fabrice's character and behaviour that constitutes his 'singularité'.

However, this uniqueness poses a certain difficulty for the reader, since it means that Fabrice cannot be related or compared to any known models or examples.[6] As a result, it is extremely difficult to make sense of him as a character, and on occasion he is apt to appear highly *invraisemblable*. Where a character has no maxim or example in mind, the reader is likely to find it that much harder to assign one to the character in question and make interpretation possible. And though of course this problem doesn't prevent the viler characters in the novel from producing an almost endless supply of naturalising maxims for Fabrice's singular behaviour, this is a solution that the scrupulous 'âmes supérieures' cannot adopt for themselves. For they recognise that the features that Stendhal picks on to describe Fabrice's character (singularity and independence from models) are such that it will be more or less impossible to ascribe any qualities to that character. Fabrice is perfect precisely because the novel manages to prevent its readers from saying what his perfection consists of.

What compounds Fabrice's singularity in the novel is his and his author's singular lack of interest in that singularity. Although he could be read as having a number of features in common with his Romantic precursors – for example, his superiority (both social and spiritual), and his proneness towards dreamy inaction in preference to decisive performance, qualities which are introduced into French literature in Chateaubriand's portrait of René – one is prevented from seeing any further similarity by Fabrice's total lack of self-absorption. Where René and Adolphe devote their lives and the narration of those lives to an overwhelming, if fruitless, introspection, neither Fabrice nor Stendhal seems to regard Fabrice's personality as being of the least interest either to itself or to the novel in which it figures. The only time that Fabrice seems to come anywhere near to such an interest is during his fight with Giletti: at the thought that Giletti might have disfigured him, Fabrice is 'saisi de rage' and his fury inspires him to deliver the fatal wound to his opponent (p. 200). But on his bizarre request for a mirror, Fabrice submits himself to a purely physical scrutiny, expressing relief that his eyes and his teeth have remained intact. Unlike Emma Bovary, who also has immediate recourse to a mirror after a major event in her life, in order to see reflected in it her new self as adulteress, Fabrice shows not the least curiosity about what the mirror reveals about his self: nothing is said as to whether the mirror reflects the face of a murderer, a dandy, or a hero. So that, if the question of Fabrice's self is raised by his fury at the thought of being disfigured and by his self-examination in the mirror, it is immediately deflected by the strictly medical content of the mirror's reflection.

Most of the attempts to characterise Fabrice are not made by the author, and still less by himself, but by the other characters in the book. The political principles of court life give Fabrice's enemies a vested interest in keeping him characterised within the bounds of a certain 'vraisemblable'. But for the majority of the other characters (who are mainly Fabrice's allies), the characterisations, which their dealings with him generate, have a quite different function. For these characters the perception of Fabrice's qualities – which include the non-qualities of the author's portrayal – are inseparable from the *effects* that those qualities have on them. If Gina finds her nephew 'singulier, spirituel, fort sérieux, mais joli garçon' (p. 16), this is part and parcel of the fact that she is 'folle de Fabrice'. Similarly, on his return home from college, his mother is first '*emerveillée* des grâces de son fils', and then '*épouvantée* de son ignorance' (p. 18, my emphases). What matters is not so much Fabrice's seriousness or his ignorance as the effect that these qualities have on others. Fabrice's naivety is not important for itself, but for the love it inspires in his aged protector, Blanès (p. 20); his bravery is noteworthy not as an entity in itself, but because it makes Gina love him (p. 304). And in most cases, the passion that Fabrice inspires in others is attributable less to any positive and intrinsic qualities (such as bravery) than to his more contentless features.

This association of passion with characterological emptiness is neatly summarised in Gina's reactions to Fabrice when the text speaks of 'cet être adoré, singulier, vif, original' (p. 419), a description in which one may read the implication that it is precisely Fabrice's singularity and originality that make him so adorable in her eyes. To the amorous gaze singularity is not a challenge to the power-seeking discourses of the *vraisemblable*, but an incitement to passion. This correlation recalls the workings of the lover's discourse, in which it is impossible ever to say anything about the beloved except 'adorable'.[7] In *La Chartreuse* the principles of the lover's discourse are at work in the representation of its hero Fabrice. In its eyes he is simply 'adorable'; he is characterised by his adorability, and he is adorable because he has no character. Even the narrative of the novel is determined by Fabrice's sheer adorability rather than by any more distinctive qualities in his personality. He is quite unlike the standard characters of realist fiction, whose 'characters' are held to be responsible for the form that their lives take; as Robbe-Grillet says of the conventional realist hero:

Son caractère dicte ses actions, le fait réagir de façon déterminé à chaque événement.[8]

But Gina is absolutely right when, after Fabrice's escape from prison, she remarks:

C'est par hasard et parce qu'il a su plaire à cette petite fille [i.e. Clélia], que la vie de Fabrice a été sauvée! *S'il n'avait été aimable, il mourait.*

(p. 415, my italics)

And exactly the same point could be made again about Fabrice's narrow escape from poisoning, where it is once more the fact that he is adored that galvanises Gina and Clélia into their separate attempts to save him.

A hero without qualities

This desirability in Fabrice is of a quite different order from the passions which provide the driving force in a Balzacian plot, and which always stem from a nameable, positive quality. It is, for instance, Goriot's paternal devotion that is responsible for his gradual descent into poverty, the jealousy of the spinster Bette that sparks off the machinations that bring about the downfall of the Hulot family. And, desirability aside, there is in fact never any question in *La Chartreuse* that Fabrice's fate depends on his character. The many prophecies in the novel (which can seem so puzzling to readers who do not know whether they are meant to take them seriously) could be regarded as a means of valorising a notion of destiny over that of nature in order to ensure that the narrative doesn't end up by inadvertently smuggling in a character for Fabrice. It may be in Fabrice's nature to believe in oracles, but the important thing is that they save him from having to make any effort of introspection to decide what his nature consists of. The predictions concerning prisons suggest that this is where he will end up, regardless of any moral or personal qualities that he might have or acquire. Indeed, he consistently sees the events that befall him as a matter of destiny rather than personality. For example, having decided that he is incapable of love, he goes on to interpret this incapacity not as a character defect, but as the lot meted out to him by fate:

Mon âme manquerait d'une passion, pourquoi cela? *ce serait une singulière destinée!* (p. 233, my italics)

Similarly, once he has fallen in love with Clélia, he regards this eventuality too as the decree of fate, and not as the consequence of particular qualities in the natures of either of them:

Il était éperdument amoureux, aussi il était parfaitement convaincu qu'il n'avait jamais aimé avant d'avoir vu Clélia, et que *la destinée de sa vie était de ne vivre que pour elle.* (p. 373, also my italics)

A belief in the workings of fate spares Fabrice both from the requirements of introspection, and from the need to probe the hearts and minds of other characters, since he always assumes that personality is irrelevant to the outcome of the situations that he finds himself in.

In fact, the lack of self-knowledge that is the corollary of Fabrice's superstition (and for which the superstition may well be a mere pretext) is one of the most striking features of this hero. On the few occasions when he bothers to give the question of his personality any thought, he is either blind or wrong. After his arrest, for instance, when he suddenly notices that imprisonment hasn't made him either miserable

189

or angry, he speculates that perhaps he may be: 'un de ces grands courages comme l'antiquité en a montré quelques exemples au monde'. And he goes on to wonder: 'Suis-je un héros sans m'en douter?' (p. 332). But these are conjectures that he does not take particularly seriously and which he certainly does not interpret as any kind of moral achievement. And in any case, it's not long before he realises that he's wrong, and that

ce n'est point par grandeur d'âme que je ne songe pas à la prison ... tant d'honneur ne m'appartient point. (p. 338)

It is significant in this context that, having rejected a false surmise, he does not go on to spell out what the real reason for his indifference to prison is.

The most notable instance of Fabrice's lack of self-knowledge occurs in the church of Saint-Pétrone in Bologna, where he prays to God for the forgiveness of his sins. He knows that he is guilty of the sin of murder, but fails to recognise that he might also be guilty on the count of simony:

quoiqu'il ne manquât ni d'esprit ni surtout de logique, il ne lui vint pas une seule fois à l'esprit que le crédit du comte Mosca, employé en sa faveur fût une *simonie*. (p. 219)

However, Stendhal does not try to attribute this blindness to any personal failing on Fabrice's part. Indeed, far from blaming Fabrice, he blames his Jesuit education, whose major achievement, he says, is to

donner l'habitude de ne pas faire attention à des choses plus claires que le jour.

If one thinks for a moment what a Jane Austen would have made of this instance of moral blindness and failure in self-knowledge, Stendhal's disinclination to pursue the nature of Fabrice's personality and personal shortcomings at this point is itself particularly striking – and much more so, in a way, than Fabrice's own lack of insight. For, rather than accuse Fabrice of personal failings, he prefers to make a comment about the Jesuits, which becomes in turn a pretext for one of the many discussions of the differences between French and Italian habits of mind that occur in the novel:

Un Français, élevé au milieu des traits d'intérêt personnel et de l'ironie de Paris, eût pu, sans être de mauvaise foi, accuser Fabrice d'hypocrisie au moment même où notre héros ouvrait son âme à Dieu avec la plus extrême sincérité et l'attendrissement le plus profond. (p. 219)

So that accusation is rapidly deflected from the self-ignorant Fabrice and directed instead towards the person who is capable of making such an accusation in the first place. Thus the Frenchman's perspicacity, however accurate (and Stendhal admits that the charge of hypocrisy against Fabrice would not have been false), is actually a mark of his own self-seeking vanity. Culpability does not consist in simony, nor yet in the failure to recognise one's being guilty of it, but in the naming of simony and hypocrisy as character traits. In the world of *La Chartreuse*, where crimes of all sorts (from murder to hypocrisy) abound, the greatest crime is nevertheless the naming of crime. Characterisation is worse than very murder because it obliterates the singularity of the 'âmes supérieures' by reducing them to the recognisable models that form the *vraisemblable*. Fabrice is saved from vulgarity and is able to remain the novel's hero precisely through the ignorance and impercipience that in other novels would be deemed to bar his promotion to the status of hero.

The story of Fabrice in *La Chartreuse* is not one of progressive self-realisation and self-discovery, with the conventional rewards of marriage and social integration. Instead, his destiny leads him through a number of transformations that say nothing about what sort of person he is, and leave him finally unmarried and in the social exile of the charterhouse. Love itself is not the fruit of perspicacity; and unlike Elizabeth Bennett, who falls in love with Darcy only when she finds out what he is really like, Clélia's feelings for Fabrice exist despite the fact that she believes him to be

[un] *homme léger* qui a eu dix maîtresses connues à Naples, et les a toutes trahies; ... [un] *jeune ambitieux* qui, s'il survit à la sentence qui pèse sur lui, va s'engager dans les ordres sacrés.

In her view,

Ce serait un crime pour moi de le regarder encore lorsqu'il sera hors de cette citadelle, et *son inconséquence naturelle* m'en épargnera la tentation; car, que suis-je pour lui? un prétexte pour passer moins ennuyeusement quelques heures de chacune de ses journées de prison.   (p. 350, my italics)

Like Fabrice, Clélia does not regard love as a matter of mutual understanding, but of destiny. Addressing her supposedly inconstant lover in her mind, she exclaims: 'Tu me perdras, je le sais, *tel est mon destin*' (*ibid.*, my italics again). Clélia knows nothing of the 'real' Fabrice, and for a long time continues (much to her anguish) to believe the rumour that he is an ambitious libertine. The physical obstacles that separate Fabrice and Clélia, and the darkness in which they eventually meet, all emphasise this absence of mutual insight between the lovers.

As far as Fabrice's feelings for Clélia are concerned, they too have nothing to do with any positive qualities that she may or may not have. He loves her simply for her 'singularité', and she resembles Fabrice himself in that her most striking feature is the impact that she has on others and on Fabrice in particular. She too exists as effect rather than essence, and Fabrice is by turns '*interdit* de la beauté si singulière de cette jeune fille' (p. 92), '*frappé* ... de l'expression de mélancolie de sa figure' and '*ravi* de la céleste beauté de Clélia' (p. 281, all my italics). Stendhal is at pains to emphasise the singularity of this celestial beauty, and whereas Gina's looks can in the end be reduced to known models, those of Clélia cannot:

L'admirable singularité de cette figure [i.e. Clélia's] dans laquelle éclataient les grâces naïves et l'empreinte céleste de l'âme la plus noble, c'est que, bien que de la plus rare et plus singulière beauté, elle ne ressemblait en aucune façon aux têtes de statues grecques. La duchesse avait au contraire un peu trop de la beauté *connue* de l'idéal, et sa tête vraiment lombarde rappelait le sourire voluptueux et la tendre mélancolie des belles Hérodiades de Léonard de Vinci.

(p. 284, Stendhal's italics)

The inexpressible singularity of Clélia's beauty outdoes the achievements of even the most melancholy masterpieces (and melancholy is always one of the highest aesthetic virtues in Stendhal). The absence of any model that would enable one to say what Clélia is like makes it just as impossible to imagine being like Clélia as it is to imagine being like Fabrice. She shares with him the quality of inimitable perfection, a quality that makes each of them adorable to the other and at the same time preserves the authenticity of the text as mimesis by placing them just beyond the grasp of the *vraisemblable*.

Mask and disguise

The counterpart to what one might call this 'degree zero' of Fabrice's characterisation in the novel is the proliferation of masks and disguises under which he is made to appear at almost every turn in the events that befall him. As well as being one of the most characterless heroes of fiction, Fabrice is also one of the most travestied. The role of these disguises has to be very carefully assessed lest they be too easily confused with the paranoid pseudonyms of Beyle himself and the hypocritical masks of Julien in *Le Rouge*.[9] The motives for Fabrice's multiple identities are neither paranoia nor hypocrisy since, as I have been arguing, he doesn't see himself as having a self either to protect or to promote. The difference between him and Julien when it comes to disguise hinges on the difference in attitude that each of them has to the idea of a model, and the figure of Napoleon in each of the novels is particularly revealing on this score.

Napoleon is of central importance to both heroes, but his significance as a figure is quite different for each of them. Julien's interest in Napoleon is as a model on which he can pattern his own personality and career; and the question which chiefly preoccupies him is how he can best *be like* Napoleon in the France of 1830. This desire makes Napoleon an imitable type and a goal. It is thus his status as a model which produces the ambition that is designed to bridge the gap between Julien's actual self (whatever that may be) and his ideal. The masks that he adopts in the course of his career (Don Juan, hypocrite, etc.) are the means whereby this ambition can be fulfilled; they are deliberately chosen by him for the purpose of self-advancement and in every case are meant to deceive. The self is supposed to become identified with its masks and their function is to present a certain view of Julien to the outside world. The fact that they frequently fail to do so does not alter the intentions that Julien has in adopting them in the first place.

For Fabrice, on the other hand, Napoleon represents neither a model nor an ideal. His interest in Napoleon is profoundly at odds with his decidedly unrepublican political beliefs, and his decision to leave for Waterloo seems quite unpremeditated in the sense that nothing has been said in the preceding pages of the novel to suggest that Napoleon has any special significance for him. (Compare this silence with the reader's introduction to Julien in *Le Rouge* – symbolically perched on a rafter and engrossed in the *Mémorial de Sainte-Hélène*.) Fabrice does not so much want to be like Napoleon as to demonstrate his liking for him. The explanation that he gives to Gina for offering his services to Napoleon is that 'il [Napoléon] avait tant d'amitié pour ton mari' (p. 30), as if his intention were simply to reward friendship in kind.[10] His dearest wish is not to copy Napoleon, but simply to talk to him: 'il était parti dans la ferme intention de parler à l'Empereur' (p. 34); and he interprets Napoleon's proclamation of war as an invitation to love rather than as an incitement to conform to a given model.

His disappointment at Waterloo is primarily due to his discovery that

La guerre n'était donc plus ce noble et commun élan d'âmes amantes de la gloire qu'il s'était figuré d'après les proclamations de Napoléon! (p. 56)

Fabrice's concept of a hero is not that of an ideal which one should aim to match; rather, heroism represents above all a promise of

amitié chevaleresque et sublime, comme celle des héros de la *Jérusalem délivrée*. (p. 55, my italics)

He goes to battle in search of love and, instead, encounters betrayal from the very companions from whom he had expected so much. They imprison him, unhorse him, take his money and end up by seriously wounding him. Whereas he had expected to find himself

entouré d'âmes héroïques et tendres, de nobles amis qui vous serrent la main au moment du dernier soupir!

and to discover friends in the battle's heroes and heroes in his friends, the reality is a series of encounters with a bunch of 'vils fripons' (p. 55). It is this *friponnerie* that necessitates his recourse to disguise. Fabrice's use of masks is simply a means of being allowed to participate in the noble fraternity of the battlefield, and their purpose is not to further any ambitious plans to conform to a model. As far as Fabrice is concerned, they are nothing more than a disposable expedient in the fulfilment of his desire. For him there are no models, and there is therefore no ambition; there is only love and the desire to express it. When things conspire to block that expression, the mask is required as a means of getting round the prohibition.

This link between masks and passion is maintained in different forms throughout the novel, both on the occasions when the mask is provided by others (which, unlike in *Le Rouge*, it frequently is) and on those where it is freely adopted by Fabrice himself. I shall begin by considering the masks that are given to Fabrice by others, an aspect of Fabrice's disguises whose significance tends to be underestimated, if not completely overlooked.[11] During the course of the novel Fabrice is provided with a whole series of borrowed identities, which he receives passively, though not unwillingly, on the advice of others. This practice begins already when Gina obtains the title and uniform of officer of hussars for the twelve-year-old Fabrice. It continues as he is passed off as Boulot, the dead hussar, by the prison-keeper's wife (pp. 36–8, 65); is instructed by Gina to call himself Cavi on his arrival in Lugano (p. 83); is identified to the Milanese police as 'Ascagne, fils du général de division Pietranera' by Gina (p. 90); is disguised by his mother and Gina as a peasant in order for him to get out of Milan safely (p. 94); is advised to adopt the role of a young ultra during his exile in Romagnan (pp. 99–100), and that of 'un grand seigneur appliqué, fort généreux, mais un peu libertin' during his time as a student of theology in Naples (pp. 133, 140); is given the passport of Giletti by Marietta and her Mammacia after his fight with Giletti (pp. 202–3); is disguised as 'un riche bourgeois de campagne' by Ludovic and the hostess of the Trattoria in Casal-Maggiore (p. 211); is described by Ludovic as his (Ludovic's) younger brother to the surgeon who attends him (p. 216); is sent the passport of a certain Joseph Bossi by Gina during his stay in Bologna; and, finally, is said by Ludovic to be the 'jeune comte Mosca, fils du premier ministre de Parme' as he and Gina make their way to Belgirate after the escape from prison (p. 413).

With the exception of the commission in the hussars, each of these roles and masks is given as a means of protecting Fabrice directly or indirectly from the police, whether they are after him because of Ascanio del Dongo's denunciation, or because of Giletti's murder, or because of his escape from prison. And the motive behind all these varied maskings of Fabrice is invariably that of passion. Gina – either in person or through the good offices of Ludovic – is the provider of most of these masks, and it is her love for Fabrice that lies behind her desire to protect him with these disguises. Even the jailor's wife, who furnishes him with the persona of the late hussar Boulot, is moved as much by pity for 'un joli garçon' as by the prospect of financial reward for helping him escape. In each case, then, Fabrice is disguised out of love, and not for the furtherance of his own ambitions.[12]

The disguises adopted by Fabrice of his own free will are those of Vasi, the barometer salesman (p. 30), and of the brother-in-law of a captain in the army, later named as Teulier (pp. 50–2), both of which enable him to take part in the battle of Waterloo; and that of a hunter–smuggler, under whose cover he is able to return to Grianta (p. 85). He presents himself to Marietta under a false name (p. 160), dresses up as a servant of his own family to visit Blanès (p. 165), and, on his journey back to Parma from Grianta, passes himself off as his own brother when he forces the *valet de chambre* to part with his horse (p. 185). The episode involving La Fausta sees him variously disguised as an Englishman (p. 238), a huntsman (p. 239) and a priest (p. 244); and the affair ends with the duel he fights with Count M*** under the pseudonym Bombace (p. 252). After Ernest IV's death he returns to Parma dressed as a peasant in the stall of a chestnut seller; and, during the separation that Clélia's vow imposes on Fabrice, he disguises himself alternately as 'un ouvrier fort pauvre' (p. 485), 'un bourgeois de campagne' (p. 489) and as a liveried servant (p. 515), all in order to be able to see Clélia. I have already indicated the motives for the Vasi and Teulier disguises, but the others are all just as

powerfully motivated by love. The return to Grianta as a hunter—
smuggler restores him to the loving circle of the female members of
his family; and the purpose of his subsequent visit to Grianta in the
guise of one of his own family servants is to consult Abbé Blanès,
whom he describes as 'son véritable père' (p. 170), and whom he loves
as such in place of his legal father, characterised as 'cet homme sévère
… *qui ne l'avait jamais aimé*' (p. 176, my italics). Fabrice's journey
back to Grianta under the name of his brother Ascanio brings him
back to Gina whom he 'aimait à l'adoration en ce moment' (p. 166),
despite the flirtation with Marietta that is going on at the same time.
The amorous motives for the multiple disguises adopted during his
affair with La Fausta are self-evident, though with the police on his
heels and a murderously jealous rival in the form of Count M***,
there is also an element of self-defence in these fantastic and somewhat
playfully enacted roles. Finally, the chestnut seller, the workman, the
provincial 'bourgeois' and the liveried servant are all a means of
bringing him closer to the woman whose love, in his own words,
constitutes his ultimate destiny.

Disguise in the pursuit of passion is never designed to deceive the
beloved about the lover, and on this score there is once again a
fundamental difference from *Le Rouge*, where the beloved is usually
the prime target of Julien's deceptions. Indeed, with Mathilde and
Mme de Fervaques, passion only comes into existence in the first place
because each is conned over who or what Julien 'really' is. The element
of deceit in the multiple maskings of *La Chartreuse* operates only
against enemies, never against friends. This applies in both the passive
and the active versions of Fabrice's disguises, where the beloved
(notably Gina, Marietta and La Fausta) frequently collude in the
process of deceit in order to protect Fabrice from the enemy. Clélia
herself never actually participates in Fabrice's travesties (mainly
because of her conviction that her feelings for him are criminal and
that she should not compound this criminality), but it is never
Fabrice's intention that she should be fooled by any of them. Rather,
these travesties share with the peephole, cut in the boarded-up window
in the Tour Farnèse, the purpose of providing a means for the two
lovers to communicate.

The effectiveness of Fabrice's masks as protection against the
enemy and the fact that they are never used to deceive the beloved can
largely be attributed to their inappropriateness. Unlike Julien, Fabrice
never disguises himself as anything that he might plausibly be taken
to be in reality. The French captain, the florid Englishman, the
peasants, servants, and so on, are for very obvious reasons of

nationality and class quite unsuitable alter egos for the Italian aristocrat that Fabrice is.[13] They function simply as covers; and, unlike the roles of Napoleon, Danton or Boniface de La Mole in *Le Rouge*, are never presented as possibilities for what Fabrice might be or become. Indeed, the extreme unsuitability of the disguises is frequently alluded to in the novel. For instance, he is twice arrested on his journey home from Waterloo because his official identity seems so very implausible:

il dut ces désagréments à son passeport italien et à cette étrange qualité de marchand de baromètres, qui n'était guère d'accord avec sa figure jeune et son bras en écharpe.   (p. 84)

Similarly, when he is forced to travel on Giletti's passport, all the identifying features listed in the document are quite wrong for Fabrice, who is a good five inches shorter and at least fifteen years younger than Giletti (p. 204). In this way, a clear demarcation between Fabrice's own person (enigmatic though it is) and the personae that he intermittently adopts is maintained consistently both by the novel and by the characters supporting the deceptions. Both Fabrice and the characters who are linked to him by love use their energies to invent roles for Fabrice that are more designed to protect than to distort him.

In contrast to the pursuit of enlightenment in a Jane Austen novel, which will involve the lovers in a contract of mutual unmasking, the lovers of *La Chartreuse* are conspicuously concerned with keeping the hero masked. For Stendhal, passion incites a desire to protect rather than reveal the person of the beloved. Mask-making keeps the 'âmes supérieures' of the novel from meddling in the dangerous business of character-making, and so contributes indirectly, but none the less very effectively, to the maintenance of Fabrice's authenticity as a character degree zero. The glaring implausibility of Fabrice's masks puts them in a quite different category from the various mistaken identities and calumnies that are so frequently imposed on him during the course of the novel. Almost all of these come from his enemies, and the characterisations are inspired by hatred and not love. Only in the Waterloo episode is Fabrice mistaken for something he is not by people who nevertheless wish him well: the 'géôlière' surmises that he is a 'gentilhomme de Milan' (p. 37), the 'cantinière' assumes that he is 'un jeune bourgeois amoureux de la femme de quelque capitaine du 4e de hussards' (p. 40), and the Flemish girls who take care of him in the inn at Zonders are convinced that he must be a prince in disguise (p. 81). Otherwise the misperceptions about Fabrice tend to come from people who are decidedly less well disposed towards him. He is mistaken for General Fabio Conti by the police (p. 87), taken by the Prince to be a republican sympathiser in cahoots with his aunt (p. 145), and the jealousy of Count M*** leads him to the conclusion that Fabrice must be the young Prince of Parma (p. 248). The outright calumnies of the court have already been discussed in the previous chapter, but their effectiveness stems from the fact that, like the portrait of Julien in Mme de Rênal's letter to the Marquis de La Mole, they are eminently plausible and only just wide of the mark. This is precisely what makes them so dangerous, and Fabrice is far better served by those who seek to mask him than by those who are out to characterise him.

Pallor

Fabrice's presence as a character in *La Chartreuse* takes, then, a variety of forms: the degree zero characterisation of sheer adorability, the mask and the misrepresentation. But none of them allows one to say what he 'really' is, or to come up with a definition of his nature and an explanation of his perfection. In this connection it is significant that the only feature of his external appearance to be mentioned in the novel is his pallor, a feature which one may read precisely as a sign of his overall lack of features. Fabrice himself sees his pale complexion as proof that he can never become a hero, but for his lovers, and for Stendhal and his readers, it may be the one sign that guarantees that he is one. Fabrice's pessimism is occasioned by his glimpse of Maréchal Ney at the battle of Waterloo. He admires the blond hair and the red face of this 'brave des braves' (p. 48), and ruefully compares this exalted figure to his own:

Jamais, moi qui suis *si pâle* et qui ai des cheveux châtains, je ne serai comme ça, ajoutait-il avec tristesse. Pour lui ces paroles voulaient dire: Jamais je ne serai un héros.   (p. 49, my italics)

But the pallor of his looks exactly matches the strangely pallid quality of his presence in the text; and this is, in Stendhalian terms, precisely the mark of his heroic superiority.

As the novel's hero, it is, paradoxically, absolutely right (*pace* Balzac) that he should be upstaged by the other, more colourful characters in the book, because in this way he is more likely to elicit from the reader the sort of response that Stendhal is seeking to produce. The effect that Stendhal seems to be aiming at can be compared to effects that he consistently admired in the sphere of painting. In particular, he regarded figurative indistinctness as a means of transforming the spectator into a creator (the terms he uses in his *Histoire de la peinture*, e.g. I, p. 19). Indistinctness is a form of understatement, and the opposite of the excessive detailing that Stendhal invariably found vulgar; and it is a principle that applies as much to literature as it does to painting. Comparing literary representations of the appeal of the women of Rome to Coriolanus with Poussin's painting of the subject, Stendhal condemns the over-explicitness of Poussin's allegorical portrayal and praises Shakespeare because

Le poète laisse à l'imagination de chaque lecteur le soin de donner des dimensions aux êtres qu'il présente. (II, p. 26)

This is precisely what the reader has to do for Fabrice in *La Chartreuse*.

If Fabrice finds himself pushed, so to speak, into the background of his own story, this is because for Stendhal the indistinctness of backgrounds often exerts the most productive effects on the imagination of readers and spectators. In painting, Stendhal tends to prefer the imprecisions of backgrounds to the sharp delineations of foregrounds. It is therefore by being such a very colourless and elusive figure that Fabrice is able to pass into what Stendhal calls 'la magie des lointains', and so be removed from 'la prosaïque réalité' of the foreground (*Histoire de la peinture*, I, p. 152). If a painting has charm for Stendhal, that charm is frequently attributed to its background:

si, dans le premier abord, nous sommes plus frappés par les figures du premier plan, c'est des objets dont les détails sont à moitié cachés par l'air que nous nous souvenons avec le plus de charme; ils ont pris dans notre pensée une teinte céleste. (*ibid.*)

What this passage is describing is the very mechanism that for Balzac and Zola (approaching the matter in quite different perspectives) constituted the novel's weak point. But the confusion and uncertainty in the arrangement of the characters may now be seen, not as the sign of a misjudgement on Stendhal's part, but as the means whereby the reader's attention can be shifted from the striking forms of the foreground to the divinely obscured ones of the background – or rather, to the background-like ones of the foreground. For Stendhal's achievement in *La Chartreuse* is very like the one he so admired in Correggio, of whom he said,

Son art fut de peindre comme dans le lointain même les figures du premier plan. (*Histoire de la peinture*, I, p. 153)

The pallor and imperceptibility of Fabrice and Clélia as 'characters' in the conventional sense are the novelistic equivalent of Correggio's technique, the means whereby Stendhal succeeds in depicting as background these central figures of the foreground.

It is a depiction whose effectiveness depends not on the accuracy of its representation of reality, but on the quality of response that it draws from the reader. The magic of a background works by removing the spectator from reality and involving him in imaginative participation in the picture:

La magie des lointains, cette partie de la peinture qui *attache les imaginations tendres*, est peut-être la principale cause de sa supériorité sur la sculpture. Par là elle se rapproche de la musique, *elle engage l'imagination à finir ses tableaux.*[14]

The blind spot that I spoke of at the beginning of this chapter can now be seen to be the effect of this backgrounding technique, and an essential feature of a strategy that requires the participation of 'imaginations tendres' rather than the naming of a recognisable reality on the part of its readers. Fabrice's authenticity is proven and ensured by his being a pretext for readerly reverie and imaginative reconstitution rather than an object to be mirrored in the infinitely repeatable discourse of the *vraisemblable*. Stendhal's treatment of his hero is the means he uses for turning the novel from a mirror reflection into the bow that plays upon the violin of the reader's soul. The dangers of specular contemplation are thus averted, for there is a risk that if the reader were to gaze too long into the mirror of the novel, he might find himself trying to match the image of the hero with his own. It is therefore by making Fabrice unrepresentable within the framework of a conventional novelistic reflection of reality that Stendhal manages to ensure that truth can never be supplanted by the imitations of readerly vanity.

9
FORGERY, PLAGIARISM AND THE OPERATIC TEXT

la Scala, véritable lieu eidétique des joies italiennes, ... une polyphonie de plaisirs.   Barthes, 'On échoue toujours à parler de ce qu'on aime'

Forgery

In Stendhal's aesthetics it is almost invariably music and painting which are presented as the superlative instances of the sort of qualities that his fiction seeks to achieve: Correggio's paintings exemplify the strategies which Stendhal adopts in the portrayal of his fictional characters; and the music of Mozart and 'le divin Cimarosa' creates the sort of emotional state in its listeners that Stendhal would like his own writing to inspire in his readers. Fiction, on the other hand, seems to provide the model for all that is opposed to these sublimities, proposing a repertoire of *vraisemblances* that feeds the vanity and the self-interested calculations of the baser forms of human action. The novel, as we have seen, is much more likely to find itself on the side of the vile Sancho Panzas than on that of the sublime Don Quixotes.

To make matters worse — and this is the issue which this chapter will be concerned with — the problem of the vilifying effects of the *vraisemblable* is compounded by the disastrous consequences wrought specifically by the material existence of writing itself within the tales told in Stendhal's novels. In *La Chartreuse* Fabrice's troubles are repeatedly associated with the written word: his brother Ascanio's denunciation of him takes the form of a written deposition lodged with the Milanese police; Mosca is powerless to persuade the Prince to commute Fabrice's prison sentence as long as Rassi refuses to give up his copy of the original order; the life-threatening continuation of Fabrice's stay in jail is due to the 'fatal billet' (as Gina calls it) so unwisely drawn up by Mosca for the Prince to sign; and, finally, Gina's role in the death of Prince Ranuce-Ernest would inevitably be brought to light if Rassi had been allowed to proceed with his case on the basis of the papers he collected as evidence. Writing is thus inextricably associated in the novel with the court and its intrigues, corruptions and misrepresentations.

In the event, however, the calamities threatened by these various pieces of writing are all averted. Fabrice is kept out of the hands of the Milanese police and the Spielberg prison, of which he has such a horror; he is saved from poison; and both parts of Rassi's evidence are eventually burned. Yet there remains one form of writing that is unquestionably catastrophic: the forged letter. The action of each of the major novels turns on a forgery of some kind; its consequences are not averted and are invariably considerable: imprisonment, separation, death. These turning points in Stendhal's novels are particularly interesting, not just because the repeated use of the same formula of forgery suggests some perennial obsession worthy of critical attention, but because, in them, forgery is tellingly linked with the practice of fictional writing. For the forgeries work only in so far as they make successful use of the strategies of fiction, developing plausible narratives, constructing lifelike characters – in short, gulling their unsuspecting reader with an illusion of reality. As the action of the novels reaches its climax and the future of their heroes is put in perilous balance, the texts confront themselves with an appalling image of their own corrupt nature. In *La Chartreuse* it is the letter Raversi has sent to Fabrice pertaining to come from Gina that lands him in prison. Raversi goes to a good deal of trouble to imitate Gina's style, to construct a plausible scenario for the letter (the invitation to spend a day with her at Castelnovo) and to have her handwriting counterfeited by an expert. Fabrice is completely taken in and walks straight into the trap that awaits him.

What happens in *Armance* is very similar, except that here the forgery leads to the death of the hero rather than his imprisonment. But the preparation of the forgery is almost identical. The forger himself is Octave's uncle, M. de Soubirane, who is described in very much the same terms as Raversi. Octave calls him 'cette âme mercenaire et basse' (p. 167) and Soubirane is as unscrupulous in his attempts to get his hands on Octave's fortune as Raversi is in hers to do Gina out of her inheritance from the Duc Sanseverina-Taxis. The narrator certainly confirms this view of Soubirane when he speaks of him as '[une] âme commune' whose former ambitions include political intrigue (p. 171). The only thing he lacks is the same degree of scheming intelligence as Raversi, but otherwise money and power both provide the chief motives for these two forgers. And the particular threat posed by Soubirane to Octave and Armance is, as with Raversi, the plausibility of the anecdotes that he can put about with such terrible consequences. Armance lives in permanent dread of the vulgar calumnies that her actions may give rise to. This fear is so great, in fact, that she prefers to deny her love for Octave rather than put herself in a position where she might become the victim of some 'histoire fâcheuse' (p. 145) that attributes to her the same base motives that inspire the purveyors of these vile reputations. But the separation of Armance and Octave is brought about in the end by a forgery whose vulgarity and plausibility is the same as those Armance had feared from social gossip. Soubirane's forgery takes the form of a letter attributed to Armance and addressed to her friend Méry, in which she says that she no longer loves Octave, but intends none the less to go through with what is undoubtedly an advantageous match. True passion is thus reduced to a form of *amour-goût* and a means of social advancement by a highly plausible account of a gradual loss of feeling on Armance's part, supposedly precipitated by the well-known 'inégalités' of Octave's temperament.

Soubirane succeeds by means of largely novelistic skills. Indeed, the very idea of engineering a separation of the two lovers through the agency of a forged letter itself comes from a novel; Soubirane's accomplice in the plot to destroy Octave's marriage is Armance's relative, the Chevalier de Bonnivet, who remembers 'un roman vulgaire où le personnage méchant fait imiter l'écriture des amants et fabrique de fausses lettres' (p. 180), and it is this novel that Bonnivet uses as a way of planting the idea in the mind of his somewhat duller associate, Soubirane. The next step is still in the realm of the novelistic and consists of coming up with the right style for the letter, a task which seems to depend on finding the appropriate fictional model to imitate. Soubirane wastes two days concocting something brilliant and witty that could have come straight out of *Les Liaisons dangereuses*, and it has to be replaced by a version more in keeping with the spirit of the times − 'plutôt pédant, grave, ennuyeux' (p. 181) − in order to clinch the deception. Only then will the professional skills of the 'calqueur', brought in by the Chevalier to imitate Armance's hand-writing, have any chance of succeeding. Octave does not doubt for a moment the authenticity of the letter, and, convinced that Armance no longer loves him, decides to go along with what he takes to be a marriage of convenience, leaves for Greece and commits suicide. This terrible deception works because the deceivers are able to pick up the threads of Stendhal's own novel (Armance's intimacy with Méry de Tersan, Octave's uneven temperament) and weave them into an intrigue that looks like a continuation of that same novel. It works to the degree that it is realistic; it is disastrous to the degree that it puts the entire action of the novel under the aegis of the *vraisemblable*, so that the sublime is grotesquely reduced to the vulgar.

The same sort of fundamental pattern lies behind the variant versions of forgery that one finds in the other novels. In *Le Rouge* the letter which Mme de Rênal sends to the Marquis de La Mole is, to all intents and purposes, a forgery; for, although she physically writes it herself, it is actually copied from the draft set out for her by her new confessor, and expresses his official, religious and utterly banal version of events and characters, rather than her own. It leads to the separation of Julien and Mathilde, the attempt on the life of Mme de Rênal, Julien's imprisonment and, ultimately, his execution. In *Lucien Leuwen* the event that separates Lucien from Mme de Chasteller is not, literally speaking, a forgery, but it has all the hallmarks and the same structure as the other forgeries. The crying baby wrapped in the blood-stained sheet is a message constructed for Lucien by Dr du Poirier, an '*intrigant* sans moralité' (p. 1058, my italics), as 'evidence' that Mme de Chasteller does not love him. Despite the element of *invraisemblance* in the episode (if the baby is Mme de Chasteller's, then how come Lucien never noticed her pregnancy?), Lucien, like Fabrice, Octave and Julien, does not stop to question the authenticity of this message. The trick works, and Lucien leaves Nancy and the world of Mme de Chasteller for Paris and the vulgar, pretentious and fundamentally prosaic world of Mme Grandet.

In most of these situations, however, the disastrous consequences of the forgery reveal an accidental loophole by which the hero is saved from the threatened plummet into vulgarity and returned to the sublime: for Julien and Fabrice the experience of love is, ironically, reserved for their imprisonment; Octave retains the nobility of his personality precisely in his decision to go through with his marriage and leave for Greece. Even Lucien was to be released from the Parisian world of vanity and to meet up again with Mme de Chasteller in Rome. They escape the corruptions of vulgarity by accident or chance – and, indeed, what other effective counter is there to the pervasive grip of the *vraisemblable* apart from the explosive force of chance and the *imprévu*? But the consequences of a forgery in 'L'Abbesse de Castro' (in Stendhal's *Chroniques italiennes*, written between *Le Rouge* and *Lucien Leuwen*, and published a year after the composition of *La Chartreuse* in 1839) have an incurable effect on the very soul of its victim, the heroine, Hélène de Campireali. In this instance the forgery is perpetrated by Hélène's mother in a deliberate attempt to separate Hélène from her lover, Jules de Branciforte: 'Son dessein était de commencer la correspondance [i.e. from Jules to Hélène] par sept à huit lettres d'amour passionné; elle voulait préparer ainsi les suivantes, où l'amour semblerait s'éteindre peu à peu' (p. 631). Despite the careful scrutiny Hélène gives to the handwriting of the first letter, she is taken in by the deceit, and thus is accomplished the prediction made at the beginning of the episode, when Stendhal announces that:

Nous allons, en effet, assister à la longue dégradation d'une âme noble et généreuse. Les mesures prudentes et les mensonges de la civilisation, qui désormais vont l'obséder de toutes parts, remplaceront les mouvements sincères des passions énergiques et naturelles.   (p. 629)

The horrible plausibility of the waning of Jules's love contaminates the noble passions and energies in the heart of the person reading of it. The 'lies of civilisation', which are the stuff of all Stendhal's forgeries, and which threaten all his other heroes, are here shown at their most devastating, capable of destroying not only the destiny but the very superiority of Stendhal's heroes.

Although forged letters were a fairly popular motif in the fiction of the period, they seem to have been a particular obsession of Stendhal's and forgeries abound in his fiction. There are the cases cited here, but there are many others too, including the numerous anonymous letters in a disguised hand: Prince Ranuce-Ernest keeps a supposedly illiterate soldier on a permanent retainer for work of this kind (suggesting that it is common currency in the state of Parma) and orders him to send an anonymous letter to Mosca about the goings-on between Gina and Fabrice; and Gina herself receives so many 'anonymous' letters from Raversi that she has to hire a secretary specially to deal with them. In *Le Rouge* there is a positive epidemic of counterfeiting: Valenod sends M. de Rênal an anonymous letter denouncing Julien and Mme de Rênal, to which Mme de Rênal herself responds by concocting an 'anonymous' letter purportedly from Valenod, to be delivered to herself; and the fifty-three letters Julien sends to Mme de Fervaques are, it is true, written by him and signed in his name, but in every other respect they are thoroughly faked. However, it is not just the abundance of these letters that is important, but the central position that the forgeries have in the structure of the novels. By providing such a dramatic turning point in the action, and by threatening such fatal consequences for the destinies of the heroes, they imply a fundamental anxiety on Stendhal's part concerning the nature and effects of fictional writing itself. The forgeries are a reminder that fiction flourishes in a climate of deceit, and that it can deceive even its most passionate readers with its plausible repetition of the lies of civilisation.

One might be tempted to think that the problem derives from the written nature of fiction, that it is writing itself that is duplicitous. For, if Italy is largely free of the corruptions of vanity, this is because the arts that flourish on its soil are those of painting and music; and, in modern Italy, a combination of opera and conversation satisfies needs that in France have to be met by the more roundabout means of the novel. In Stendhal's idealised Italy there is no place — because no need — for fiction, which carries all the negative connotations of being a mediated and surrogate form of other, more direct aesthetic experiences. Much is made in the early part of *La Chartreuse* of Fabrice's near-illiteracy, an essential feature of his (non-)education. His idyllic and nostalgically recalled childhood at Grianta is spent fighting with the village boys 'et n'apprenant rien, pas même à lire' (p. 15). Books are associated with his unloving father, who insists that Fabrice learn his Latin from the pompous genealogy of the Valserra family. Gina gaily sabotages Fabrice's formal education at the Jesuit college in Milan (where, in any case, he is described as being 'ignorant à plaisir, et sachant à peine écrire', p. 16), by taking him out of school from Saturday to Wednesday or Thursday of each week in order to initiate him into the far more essential and enjoyable ways of her salon and the social life of Prince Eugene's Milan. The superior wisdom of the Abbé Blanès seems to be confirmed by his disdain for the world of letters; charged with the responsibility of completing the education of Fabrice, he dismisses the value of the whole enterprise when he asks, 'Que sais-je de plus sur un cheval ... depuis qu'on m'a appris qu'en latin il s'appelle *equus*?' (p. 20). The implication is that language is an obstacle to the immediate perception and experience of the real world.

Napoleon (another father figure in the novel) also seems, at any rate indirectly, to endorse this impression that writing is a futile and devious distraction. For not the least of his achievements on his entry into Milan is to put an end to a degenerate way of life in which 'leur grande affaire [i.e. of the Milanese republicans] était d'imprimer des sonnets sur de petits mouchoirs de taffetas rose quand arrivait le mariage d'une jeune fille appartenant à quelque famille noble ou riche' (p. 5). These printed handkerchieves are a stark contrast to the caricatures of Gros and the music-making of the French soldiers in the villages of Lombardy, which are the artistic forms in which 'la masse de bonheur et de plaisir' erupts in Italy. The written word of the Austrian press is powerless in the face of a gaiety that is associated exclusively with drawing, dance and the violin: 'presque chaque soir quelque tambour, jouant du violon, improvisait un bal' (p. 8). The ink left over from the literate days of Austrian rule, no longer needed to write descriptions of the French army as a bunch of brigands, or to celebrate a society wedding with a sonnet, is now used instead to dye the string that holds Robert's shoes together, and so prepare him for dinner with the del Dongo family and the first meeting with his future mistress. In a word, then, writing and literacy would seem from these examples to be condemned as devious and degenerate by the utopian standards of Stendhal's Italy.

Plagiarism

And yet it is actually the most passionate characters in the novel who resort most frequently to the written word. It is not at all the most dangerous and deceptive writers who prove to be the most prolific. The dreary Count Zurla-Contarini – 'un imbécile bourreau de travail, qui se donne le plaisir d'écrire quatre-vingts lettres chaque jour' (p. 121) – is the only person in the book who actually keeps count of the number of letters that he writes, no. 20715 being addressed to Mosca. But Gina, Mosca and Fabrice repeatedly have recourse to letter-writing, to communicate not just with the outside world, but particularly, and indeed primarily, with each other. Letters are used in the novel for a multitude of purposes: to inform, warn, excuse, persuade, denounce, advise, deceive, plead, grant, reproach, reprieve, mock, condemn, resign, refuse, congratulate, beg for pardon, bid farewell, or to announce the end of an affair.[1] But between the passionate characters themselves writing is used in the first instance just to compensate by its very existence for the distance or the obstacles imposed by separation. Under these circumstances the negative value of mediacy associated with the writing of the forgeries is reversed, and rather than forming an unnecessary detour – like the word *equus* in relation to a real horse – letters between lovers seem actually to create or restore a lost contact.

For instance, no sooner has Fabrice said goodbye to Aniken's family in Zonders than he takes up his pen to write them a letter. And, in fact, typically for these occasions, he doesn't just write one letter, but several. The 'braves jeunes gens' who escort Fabrice to safety return to Zonders 'avec des lettres où Fabrice, un peu fortifié par l'agitation de la route, avait essayé de faire connaître à ses hôtesses tout ce qu'il sentait pour elles. Fabrice écrivait les larmes aux yeux, et il y avait certainement de l'amour dans la lettre adressée à la petite Aniken' (p. 82). The content of these letters is not revealed, for what matters most about them is not what they say, but the fact that they have been written in the first place – all the more so in this instance, since Aniken's Flemish-speaking family are incapable of understanding a single word of French (always assuming that this is the language in which Fabrice writes to them). Again, on returning to his hotel in Paris, Fabrice finds not just one, or two, but twenty letters from his mother and his aunt imploring him to return and begging him to write. Fabrice's departure from Grianta and the adoring circle of his mother and aunt provokes a compensatory supply of letters, whose mere existence and number are enough to convey to him that he continues to have a place in that circle. In the same way, the passion that begins in Gina's box at the opera house in Milan is maintained and fuelled by Mosca's assiduous correspondance with her after his recall to Parma and her return to Grianta. And these letters, about which we are told little beyond the fact that they are 'amusantes' and 'aimables', nevertheless have the effect not only of keeping their author in the forefront of Gina's mind, but also of inducing in her 'une amitié tendre' for him (p. 112). This friendship is the fruit of the apparently tortuous and circuitous medium of the written word, itself the only medium available for the expression of the passionate energies of the 'amour fou' to which Mosca has fallen prey.

However, although these letters are clearly able to perpetuate the functions initiated by evenings of conversation in La Scala, they still share many of the characteristics associated with that vulgar and devious surrogate for the pleasures of the opera and of conversation – the novel. In order to be successful in overcoming the obstacles imposed by separation, the written word has, paradoxically, to exaggerate the very deviousness which originally seemed to make it such a negative and destructive enterprise. Not only does Mosca adopt the written word, but in addition, instead of addressing his letters directly to Gina at Grianta, he has them delivered to a number of different places around Lake Como, from where Gina has to collect them. The ostensible excuse for this strategy is that it helps to 'éviter les commentaires du marquis del Dongo qui n'aimait pas à payer des ports de lettres' (p. 111), but since Mosca is using the services of a courier it has the added bonus of encouraging Gina to reply. It is as if the more circuitous the route by which communication takes place, the more effective it is likely to be.

More strangely still, the deviousness of these successful communications frequently takes the specific forms adopted by the forgeries: anonymity and/or a disguised hand. One of the letters that Gina sends to Fabrice in Paris advises him not to sign 'les lettres que tu écris pour donner de tes nouvelles' (p. 83). And the two letters that Fabrice writes after the Giletti episode are unsigned and written in a hand other than his own, namely the 'pauvre écriture de cocher' of Ludovic (p. 213). Furthermore, it is not just passion, but literature itself, that is implicated by these tricks, for the two poets in the novel are both experts in anonymity and disguise. Ludovic is living in retirement on a pension granted to him by Gina, his former employer, to enable him to devote himself to writing poetry. And although Ludovic's poems are actually somewhat mediocre, exactly the same combination of forgery and poetry is made in the figure of Ferrante Palla, who is not mediocre but, in Gina's words, 'l'un des plus grands poètes du siècle' (p. 389), and whose poetry, according to Mosca, is 'aussi beau que le Dante' (p. 117). Even so, Ferrante Palla can outdo Raversi herself when it comes to anonymous writing and forged letters. The two poems which he contributes as 'œuvres de circonstance' to the action of the novel are both anonymous: one of the few letters that Gina manages to get smuggled to Fabrice in prison contains 'un sonnet magnifique' written in an unknown hand and in which 'une âme généreuse exhortait Fabrice à prendre la fuite, et à ne pas laisser avilir son âme et dépérir son corps par les onze années de captivité qu'il avait encore à subir' (p. 382); and after Fabrice's escape, 'tout Parme répétait un sonnet sublime. C'était le monologue de Fabrice se laissant glisser le long de la corde, et jugeant les divers incidents de sa vie' (p. 426). But the most devious piece of all Ferrante Palla's writing is the unsigned letter of farewell that he sends to Gina before leaving for America. Materially speaking, it is hard to imagine a more duplicitous letter: it consists of a request purporting to come from a former chambermaid, asking Gina to get her a job at the court. However, Gina sees at once that it is neither the handwriting nor the style of the maid in question. It is a poor pretence in one sense, but the real message is not contained in this letter at all, but is wrapped around a small image of the Madonna inside the first letter. It consists of a sheet of printed paper that looks as though it has been torn out of a book. Thus, two extremely elaborate layers of disguise – the letter from the chambermaid and the printed piece of wrapping paper – have to be penetrated before Ferrante Palla's letter of farewell can be read.[2]

Clearly, neither the most sublime poetry since Dante, nor the most passionate outpourings of superior souls (and the letter of farewell is nothing if it is not this) can be decisively distinguished from the basest forms of forgery and deceit. Forgery is formally indistinguishable from the kind of writing which (in spite of the negative connotations of the term as used in chapter 1 above) I have provocatively – and perhaps not very accurately – called 'plagiarism' in honour of Stendhal's notoriety as a plagiarist. There is nothing that intrinsically sets poetry apart from vulgarity and corruption. The only difference – but it is a crucial one – between poetry and other positive forms of writing on the one hand, and the worst deceptions and frauds on the other, lies not so much in the manner in which they are *written* as in the manner in which they are *read*. Gina is not taken in by the written impersonation of the maid in the way that Fabrice is taken in by Raversi's impersonation of his aunt, for Ferrante Palla's letter is not meant to deceive Gina but 'l'œil profane' which he fears might intercept it. Similarly, the anonymity and disguised hand which Ludovic recommends for the letters that Fabrice sends back to Parma are precautions that need to be taken against the possibility of the letters falling into the hands of the police and the Prince. It is Raversi as potential interceptor, not Gina, the actual recipient of the letters, who is supposed to be deceived by the forgery. In the same way, the anonymity of the sonnet that circulates in Parma after Fabrice's escape does not prevent the cognoscenti from immediately recognising the style of Ferrante Palla. Nor should it, since it is presumably only the ignorant and unlettered Rassis of the court who fail to see beyond the appearance of anonymity. In a sense, then, these writerly deceptions are rather like the physical disguises adopted by Fabrice, in that their ultimate purpose is not to deceive but to protect. They help to promote the contact between author and recipient in exactly the same way that Fabrice's disguises provided a means of bringing him closer to the people he loves.

The forgeries, on the other hand, work only as long as their deceptions are not penetrated. Whereas Gina sees at once that the letter from her chambermaid is not what it appears to be, Fabrice never suspects for a moment that the letter inviting him to spend the day at Castelnovo is not from Gina. It is, however, possible to undo the threats posed by the forgeries simply by reading round, or through the disguise. Mosca manages to do this in the case of the anonymous letter sent to him by the Prince. The insinuations made in the letter concerning the 'amour des plus singuliers' between Gina and Fabrice purport to come from a 'woman of a certain age', and have the desired effect of plunging Mosca into 'des angoisses qui eussent fait pitié à son plus cruel ennemi' (p. 151). Seeing through the letter to the Prince behind it may not assuage the torture, but it does make the letter less of a threat.

The writing of both the forgeries and the letters between the lovers involves impersonation, or what one might call a certain two-voicedness. In the case of the forgeries, though, the aim is to close the gap between the two voices, so that one disappears behind the other, Raversi's behind Gina's, the Prince's behind that of the 'woman of a certain age'. In the letters between the lovers, by contrast, the writing actively encourages its reader to hear the voice of Fabrice behind that of the uneducated coachman, and of Ferrante Palla behind the pieties and ambitions of the former chambermaid. One may infer from this that Stendhal sees all writing as a devious, round-about thing, whose tortuous path will inevitably involve passing through another voice. There would seem to be no original, purely spontaneous form of writing that could bypass the route taken by the despicable strategies of forgery and imitation. Even the sonnets on pink handkerchieves that stand for all that is degenerate and vile in Milan under Austrian rule reappear at the end of the novel as an index of the sublimest of passions when Fabrice sends Clélia a sonnet by Petrarch (not even a composition of his own) which he has printed on a silk handkerchief. Far from being a sign of degeneracy, his murmured reference to it at the Princess's birthday reception is enough to convince Clélia that 'Cette belle âme n'est point inconstante' (p. 503). There is no suggestion here that the handkerchief might not be an appropriate form of communication between passionate characters. So that the only difference between good and bad forms of writing depends in the end on whether the detour through the other voices is honestly sounded and allowed to be heard.

If one examines the nature of the different strategies developed by Fabrice and Clélia in order to communicate with each other, one finds that forms involving a dual voice are the ones they habitually strive for and obviously prefer. Fabrice's time in prison is largely devoted to the search for an ideal means of communication with Clélia, and this, as many critics have pointed out, leads him to a rediscovery and a re-evaluation of language itself.[3] But what has not been sufficiently appreciated in these critical discussions is that the quest which begins with what one might take to be the most simple and straightforward form of communication – the glance – ends with the use of the most arcane and circuitous – the St Jerome marginalia and the afore-mentioned sonnet. The glance that Fabrice and Clélia exchange on Fabrice's entry into the Farnese prison initiates their passion for each other, but it is felt by each of them to lend itself to gross misinterpre-tation. Clélia convinces herself that Fabrice must have found her 'bien ridicule', and worse, 'une âme basse', for not having responded to his gesture (p. 282). The language of the glance is, of course, essential to the lovers, and Fabrice is totally absorbed by the need to find a way of keeping it going after the wooden screen has blocked up his window: 'Si je parviens seulement à la *voir*, je suis heureux ... Non pas, se dit-il; il faut aussi *qu'elle voie que je la vois*' (p. 336, my italics). But it is a need that leads to another stage in the quest for communication — the language of signs.

Far from being direct and immediately expressive, however, communication by sign also proves to be open to more than one interpretation, as Fabrice sees to his horror after his attempt to convey to Clélia by signs and gestures his intention to saw through the screen: 'Hé quoi! se dit Fabrice étonné, serait-elle assez déraisonnable pour voir une familiarité ridicule dans un geste dicté par la plus impérieuse nécessité?' (p. 337). The gesture, which is supposed to convey to Clélia Fabrice's wish that she should look towards his window when she is attending to her birds, and his intention to do everything humanly possible to carry on seeing her, is suddenly seen to be susceptible of another, unspeakably vulgar interpretation. The supposedly natural language of signs actually threatens to put an end to the very communication that it was designed to promote. For Clélia's part, these signs are hopelessly inadequate in helping her to decipher the nature of Fabrice's feelings for his aunt (the issue that preoccupies her the most). The limits imposed by this form of communication mean that she cannot be disabused of her conviction that Fabrice is in love with Gina: 'Sa coquetterie de femme sentait bien vivement *l'imperfection du langage employé*: si l'on se fût parlé, de combien de façons différentes n'eût-elle pas pu chercher à deviner quelle était précisément la nature des sentiments que Fabrice avait pour la duchesse!' (pp. 341–2, my italics). Equally, for Fabrice, the restriction of the language of signs makes it impossible for him to put the score right on this question, and this impossibility leads to a further *malentendu* in the form of Clélia's belief that Fabrice is an inveterate womaniser who has turned his attentions to her because she is the only woman available in the confines of the prison. The language of signs is repeatedly characterised as imperfect by the text, and the next stage, which introduces the written word, sees a significant improvement in the communication between the two lovers.

This strategy begins when Fabrice traces letters on his hand with a piece of charcoal that he finds in his stove. He spells out his messages letter by letter, and the most important of these is both a declaration of love ('Je vous aime, et la vie ne m'est précieuse que parce que je vous vois', p. 352), and a request for pencil and paper, i.e. the means of further written communication. Although Clélia is said to long for the chance to elucidate Fabrice's feelings by means of the spoken word, Fabrice explicitly prefers even this extremely cumbersome form of the written word to all the conversations that he might have been able to have with Clélia in the salons of Parma, where the social forms of the spoken word would divide and distance them from each other far more than the unwieldiness of their improvised alphabets. But even these alphabets are used merely as a means of procuring a more satisfactory means of written communication − letters. No sooner has Clélia provided paper and pencil for Fabrice than he sits down to write 'une lettre infinie à Clélia' that is far more expressive of his feelings for her than the bald declaration 'Je vous aime' (p. 353). The transparency of the glance and the direct iconicity of the gesture are rejected in favour of the length and the wordiness of prose, even though it requires the most convoluted and ingenious schemes to deliver it to its recipient. The written word circulates between the lovers in a whole variety of forms − lowered on a rope, pinned to a shawl, hidden in a basket of fruit − exposing them both to the dangers of discovery every time.

This danger leads to yet another version of the written word, namely the use of the already written. Clélia's own improvised alphabet is written on the pages of a book that she tears up for the purpose, and her warning to Fabrice about the risk of poison is written in the margin of a breviary that she has sent to him and from which Fabrice in turn tears a number of pages in order to make his own alphabet. A variant of this stragegy is Clélia's recourse to her piano and her playing of tunes from fashionable operas, under cover of which she is able to sing messages to Fabrice − in the margins, so to speak, of the recitatives on which she improvises: 'elle se précipita à son piano, et, feignant de chanter un récitatif de l'opéra alors à la mode, elle lui dit, en phrases interrompues par le désespoir et par la crainte d'être comprise par les sentinelles qui se promenaient sous la fenêtre ...' (p. 351). There follows the warning that Barbone has returned to the citadel and intends to take his revenge by poisoning Fabrice. This is a device which Fabrice also uses later on, during his second stay in the tower when he accompanies himself on an imaginary guitar and sings out 'quelques mots improvisés et qui disaient: *C'est pour vous revoir* que je suis revenu en prison' (p. 469, Stendhal's italics). I shall be returning below to the significance of music implied by these and other episodes, but before doing so, I should like to deal with what one might call the masterpieces of this particular form of communication: the written record kept by Fabrice in the margins of the copy of St Jerome and the sending of the sonnet by Petrarch. In both these instances communication takes place by means of an

213

exploitation of existing forms of the written word, and is effected in the most peculiar and devious manner.

The St Jerome writings constitute the most circuitous of the communicative strategies, and are further complicated by the fact that their intended recipient, Clélia, is in physical terms their interceptor. This is also the case with the letter that Fabrice sends to Fabio Conti, asking pardon for having escaped, where the essential message is hidden behind the apparent meaning of the text, and the true interlocutor is not the stated one:

> Peu lui importait ce qu'il écrivait, Fabrice espérait que les yeux de Clélia verraient cette lettre, et sa figure était couverte de larmes en l'écrivant. Il la termina par une phrase bien plaisante: il osait dire que, se trouvant en liberté, souvent il lui arrivait de regretter sa petite chambre de la tour Farnèse. C'était là la pensée capitale de sa lettre, il espérait que Clélia la comprendrait.
>
> (p. 421)

In the case of the marginalia, the copy of St Jerome has been returned to its original owner, Don Cesare, who does little more than glance through its pages before returning it to its shelf, 'Mais un autre œil que celui du bon aumônier avait lu cette page depuis la fuite' (p. 422). The reference to this other eye recalls the 'œil profane' alluded to in Ferrante Palla's letter to Gina, incidentally confirming once again both the fact that positive forms of writing are indistinguishable from negative ones[4] (Clélia is in the reading position of the police spies who might intercept the letter to Gina), and also the fact that the perception of two-voicedness is the vital element in successful communication. Fabio Conti sees only the overt plea for pardon, but Clélia understands the hidden significance in the concluding sentence, which contains the letter's true message.

In the case of the marginal jottings, their apparent concern is with an *'amour divin'*, but 'ce mot divin en remplaçait un autre qu'on n'osait écrire'. Don Cesare, even supposing that he bothers to look that closely, sees just a record of the thoughts of a young priest with mystical tendencies; only Clélia knows what word the adjective 'divin' is standing in for, and how to interpret the meaning of the 'voix entendue à travers les airs [qui] rendait quelque espérance et causait des transports de bonheur' (p. 422). The sonnet which concludes these mystical musings produces the same effect of 'transports de bonheur' in Clélia herself when she hears behind it the second voice of Fabrice's more secular passion: 'Comment dire son ravissement au milieu de la sombre tristesse où l'absence de Fabrice l'avait plongée, lorsqu'elle trouva sur les marges de l'ancien saint Jérôme le sonnet dont nous

214

avons parlé, et les mémoires, jour par jour, de l'amour qu'on avait senti pour elle!' (p. 423). Fabrice's highly duplicitous writing proves to be the best assurance she could possibly have of the nature and extent of Fabrice's feelings for her. The languages of the glance and the sign, the letter-by-letter message that said 'Je vous aime', even the 'lettre infinie', all failed to produce that assurance which only the two-voiced deceptions of the St Jerome marginalia are able to give.

Moreover, Clélia's enraptured response to this multilayered communication is to add another layer of her own. She at once learns the sonnet by heart, and then sings it: where Fabrice entrusts the language of religious mysticism with the task of expressing his love, Clélia brings the language of music to the language of the sonnet in order to express hers. Passion seems actively to encourage the accumulation of these layers of different languages, whose very diversity and multiplicity serve both to conceal and to reveal the existence of passion: to conceal it from Fabio Conti, Don Cesare and the sentries on duty, to reveal it to Clélia and the memory of Fabrice to which she addresses the sung version of the sonnet. Clélia uses Fabrice's words to send back to him, or at least to his memory, a musically disguised message about her own feelings for him.

Before dealing with the implications of the lovers' use of language for Stendhal's own prose, there remains one final moment in Fabrice's search for a communicative language that needs to be examined – the sermons, which are not only the last of the many different means that he employs in his attempts to communicate with Clélia, but also the only one that actually brings them together. It is the effect upon Clélia of Fabrice's final sermon that leads to the assignation at the door to the orangery and the words of welcome with which she marks her surrender to passion, 'Entre ici, ami de mon cœur.' A striking feature of this episode is the way in which the sermons build on the musical elements of the lovers' earlier attempts to create a language for communication by persistently, if discreetly, associating Fabrice's eloquence in these sermons with opera. The original idea for them comes from Gina, who recommends that Fabrice exploit his talent for improvisation by giving a series of sermons that will help to dispose the Prince in his favour. 'Tu *improvises* si bien en vers', she says to him (p. 512, my italics), a talent which becomes more and more explicitly linked to an image of Fabrice as a successful operatic singer. His improvisatory skills make him a deserving rival to 'un ténor qui faisait fureur et remplissait la salle [i.e. at the opera] tous les soirs' (p. 514). On the night that Fabrice decides to preach at the little church of the Visitation, the poor tenor sings to an almost empty house while

Fabrice performs in a church packed with 'les jeunes gens à la mode et ... les personnages de la plus haute distinction' (p. 515), whom one would otherwise have expected to find in their boxes at the opera house. His appeal to this audience is distinctly profane, evoking idolatrous cries of admiration and furious applause. The consensus of this highly urbane gathering is that 'il l'emporte même sur le meilleur ténor de l'Italie' (p. 517), a judgement that implies that his success comes from simply having outsung the visiting tenor. Fabrice's last sermon has all the features of a last night, and it takes the form of a series of improvisations (improvisation being a singer's skill) on the theme of 'pity'. The cognoscenti find the performance 'singulier', but praise it for 'le pathétique', in other words, for the very quality that so moves Fabrice and Clélia themselves in the arias from Pergolesi and Cimarosa sung by Madame P... at the reception for the Princess's birthday.

This final operatic form that Fabrice's wooing of Clélia takes shares with all the others the strategy of two-voicedness in that it uses the public language of the pulpit to convey a very private and secular message. But by characterising it as an operatic triumph, Stendhal is explicitly linking it to a genre which, as I shall be showing, requires the collaboration of two voices at every level of both composition and performance. Opera is, in short, the epitome of polyphony, and there seems little doubt that the sermons' orchestration of a kind of operatic polyphony is what makes them the culmination of Fabrice's quest for communicative perfection, before he relinquishes language of all kinds in favour of the silence of the charterhouse.

What all these examples suggest is that passion does not have its own particular language in Stendhal, for Fabrice and Clélia do not discover or invent a new language. What they learn, rather, is how to exploit the multiplicity of existing languages in such a way as to make passion legible to the right recipient. The words that spell out Fabrice's passion to Clélia do nothing of the kind in the eyes of Don Cesare, since the words in themselves are of little importance, and originality is an irrelevant requirement. For this reason, too, there is nothing negative or inauthentic in Fabrice's repetition of the sonnet by Petrarch (the one on the silk handkerchief). Unlike Julien quoting from Rousseau in Mathilde's bed, there is no attempt on Fabrice's part to pass off the literary text as his own. Julien's use of Rousseau is fraudulent because he blurs the voice of the literary text with his own, whereas Fabrice makes the sonnet convey his passion by deliberately distinguishing his own voice from the text of the poem. This he does by simply changing one word in it (the poem is not given in full and we are not told what the word is – just of the fact of the alteration), so that Fabrice's own voice can be heard behind that of Petrarch in such a way as to make his feelings perceptible to the right reader of the poem.

Part of the interest of the privileging of this strategy in Stendhal is that it gives a new twist to the vexed issue of his plagiarism. Without wanting to raise the whole question of its role in the *Vies de Haydn, de Mozart et de Métastase*, which is said to be the most flagrantly plagiarised of his texts,[5] plagiarism is a question of special importance to the novel, where the demands of realism make authenticity an essential requirement of the writing. As the 'Projet d'un article sur *Le Rouge et le Noir*' makes clear, genuine success in the novel depends on finding a way of not repeating existing forms of fiction, of not copying the 'roman pour les femmes de chambre', nor the Parisian 'roman de bonne compagnie', nor yet the novels of Walter Scott. But if passion, where the demands of authenticity are just as great as they are in fiction, if passion can accommodate and even flourish on a repetition of the already written, then what about the novel? Within *La Chartreuse* the lovers' quest for effective communication would seem to point to an unconventional conclusion, namely that repetition in itself is neither positive nor negative, neither vulgar nor sublime. The only thing that counts is, first, how the speaker positions himself (or herself) in relation to the language he (or she) uses, and second, how he positions his readers in relation to that, or, rather, those languages. The novelty or otherwise of the discourse itself is irrelevant, and for this reason it makes little difference whether Fabrice composes his own sonnets or copies them out from Petrarch. The important thing is that in both cases there is a deliberate sounding of more than one voice, and a careful positioning of the desired reader to enable her to hear all the voices at work in the texts. By the same token, the unwanted readers are manoeuvred to one side, where only one voice and one language can be heard. If Stendhal's novels are to share the qualities of the language of passion, then their main concern must be to point up the many languages and voices that they draw on, and to create the means whereby that polyphony may become audible to the happy few destined to read them. Stendhal had little to say about the novel from this point of view, but a detour via his remarks on the opera should help to clarify the nature of his preference for the principle of two-voicedness, and suggest how this might be applicable to the writing and reading of his fiction.

La Chartreuse de Parme
The operatic principle

Stendhal's enthusiasm for the opera is well known and amply recorded in all his writings. In part it has to do with his general preference for the Italian climate and way of life over the French. This is how he describes the place and the appeal of opera within the divine indolence of Italian culture and civilisation:

La chaleur extrême, suivie, le soir, d'une fraîcheur qui rend tous les êtres respirants heureux, fait, de l'heure où l'on va au spectacle, le moment le plus agréable de la journée. Ce moment est, à peu près partout, entre neuf et dix heures du soir, c'est-à-dire quatre heures au moins après le dîner.

On écoute la musique dans une obscurité favorable. Excepté les jours de fête, le théâtre de la Scala, de Milan, plus grand que l'Opéra de Paris, n'est éclairé que par les lumières de la rampe; enfin on est parfaitement à son aise dans des loges obscures, qui sont de petits boudoirs.

Je croirais volontiers qu'il faut une certaine langueur pour bien jouir de la musique vocale. Il est de fait qu'un mois de séjour à Rome change l'allure du Français le plus sémillant. Il ne marche plus avec la rapidité qu'il avait les premiers jours; il n'est plus pressé pour rien. Dans les climats froids, le travail est nécessaire à la circulation; dans les pays chauds, le *divino far niente* est le premier bonheur. (*Haydn*, pp. 393–4)

The Italian climate and culture impose the leisure without which neither passion nor the arts are possible. And the obscure intimacy of the *loge* at the opera makes the perfect breeding ground for passion: Mosca falls in love with Gina in her box at La Scala, and it is at the Italian Opera in Paris that Mathilde's *amour de tête* for Julien has one of its rare 'instants d'enthousiasme' and drives her nearly to distraction with emotion (*Le Rouge*, p. 341). But the decisive quality of the opera that gives it pride of place in Stendhal's pantheon of the arts is the way in which it combines the two languages of words and music.

Without music, the words are nothing, the flattest prose: 'les paroles que l'oreille entend sont toujours de la prose dans les moments passionnés où le chant succède au récitatif; et jamais un aveugle ne s'aviserait d'y reconnaître des vers' (*Vie de Rossini*, I, pp. 193–4). Yet without words, the power of music is hugely diminished, and a Mozart symphony in the hands of an Italian orchestra is usually little less than a massacre. (This is certainly the case at the Princess's reception in *La Chartreuse*.) The distinctiveness of the two components of operatic language is essential to the genre, and Stendhal is scathing in his condemnation of the operas of Gluck, which he dismisses as merely 'la déclamation chantée ... la plus triste chose du monde' (*Rossini*, I, pp. 34–5). In opera the task of the music is to say things that the words alone don't and cannot say: 'Ce n'est pas, comme on le croit en Allemagne, l'art de faire exprimer les sentiments du personnage qui est en scène par les clarinettes, par les violoncelles, par les hautbois; c'est l'art bien plus rare de faire dire par les instruments la partie de ces sentiments que le personnage lui-même ne pourrait nous confier' (I, pp. 73–4). Word comments on music and, more importantly, music comments on, and transforms, the words: 'la musique répète sans cesse les mêmes mots, à chaque répétition elle donne à la même parole un sens différent' (I, p. 193). Music works on the text of the libretto in the same way that Fabrice's repetition and inflection of the words of Petrarch transform their significance for Clélia.

This two-voicedness is a feature of the opera, not just in the way that music works on the language of the libretto, but at many other levels too. The role of the singer is especially important in this perspective; first, in the improvised embellishments he adds to the score, and second, in the particular accent or inflection of his or her own individual voice. One of the things that Stendhal laments most in the nineteenth-century development of the opera is the decline in the habit of embellishment or fioriture. The contemporary tendency, he says, is to make the voice nothing more than the 'rival heureux d'un violon' (II, p. 90), and he continues this theme in his assertion that 'l'art du chant est tombé à ce point de misère qu'il n'est plus aujourd'hui que l'exécution *fidèle* et inanimée de la note ... L'on a banni l'invention du moment, d'un art où les plus beaux effets s'obtiennent souvent par l'improvisation du chanteur' (II, p. 91, Stendhal's italics). He concludes, significantly, that it is the vanity of Rossini which is largely responsible for this deplorable decline. This is because, when the famous Velluti sang for the first time in one of Rossini's operas, *Aureliano in Palmira*, his improvisations and embellishments of the cavatina written for him became so extensive that Rossini was thoroughly piqued at not being able to recognise his own composition underneath any more:

Arrive enfin le grand jour de la première représentation: la cavatine et tout le rôle de Velluti font fureur; mais à peine si Rossini peut reconnaître ce que chante Velluti, il n'entend plus la musique qu'il a composée; toutefois, le chant de Velluti est rempli de beautés et réussit merveilleusement auprès du public, qui, après tout, n'a pas tort d'applaudir ce qui lui fait tant de plaisir.

L'amour-propre du jeune compositeur fut profondément blessé; son opéra tombait et le soprano seul avait du succès.   (II, p. 95)

Rossini had a point to the extent that an over-improvised text ceases to be a two-voiced text, and instead the singer becomes 'l'auteur véritable des airs qu'il chante' (II, p. 110). Be that as it may, however, the upshot of this wounding of Rossini's *amour-propre* is that, by writing his own embellishments into the score, he was able to compose in such a way as to exclude all possibility of singers introducing their individual fioriture. An attack of Parisian vanity (and Stendhal frequently comments on Rossini's Frenchness and his popularity in Paris) leads to the suppression of the second voice at this particular level of the operatic text.

Nevertheless, leaving aside the question of the singer's own improvisatory discourse, the very presence and existence of the singing voice is enough in itself to inflect and transform the musical text. Despite his pessimistic remarks about its progressive mechanisation, the human voice is for Stendhal superior in every way to all the instruments of the orchestra. First, there is its diversity. Where, for Stendhal at least, a violin is just a violin, a piano just a piano, 'Les voix humaines n'ont pas moins de diversités entre elles que les physionomies. Ces diversités, que nous trouvons dans les voix *parlées*, deviennent cent fois plus frappantes encore dans les voix qui chantent' (II, p. 120, Stendhal's italics). Every voice, regardless of its technical sound quality, has its own expressive register, and it is impossible for the human voice to be '*sans passion*' (II, p. 132). This passion, whatever its nature, is bound to bring a whole variety of inflections to the operatic score. The intrinsic sound quality of the voice, the musical ability of the singer are nothing beside the sheer expressivity of the singer's own style. The words that the singer utters are far less important than the emotional accent that she brings to them: 'C'est ainsi que l'on peut voir avec plaisir un excellent acteur tragique jouant dans une langue dont on comprend à peine quelques paroles. Je conclurai de ces observations que l'*accent* des paroles a beaucoup plus d'importance en musique que les paroles elles-mêmes' (II, p. 134, Stendhal's italics). For Stendhal, the supreme exponent of the singing art was Mme Pasta,[6] whose talent put her, in his eyes, on the same plane as Correggio or the sculptor Canova. Where she excelled was precisely in her power of inflection: 'Pour madame Pasta, la même note, dans deux situations de l'âme différentes, n'est pas, pour ainsi dire, le même son' (II, p. 149). Moreover, these inflections are never the same, even in repeated performances of the same text, but always follow 'les *inspirations actuelles* de son cœur' (Stendhal's italics). Mme Pasta's skills make her far more than a faithful executant of Rossini's *Tancredi*, for they have a creative force of their own:

'J'appelle *créations* de cette grande cantatrice certains moyens d'expression auxquels il est plus que probable que le maestro qui écrivit les notes de ses rôles n'avait jamais songé' (II, p.151, Stendhal's italics). If we recall Fabrice's rendering of Petrarch's sonnet, it becomes possible now to argue with even more assurance that the nuances of his individual rendering of it are the equivalent of Mme Pasta's performance of *Tancredi*, and his alteration of the single word is an analogue of Velluti's fioriture in Aureliano's cavatina.

So the opera is bi-vocal, not only in the sense that it brings together the two languages of music and of prose, but also in the more literal sense that the singer's role is a working of – or, as Roland Barthes would say, a friction between[7] – the singing voice and the already dual language of the operatic score. True bi-vocality will be lost if it is merely repeated; it always requires the continuing and ever-renewed co-operation of another voice. This perhaps explains Stendhal's decided preference for the *opera buffa* over the *opera seria*. *Opera seria* is obviously two-voiced in the senses that I have discussed so far – in its combination of words and music and in the vocal involvement of its performers. But in the uniformity of its discursive tone – 'la passion continue' (II, p.96) – it tends to collapse back into the monologic, wearying and boring its audience with its unremitting sublimity. In the *opera buffa*, on the other hand, the alternation of tone between the passionate and the comic is alone capable of inspiring the 'plaisir fou' for which Stendhal prizes it so highly:

Dans le véritable opéra buffa, la passion ne se présente que de temps à autre, comme pour nous délasser de la gaieté, et c'est alors, pour le dire en passant, que l'effet de la peinture d'un sentiment tendre est irrésistible; il a les charmes réunis de l'imprévu et du contraste. Comme à l'Opéra, quand la musique est bonne, l'âme ne peut pas être à demi occupée d'une passion, la passion continue nous occuperait trop, nous fatiguerait, et adieu pour toujours le plaisir fou de l'opéra buffa.   (I, pp.95–6)

It is this tonal polyphony that makes the Mozart of *Don Giovanni* and *Le nozze de Figaro*, and, even more so, the Cimarosa of *Il matrimonio segreto* the greatest operatic composers, after whom Rossini (whose talent was for the *opera seria*) appears very much a second best for Stendhal.

But to be complete, even the *opera buffa* of Cimarosa sung by Mme Pasta or Velluti would still require the addition of yet another voice – that of the audience. Both as collective cultural context for the performance of the arts, and as the sum total of individual experiences of and responses to them, the audience's role is as essential in

Stendhal's view and as creative as the nuances brought to a score by the most inspired singers of Naples or Milan. Collectively, the audience provides the cultural atmosphere without which no work of art can have meaning. For reasons of climate, but also of politics, Italy has a highly developed appreciation of the arts, which is responsible for bringing them into existence in the first place. This helps to create a cultural climate of receptiveness, without which individual works of art go cold and cannot survive. In the 'Lettre sur l'état actuel de la musique en Italie' Stendhal deplores the habit of removing works of art from the original context in which they were produced, for they are then deprived of the public that gives them life: 'vous avez beau emporter à Paris la *Transfiguration* et l'*Apollon*; vous avez beau transporter sur toile la *Descente de croix* peinte à fresque par Daniel de Volterre, toutes ces œuvres sont des œuvres mortes: *il manque à vos beaux-arts un public*' (*Haydn*, p. 375, my italics). In their acquisitiveness the French fail to see that they are leaving behind the public that gives lifeblood to the pictures that they want for their own: 'Vous ne vous êtes pas aperçus, messieurs les voleurs, que vous n'emportiez pas, avec les tableaux, l'atmosphère qui en fait jouir' (p. 374). In Stendhal's view, the value that Parisians put on *esprit*, their proclivity to vanity, and their tendency to judge rather than enjoy, mean that they can only fully appreciate the arts of comedy, the *chanson* and 'les livres d'une morale piquante' (p. 375). As a result, they are ill-equipped to make a proper response to the Italian arts of painting and opera, and simply miss out on the pleasures that form the delight of an Italian audience. Worse still, their lack of the necessary qualities of appreciation can have a devastating effect on the very substance of the arts themselves. Outside their native Lombardy, the paintings of Carracci are simply invisible; and singers, who in Naples or Milan would be 'électrisés par un public sensible et capable d'enthousiasme' (p. 378), are distinctly lacklustre in a Parisian cultural climate. For although the French are technically superior to the Italians when it comes to musical expertise, their audiences lack the fire that even Italian singers need to fuel their talents. Stendhal remarks morosely that 'J'ai trouvé froids tous les grands chanteurs que j'ai vus à l'Odéon: Crivelli n'est plus le même qu'à Naples … Ce malheur-là n'est pas de ceux qui se réparent avec de l'argent, il tient aux qualités intimes du public français' (p. 380). In short, then, an ideal audience constitutes an electrifying voice of its own, which has an essential part to play in the dialogue of which opera consists.

This dialogue exists equally, and equally essentially, at the level of the individual spectator. Indeed, a proper response to music or painting, or to any other art, can only be individual. The collective cultural atmosphere provides a context not only for the production and performance of the arts, but also for the individual's response to them. In his *Histoire de la peinture en Italie* Stendhal always assumes that the viewer of a painting will be alone and he seeks to validate his comments on the paintings he reviews by saying that he had always been alone when he had seen them. Furthermore, he envisages for the very book he is writing 'un lecteur unique, et que je voudrais unique dans tous les sens' (I, p. 174). One of the most important differences between France and Italy is that in Italy individual responses are encouraged, whereas in France only collectively endorsed opinions are allowed: 'l'enthousiasme musical de Paris n'admet ... aucune discussion; cela est toujours délicieux ou exécrable', and everyone is influenced by the reactions of his neighbour. In Italy, however, 'comme chacun est sûr de ce qu'il sent, les discussions sur la musique sont infinies' (*Haydn*, p. 380). These discussions are themselves a further dialogue of different viewpoints, illustrating at yet another level the fact that the arts both require and provoke dialogue at every turn.

This individual dialogue is particularly vital to the possibility of representation in the arts, since as this book has been arguing, representation for Stendhal is inseparable from response. This issue is obviously of special relevance to the novel, which, of all the arts, and even within literature itself, is the genre whose definition depends most crucially on a representational function. In music, by contrast, the question of referential representation never arises, and the solution it offers to the requirements of realism and authenticity takes a very different form, and one which promises to have implications for its operation within the apparently descriptive format of fiction.

Music, on the face of it, is the least descriptive of all the arts. 'On a beau faire,' says Stendhal in his *Haydn*, 'la musique, qui est le plus vague des beaux-arts, n'est point descriptive à elle seule' (p. 98). Not only is it a-descriptive, but in the form of opera it is highly and, to a Frenchman at least, scandalously *invraisemblable*. Judged with the cold eye of reason, the libretti of Metastasio, like the paintings of Raphael in the Vatican palace, are liable to produce the reaction: 'Ce n'est pas dans la nature':

Je crois voir un Français, homme d'esprit, bien sûr de ce qu'il doit dire sur tout ce qui peut occuper l'attention d'un homme du monde, arrivant dans le palais du Vatican, à ces délicieuses loges que Raphaël orna de ces arabesques charmantes qui sont peut-être ce que le génie et l'amour ont jamais inspiré de plus pur et de plus divin. Notre Français est *choqué des manques de vraisemblance*: sa raison ne peut admettre ces têtes de femmes portées par des corps de lions, ces amours à cheval sur des chimères. *Cela n'est pas dans la nature*, dit-il d'un ton dogmatique; rien de plus vrai.   (p. 329, my italics)

This acknowledgement of the unrealistic quality of Raphael's chimeras is enthusiastically made by Stendhal, who sees in that unrealism the very condition of the enjoyment of his art. It is the unfortunate 'gens raisonnables' who erroneously 'ont appelé, dans Métastase, manque de vérité ce qui est le comble de l'art' (*ibid.*). For it is only when they are freed from all referential ties to reality that the sensual arts of music and painting can begin to make their effects. The message that Stendhal attributes to Metastasio's operas is an undiluted incitement to pleasure:

Il [Metastasio] semble dire aux spectateurs: 'Jouissez, votre attention même n'aura pas la moindre peine; laissez-vous aller à l'oubli, si naturel, du plan d'une pièce dramatique; ne songez plus au théâtre; soyez heureux au fond de votre loge; partagez le sentiment si tendre qu'exprime mon personnage.' Ses héros ne retiennent presque rien de la triste réalité.   (p. 328)

The exclusion of dismal reality induces in the spectator a pleasure whose very intensity makes it more likely in turn that he will be able to ignore the vulgar corruptions of the *vraisemblable*. Neither reality nor the *vraisemblable* plays any role in the Italian response to the paintings of Raphael. Instead of demanding a mirror held up to nature, the Italian's strategy is to visit them at the magical hour of nine in the evening in the company of a group of 'femmes aimables'. Refreshed by ices, and relaxing on a divan, the Italian simply gives himself over to the contemplation and enjoyment of 'les formes charmantes que Raphaël a données à ces êtres qui, *ne ressemblant à rien que nous ayons rencontré ailleurs*, ne nous apportent aucune de *ces idées communes* qui, dans ces instants rares et délicieux, nuisent tant au bonheur' (p. 330, my italics). Reality and the 'idées communes' which it activates are death to the happiness that comes from the uninhibited enjoyment of music or painting.

And yet these apparently purely hedonistic responses are precisely the means whereby pictorial and musical representation operates. Stendhal describes the musician as the artist 'qui peint de plus près les affections du cœur humain', but this painting is achieved not by directly representing the 'affections', but 'en faisant agir l'imagination et la sensibilité de chacun de ses auditeurs, ... en mettant, pour ainsi dire, chacun d'eux de moitié dans son travail' (p. 211). The listener's work consists in the imaginative production of images, which are the form taken by his response to the music, and it is these emotionally produced images which constitute the representational element of aesthetic experience: 'Il n'y a de réel dans la musique que l'état où elle laisse l'âme' (*Rossini*, I, p. 22). This 'état d'âme' and the images that go with it are different in every individual, in accordance with his or her temperament and experiences:

> La musique, qui met en jeu l'imagination de chaque homme, tient plus intimement que la peinture, par exemple, à l'organisation particulière de cet homme-là. Si elle le rend heureux, c'est en faisant que son imagination lui présente certaines images agréables ... Or il est évident que ces images doivent être différentes, suivant les diverses imaginations qui les produisent.
>
> (*Haydn*, p. 204)

In other words, the truth of an aesthetic representation is guaranteed precisely by this diversity, a stark contrast to the *vraisemblable*, where repetition and conformity constitute the guiding principle of what passes for representation. The plausible accounts of the real provided by the *vraisemblable* are actually only a reiteration of what Stendhal calls 'idées communes'. They merely repeat the *déjà-dit* and in doing so invite further imitative repetition by way of readerly response. Prince Ranuce-Ernest is a living and ludicrous example of the imitative effects of the *vraisemblable*: smiling bountifully and talking nobly in the manner of the Louis XIV portrayed in the painting beneath which he stands, he is also wearing the tail-coat prescribed by the conformist demands of Parisian fashion in bizarre combination with a pair of red trousers derived from portraits of Joseph II. The attempt to imitate simultaneously three such different models produces a grotesque mishmash of quite incompatible styles, and is in total contrast to the truly representational response that comes from the unique imaginations of ideal readers and spectators.

This unique response is the spectator's own personal equivalent (rather than dutiful imitation) of the passions that originally inspired the music or the painting in question; and here Stendhal is un-equivocally elitist. The music of Pergolesi, for instance, is simply meaningless for 'les neuf cent quatre-vingts personnes sur mille qui n'ont jamais senti les choses qu'elle peint' (*Haydn*, p. 350). It is therefore only the listener's own experience of particular passions that turns a work of art into a representation. If one hasn't in one's own life had the equivalent of the experience implied by, say, 'Saint-Preux arrivant dans la chambre de Julie' (p. 328), then, faced with Rousseau's novel, one would be

> comme nous devant un sauvage Miâmi, qui nous nommerait, en sa langue sauvage, un arbre particulier à l'Amérique, qui croît dans les vastes forêts

qu'il parcourt en chassant, et que nous n'avons jamais vu. C'est un simple bruit que ce que nous entendons, et il faut convenir que si le sauvage prolonge son discours, ce bruit-là nous ennuiera bientôt. (p. 350)

Representation takes place only in the very diverse souls of the happy few whose individual experiences enable them to understand, albeit only in the terms of those experiences, the passions whereof Rousseau or Pergolesi speak.

This means that the work of art, whatever its form (painting, music, literature of whatever school or genre), should not itself try to take on the task of representation; rather, it should aim to evolve strategies which leave space for the reader to complete this task. For representation to be possible, art does best to omit the details of what it wants to describe. As the *Histoire de la peinture* repeatedly implies, Correggio's technique of chiaroscuro is a far more effective means of representation than the painstaking reproduction of veins and muscles in the paintings of Michelangelo, precisely because it requires the spectator to complete the picture in a way that the meticulous fidelity of Michelangelo does not. Michelangelo blocks readerly participation by exactly the same means used by Rossini to prevent singers from introducing their own fioriture into his score – by being too complete. The blurred outlines of Correggio's figures bring the viewer far closer to the truth of nature than the sharply defined anatomies reflected in Michelangelo's mirror.

This is the reason why Stendhal thought so highly of the poetry of Metastasio. Not only did Metastasio steer clear of the 'tristes réalités' of everyday life, but the reticence of his style made him an ideal librettist for the operatic compositions of Pergolesi and Cimarosa. His poetry creates a space in which the language of music is able to dialogue with it; and he was one of the rare poets who knew that reticence is particularly necessary in the moments of greatest passion: 'le poète ne doit être éloquent et développé que dans les récitatifs. Dès que la passion paraît, le musicien ne lui demande qu'un très petit nombre de paroles; c'est lui qui se charge de toute l'expression' (pp. 354–5). The proof of the superiority of Metastasio's genius is that he invites dialogue (from the composer, from the reader), but not imitation:

malgré des milliers d'essais tentés depuis près d'un siècle pour produire une seule *aria* dans le genre de Métastase, l'Italie n'a pas encore vu deux vers qui puissent lui faire l'illusion d'un moment. Métastase est le seul de ses poètes qui, littéralement, soit resté jusqu'ici inimitable. (p. 358)

The strategies which provoke readerly dialogue simultaneously exclude the possibility of imitative reproduction; and, indeed, the implication seems to be that dialogic response and imitative reproduction are mutually exclusive reactions to a text, so that the greater the scope for dialogue, the less the scope for imitation, and vice versa. Metastasio invites Fabrice's impassioned inflection of his poem (for the sonnet that, with his characteristic carelessness, the author of *La Chartreuse* attributes to Petrarch has been identified as being by Metastasio)[8] and not the imitative pose or the fashionable emulations of the Prince.

The operatic text

The operatic principle of two-voicedness runs through Stendhal's thinking on all the Italian arts; and although the novel is perhaps the least Italian form of literature, the notion seems to make particular sense of the sort of writerly values that have emerged from this chapter's discussion of *La Chartreuse*. In these final pages I shall be looking at the advantages of seeing the operatic principle at work not only within the fictional world of the novel, but also as a constitutive element of the writing of the text itself.

In representing the operatic qualities of polyphony (as, for example, in Fabrice's sermon), Stendhal seems to be inviting inferences about his own writerly eloquence. Certainly, the novel presents itself as having fundamentally dialogic relations both with its origins and with its readerly destination. As regards the origins, *La Chartreuse*, of course, has its beginnings in the written fragment entitled 'Origine des grandeurs de la famille Farnese'. Like all Stendhal's fiction, it is a reworking of an already existing text.[9] What the *affaires Berthet* and *Lafargue* were to *Le Rouge*, the Farnese manuscript is to *La Chartreuse*. But leaving aside the real textual genesis of the novel, *La Chartreuse* is interesting because, unlike *Le Rouge*, it actually proclaims itself as a response to the written word.

Le Rouge cites 'l'âpre vérité' as its sole source and justification, whereas the epigraphs to part I and chapter 2 of *La Chartreuse* (and there are only three epigraphs in the whole novel) point to origins in the *'luoghi ameni ... en qui Dieu nous escrit'* − to conflate the two quotations. That is to say, the first epigraph from Ariosto, 'Gia mi fur dolci inviti a empir le carte / I luoghi ameni' (which the notes translate as 'Jadis les lieux charmants me furent de douces invitations à écrire'),[10] places the original stimulus to write in the 'luoghi ameni' which the Ronsard epigraph to chapter 2 defines specifically as a form of writing. Ronsard's elegy describes nature as consisting of a series of written messages in which God attempts to communicate with man; the poet writes of 'les cieux / En qui Dieu nous *escrit*, par *notes* non obscures', of 'les astres du ciel qui sont ses *caractères*', and regrets that the earthly preoccupations of men mean that they 'Méprisent tel *écrit*, et ne le *lisent* pas' (all my italics). This view of nature as a written text is corroborated within the novel itself, where the *luoghi ameni* of the Italian landscape, to which Gina and Fabrice are especially responsive, are always described as a language. On Lake Como Gina is rejuvenated by 'le *langage* de ces lieux ravissants' (p. 28, my italics); and as Fabrice makes his way back to Parma through the forests surrounding the same Lake Como, with such imprudent disregard for his safety, the forests are said to *speak* to the soul, and Fabrice is described as listening to their *language*:

Fabrice se laissait attendrir par les aspects sublimes ou touchants de ces forêts des environs du lac de Côme. Ce sont peut-être les plus belles du monde; je ne veux pas dire celles qui rendent le plus d'*écus neufs* [Stendhal's italics], comme on dirait en Suisse, mais celles qui *parlent* le plus à l'âme. *Ecouter ce langage* [my italics] dans la position où se trouvait Fabrice, en butte aux attentions de MM. les gendarmes lombardo-vénitiens, c'était un véritable enfantillage. (pp. 182–3)

If Stendhal's novel is born of the 'lieux ravissants' in which its hero first sees the light of day, it is less as a direct representation of them than as a response to the language that they speak. The pages of Stendhal's novel are offered as a reply to the 'dolci inviti' of the Italian landscape, not as a cold and faithful description of it.

It is in the same spirit of invitation to response that the novel presents itself to its readers. In view of Stendhal's comments on audiences in *Haydn*, the dedication TO THE HAPPY FEW must be taken to exclude the 'gens raisonnables' who will only ask if it is 'dans la nature'. They form the 980 people out of every thousand for whom the text, like the music of Pergolesi, is bound to appear unintelligible. The remaining twenty must be numbered among the happy few just because they will not be trying to match up what Stendhal writes with 'idées communes' about what is or is not likely to be found in nature. In its concluding dedication, therefore, *La Chartreuse* indicates its intention of engaging with the imaginations of its readers, offering its pages primarily as its own 'dolci inviti' to readerly reply.

The dialogic qualities of the opera are also evident within the novels themselves. There is the conflict of different discourses which I have discussed in earlier chapters; and in *La Chartreuse* in particular, there is a mixing of novelistic styles or sub-genres that a number of critics have commented on. Many have seen *La Chartreuse* as a divided text, telling two different stories, composed of two different techniques. One has only to think of Balzac's account of the novel as the combination of the story of the Duchess Sanseverina with the story of Fabrice, of Maurice Bardèche's division of the novel into the satiric and the poetic, or of Gilbert Durand's characterisation of it as a mixture of epic and romance.[11] The abrupt switches of tone that all these critics have remarked on may be regarded as the written equivalent of the style of the *opera buffa* with its sudden and unexpected shifts from the passionate to the comic. But – and this point is vital – if Stendhal's novel is to be read as opera, this reading cannot be undertaken as a simple rejection of realism and the traditional requirements of fiction. The operatic is not a mere alternative to the novelistic, but only makes sense when viewed as a solution to the generic demands of mimesis. The polyphonies of the text itself are as much an exploration of the nature of representational discourse as a sign of dissatisfaction with it. Similarly, the dialogue with the reader is an attempt to achieve a more satisfactory and more authentic form of representation than those offered by a naive model of mimesis as mirror, rather than an outright rejection of the notion.

CONCLUSION

It is not just *La Chartreuse* which may be classed as an operatic text, for one perhaps makes the most sense of Stendhal and does him the greatest justice if one regards *all* his novels as opera, as fictional equivalents of the *opera buffa*. This is not because of the existence of the formal parallels that I have identified in the foregoing chapter, but because the operatic principle as I have discerned it in Stendhal is ultimately a novelistic principle, and may be seen as Stendhal's overall response to the exigencies implied by the contemporary conception of the novel as a mirror.

It is a response through which Stendhal gestures both backwards and forwards in the history of the genre. In the backwards sense it shows how far Stendhal remained a man of the eighteenth century, nostalgically harking back to values and a way of life which the nineteenth century had no place for. His belief that the mirror of the nineteenth century was capable only of reflecting a sad and prosaic reality drove him to find a solution which could accommodate the pre-Revolutionary and fundamentally aristocratic qualities of 'le romanesque' and 'la grâce'.[1] The anachronistic appeal to the sublime which Stendhal's operatic model promotes is, in this sense, frankly regressive: as he himself admitted, 'En musique, comme pour beaucoup d'autres choses, je suis un homme d'un autre siècle' (*Haydn*, p. 399). The musical qualities of Stendhal's fiction are therefore the most eloquent testimony that there was a part of him which belonged to the pre-realist century of his childhood, and not to the realist one of his maturity, and which could be called on to counter the unpleasanter demands of contemporaneity.

On the other hand, the operatic principle can also be seen as way ahead of its time in the sort of solution that it proposes to the problems implied by the mirror model of fiction. Stendhal seems to have had an unusually modernist, twentieth-century sensitivity to the discursive nature of positivist or empiricist procedures. Not only did he see that the mirror was positioned inside the world of which it purported to provide a reflection; but he also pointed out that the mirror is on the move within that world, strapped to the saddle-bag of a moving perspective. So that, on both counts, its objectivity and its impartiality are already under suspicion. But more importantly, and more modernistically, because he saw that what passes for empirical representation always has a strategic function, he was able to demonstrate that it therefore also had a discursive function. Representations are deployed as a means of gaining advantage for oneself and denying it to others; and they are ways of talking that can be more or less successful, more or less disastrous in determining more or less advantageous perceptions of reality. Stendhal's novels turn the mimetic language of realism into dialogic polyphonies of discourse. In every representational account the reader is invited to hear a particular discursive register being adopted for particular political purposes.

The operatic principle is indeed essentially related to the mimetic concerns at the heart of all fiction. As polyphony within the text, it thematises both the exigencies of representation and the impossibility of ever satisfying them. As dialogue with the reader, it bypasses mimesis at one level and enacts it at another — in the hearts of the happy few. To read Stendhal, one has to be both Mosca and Fabrice: to have the acumen of the diplomat and hear the multiple play of voices in the text; and at the same time, like Fabrice, to throw diplomacy and prudence to the winds and indulge in the 'enfantillage' of listening to the language that it addresses to the soul, where representation will eventually take shape.

And yet, as a reader, one cannot be simultaneously both a passionate *enfant* and a discerning diplomat. Stendhal's novels are implicitly proposing a model of reading that it is impossible to reproduce in acts of reading because of this mutually contradictory requirement. The novels impose a double bind of the most intractable kind. But it is a double bind that, far from spelling defeat for its victim, is actually promising a solution. Its fundamental contradictoriness is a sign that the very reading that allows representation to take place cannot itself be represented. The passionate ironist is an oxymoron that exceeds even the illogic of the lover's figuring of the beloved as both tender and 'romaine'. Representation is therefore paradoxically guaranteed by the unrepresentability of the medium through which it is enacted: the oxymoronic passion/irony of its reader. The reader who enables mimesis cannot her-/himself be mimetically figured, cannot consequently be emulated, and so renders unthinkable any possible imitation of the ideal reader by real readers ...

Nevertheless, to read Stendhal adequately as a realist means that real readers must at least try to undertake the impossible task of reading with both sublime responsiveness and ironic discrimination. For it is in this way that conceptions of realism may be opened up to permit reconsideration of what it means to read realism, of how realism might be affected by reading, and reading by realism. But just as I have avoided constructing an imitable reader-figure in the novels, so too should we be wary of producing too neat and reproducible a definition of any new realism in our desire to revise those that we already have. So, at the risk of appearing to reverse the thrust of the claim with which I began this book, I should like to conclude by suggesting that the misrecognition of Stendhal's contribution to the realist tradition has not, after all, been a mistake or an injustice. Although his novels require us to rethink realism, that rethinking should not necessarily lead to a retrospective over-centralising of Stendhal's place in it. To give him too central a place in that tradition would mean, by implication, accusing him of having finally fallen in with the age of platitude, and would imply that he had written in a manner that inspired imitation and emulation rather than *rêverie*. The abortive paternity of his heroes may be sad to read of in the novels; but it is actually a triumph in their author. The lack of any literary issue from Stendhal is proof that his writing did manage to achieve the prevention of filial emulation, and suggests that he ended up being in France what he himself admired Metastasio for being in Italy: 'le seul de ses poètes qui, littéralement parlant, soit resté jusqu'ici inimitable' (*Haydn*, p. 358).

NOTES

Preface

1 René Wellek, 'The concept of realism in literary scholarship', in *Concepts of Criticism*, pp. 240–1. There have been some recent exceptions to the situation I am describing, not least in the Cambridge Studies in French: e.g. Marian Hobson, *The Object of Art*, Diana Knight, *Flaubert's Characters: The Language of Illusion*, and Christopher Prendergast, *The Order of Mimesis*.
2 Jean Ricardou, 'Fonction critique', in *Tel quel. Théorie d'ensemble*.
3 Robert Alter, *Partial Magic: The Novel as a Self-Conscious Genre*.
4 Patricia Waugh, *Metafiction: The Theory and Practice of Self-Conscious Fiction*, p. 2.
5 Alain Robbe-Grillet, *Pour un nouveau roman*. See esp. the essay 'Sur quelques notions périmées'. Leo Bersani argues along broadly similar lines in *A Future for Astyanax: Character and Desire in Literature*.
6 Roland Barthes, 'L'effet de réel', in *Le Bruissement de la langue*.
7 Fredric Jameson, *The Prison-House of Language*.

1 Mimesis and the reader: some historical considerations

1 See Stendhal's *Vie de Henry Brulard*, chapters 5 and 6, for his portrait of Romain Gagnon.
2 Erich Auerbach, *Mimesis*, p. 408.
3 'Balzac and Stendhal', in *Studies in European Realism*.
4 See *Brulard*, pp. 552 and 593.
5 'Projet d'un article sur *Le Rouge et le Noir*', p. 704.
6 Michel Foucault, *Les Mots et les choses*, p. 229. Foucault's formulation may seem a little melodramatic when one thinks of the sort of continuity asseverated by Barthes in *Le Degré zéro* who argues that in the period from 1650 to 1848 the same mode of 'bourgeois' writing remained dominant, since the Revolution changed nothing in the bourgeois ideology which informed it, and he places its end in the middle of the nineteenth century (see pp. 41–5). Paul Bénichou ignores rupture altogether and his chronicling of what his subtitle calls 'l'avènement d'un pouvoir spirituel laïque dans la France moderne' treats a phenomenon that runs from 1750 to 1850.

See *Le Sacre de l'écrivain*. Foucault's conception does, nevertheless, endorse the sense of a break that Stendhal himself seems to have had and which much of the contemporary discussion of fiction seems to presuppose.

7 For an account of Stendhal's literary education, see his *Vie de Henry Brulard* and also Victor Del Litto, *La Vie intellectuelle de Stendhal: genèse et évolution de ses idées (1802–1821)*.

8 Not that it is a question of dating and therefore hypostatising the break itself, which is something that can only be adduced from its effects. 'In the Hôtel de La Mole' is the chapter-heading that Auerbach uses for his discussion of the rise and development of modern realism, thus confirming Stendhal's centrality to the phenomenon, whatever his supposed shortcomings. See *Mimesis*, chapter 18.

9 Georges Blin's classic study of Stendhal, *Stendhal et les problèmes du roman*, does, however, seek to rescue Stendhal's realism from the distorting criteria of a traditionally conceived objectivism, precisely through his emphasis upon the subjective, or what he also calls the 'relativist' quality of Stendhal's realism. Blin remains essential reading for anyone interested in Stendhal, but although the subtitle he claims to have considered using for his book – 'limites et moyens du réalisme dans les romans de Stendhal' (p. 5) – would apply equally well to my own account of Stendhal, his approach leaves only incidental room for the role of the reader in Stendhal's realism, and totally ignores any consideration of the problematic nature of language in his writing.

10 M. H. Abrams, *The Mirror and the Lamp*, p. 16.

11 Or at least pre-Romanticism. See D. G. Charlton, *The French Romantics*, esp. Roger Fayolle, 'Criticism and theory', vol. 2.

12 There are some modern parallels to aspects of this dual pragmatic tradition in the reader-oriented criticism of Wolfgang Iser's 'reader response' and Hans Robert Jauss's 'reception aesthetics'. See Wolfgang Iser, *The Act of Reading*, and Hans Robert Jauss, *Toward an Aesthetic of Reception*. See also Jane P. Tompkins (ed.), *Reader-Response Criticism* for a representative anthology of contemporary reader-oriented criticism, and in particular her own essay 'The reader in history: the changing shape of literary response', which maps the changing forms and fortunes of the pragmatic theories that Abrams talks about.

13 'Salon de 1827', *Mélanges III: Peinture*, p. 101. See also *Racine et Shakespeare*, *passim*, and *Histoire de la peinture*, II, pp. 107–13.

14 *ibid.*, Stendhal's emphasis. Although Stendhal allows the concept of the useful to creep back into his argument here, there remains an important distinction whereby the socially useful in the real world is transformed by art into the aesthetically pleasurable without necessarily feeding anything useful back into the social system.

15 See the essay of that title in *Mélanges II: Journalisme* and his comments in the Civita-Vecchia copy of *Le Rouge*.

16 'Walter Scott et la Princesse de Clèves', *Mélanges II: Journalisme*, pp. 221–4 (p. 223).

17 In particular Peter Brooks, whose important study of the eighteenth-century novel in *The Novel of Worldliness* is essential reading on this subject. See also Marian Hobson, *The Object of Art*.

18 Antoine-François Prévost, 'Avis de l'auteur', *Histoire du Chevalier des Grieux et de Manon Lescaut*, p. 363.

19 Geoffrey Bennington's *Sententiousness and the Novel: Laying Down the Law in Eighteenth-Century French Fiction* shows that this remark too is a topos from contemporary thinking about pedagogy. His discussion concentrates largely on what he calls the 'scene of education' as staged and enacted in novels (and worldly novels in particular). See chapters 2–3.

20 Denis Diderot, *Œuvres esthétiques*, pp. 29–30.

21 As demonstrated by Vivienne Mylne, *The Eighteenth-Century French Novel: Techniques of Illusion*.

22 For a full discussion of the novel of worldliness, see Peter Brooks's book on the subject. No discussion of this topic can avoid being indebted to, and indeed highly dependent on, his work.

23 Stendhal speaks very affectionately of *Jacques le fataliste*, and it was his hope that with *Le Rouge* he might have earned himself a place on the shelf 'accanto all'immortale *Tom Jones*' ('Projet d'un article', p. 726).

24 I disagree therefore with Stephen Gilman's account, which presents the bow metaphor as a development that follows the mirror one in Stendhal's thinking. See Stephen Gilman, *The Tower as Emblem*. His discussion is nevertheless worth reading as he is one of the few critics to address themselves to the significance of these metaphors in Stendhal's writing.

25 For a survey of fiction in this interim period, see André Le Breton, *Le Roman français au dix-neuvième siècle. I: avant Balzac*. In Le Breton's view, the reason for the turn that the French novel – such as it was – took in this period is that the concrete reality of the Revolution and its consequences were too close and too overwhelming for the novelist to be able to contemplate them with the detachment and the objectivity that the genre would require. See his chapter 1.

26 See *Histoire de l'édition française*, tome II: *Le Livre triomphant 1660–1830* (1984), and in particular the essay by Françoise Parent, 'De nouvelles pratiques de lecture' (pp. 606–21), which deals, amongst other things, with the introduction of the 'cabinet de lecture' in the early nineteenth century.

27 See Bernard Weinberg, *French Realism: The Critical Reaction, 1830–1870*, esp. pp. 117ff. This thorough and enormously useful account of its subject is an indispensable adjunct for any discussion of the sort of issue I shall be dealing with here. Also immensely helpful is Marguerite Iknayan, *The Idea of the Novel in France: 1815–48*.

28 See Weinberg, *French Realism*, pp. 3–4, and Edouard Maynial, *L'Epoque réaliste*, p. 16, respectively.

29 *Mercure français du xixe siècle*, XIII:b, quoted by E. B. O. Borgerhoff, '*Réalisme* and kindred words: their use as terms of literary criticism in the first half of the nineteenth century', p. 839.

30 Victor Hugo, *Théâtre complet*, vol. 1, pp. 409–54 (p. 436).

31 'Testament', reproduced in *Romans*, vol. 1, p. 751.

32 Honoré de Balzac, 'Avant-propos de la *Comédie humaine*', in *La Comédie humaine*, pp. 7–20 (p. 11).

33 'Etudes sur M. Beyle (Frederic Stendalh [*sic*])', p. 1214.

34 Auguste Comte, *Cours de philosophie positive (première et deuxième leçons)*, vol. 1, p. 13. This 'leçon' was in preparation during the 1820s and was delivered in its definitive version in 1829.

35 See *Mélanges III: Peinture*. Janin's review in the *Journal des débats* is reproduced in Castex's appendix to *Le Rouge*, 'L'Accueil des contemporains'.

36 See Marguerite Iknayan's *Concave Mirror: From Imitation to Expression in French Esthetic Theory 1800–1830* (esp. p. 209 and *passim*), which shows the links between the debates about painting and those about the novel in the realist period. Weinburg also discusses the similarity of the arguments in the two spheres.

37 Alfred de Vigny, 'Réflexions sur la vérité dans l'art', in *Œuvres complètes*, p. 144. Iknayan discusses the revival of interest in Platonic theories of art in *The Concave Mirror*. See esp. her two chapters on 'The real and the ideal'.

38 George Sand, 'Préface de l'édition de 1832', *Indiana*, p. 6.

39 George Sand, 'L'Auteur au lecteur', *La Mare au diable. François le Champi*, p. 12, my italics.

40 See Christopher Prendergast's chapter on Stendhal in *The Order of Mimesis*, 'Stendhal: the ethics of verisimilitude' for a discussion of some of the consequences of this accusation of immorality.

41 *Quotidienne*, 24 July 1839. Quoted by Weinberg, *French Realism*, p. 15.

42 See David Bellos, *Balzac Criticism in France 1850–1900*, p. 46. This book charts the limits and fortunes of the critical vocabulary associated with realism, and while its immediate concern is with the work of Balzac, it nevertheless offers an outline of the overall critical framework into which all the novels of the period were received.

43 Benjamin Constant, *Adolphe*, p. 11.

44 Imitation as *imitatio* only acquired its predominantly pejorative sense in the modern period, and any use of the term in the context of the nineteenth century is bound to be highly anachronistic. Just how anachronistic can be seen by referring to Terence Cave, *The Cornucopian Text: Problems of Writing in the French Renaissance*. See esp. his chapter 2, 'Imitation'.

45 Christopher Prendergast provides a masterly exposition of these discussions in chapter 2 of his *Order of Mimesis*.

46 Tzvetan Todorov, 'Introduction au vraisemblable', in *Poétique de la prose*, p. 94.

47 Roland Barthes, *S/Z*, p. 61.

48 I owe this nice point to the article by Grahame C. Jones, 'Réel, Saint-Réal: une épigraphe du 'Rouge' et le réalisme Stendhalien'.

49 Emile Zola, *Les Romanciers naturalistes*, p. 80.

50 Letter dated 22 November 1852, *Correspondance*, tome III, 1927, p. 53.

51 Elme-Marie Caro, 'Etudes morales sur le xixᵉ siècle', *Revue Contemporaine*, 31 March 1854. Quoted by Weinberg, *French Realism*, p. 128. All italics mine.

52 Aaron Scharf provides a succinct account of the origins and development of photography in his *Art and Photography*, which is primarily devoted to a discussion of the effects on the visual arts of the advent and spread of photography. Talbot's technique, originally called the calotype, was evolved at about the same time as the daguerrotype. It is a process in which the picture emerges during development rather than at the time of shooting, and involves a negative proof from which an unlimited number of positive prints can be printed. Eugène Disderi's *cartes de visite* constituted another variant on the multiplication theme: a single sitting would produce a series of portrait poses. See Claude Nori, *La Photographie française: des origines à nos jours*.

53 For a full account of these developments, see *Histoire générale de la presse française, tome II: de 1815 à 1871*, Claude Bellanger *et al.* (eds.), and *Histoire de l'édition française*, vol. 2.

54 See John and Muriel Lough, *An Introduction to Nineteenth-Century France*. Chapter 4, 'The writer and his public', deals with this phenomenon. See also *Histoire de l'édition française*, vols. 2 and 3.

55 See Ruth Amossy and Elisheva Rosen, *Le Discours du cliché* for a discussion of the technical origins of the word. They emphasise 'l'ancrage socio-historique du cliché', and point out that 'En tant que métaphore (usée) et que concept, il est né au lieu même où la production de masse s'empare de l'écriture et où l'économie capitaliste montante se soumet la parole' (p. 5).

56 Both quoted by Iknayan in *The Concave Mirror*, pp. 129–30.

57 Roland Barthes, *La Chambre claire*, p. 137. I shall be discussing this book in more detail below.

58 *Œuvres intimes*, II, pp. 54 and 554. See also p. 1348, note 6 for a discussion of Stendhal's error.

59 Lady Eastlake. Quoted by Beaumont Newhall, *Photography, Essays and Images*, p. 94.

60 Charles Baudelaire, 'Salon de 1859', *Œuvres complètes*, tome II, p. 616.

61 Champfleury's defence of realism is careful to separate the mechanical reproduction of the daguerrotype from the individual interpretation in the artist's copying of nature. See Champfleury, *Le Réalisme*, pp. 91–4.

62 See Madeleine Varin d'Ainville, *La Presse en France: genèse et évolution de ses fonctions psycho-sociales* for this distinction. Her book is a highly

illuminating discussion of the social and cultural significance of the press at the various stages of its development.

63 See Udo Schöning, *Literatur als Spiegel*, pp. 18–19.

64 I shall be returning to a discussion of Stendhal's use of the Berthet case in chapter 3. Both Madeleine Varin d'Ainville and Bellanger *et al.* provide useful accounts of the popular press and the growth of the *fait divers* in this period.

65 In *Illuminations*.

66 Albert Pingaud, 'Préface' to *Vie de Napoléon*, pp. xii–xiii.

67 Roland Barthes, 'Le troisième sens', in *L'Obvie et l'obtus*, pp. 43–61.

68 In Walter Benjamin, *One Way Street and Other Writings*, p. 243.

69 This concept of mimetic illusion as created by analogy was fairly common in the eighteenth century, particularly in the sphere of music. See Marian Hobson, *The Object of Art*, pp. 273–97, and esp. p. 283, where she quotes Rousseau's claim that 'à un très-petit nombre de choses près, l'art du musicien ne consiste point à peindre immédiatement les objets, mais à mettre l'âme dans une disposition semblable à celle où la mettoit leur présence' (*Correspondance complète*, ed. R. A. Leigh, Geneva–Banbury, 1965– , vol. 2, p. 160). Paul Ricœur's notion of 'la triple *mimésis*' also includes the reader as the third stage of the mimetic process, but his argument is focussed specifically on the concepts of time and narrative. See Paul Ricœur, *Temps et récit. Tome I*.

70 For a comprehensive account of the use and extent of the mirror metaphor in the period, see Udo Schöning, *Literatur als Spiegel*, which discusses Stendhal at some length as the most prolific user of the metaphor, not only in terms of frequency, but also in range and sophistication. Schöning recognises that Stendhal is unique in his awareness of the reader's reception of mirror reflections, but does not pursue his analysis of this awareness beyond its relevance to Stendhal's aesthetics of readerly *plaisir*. See chapter 3 of his book.

71 See the opening essay in Nathalie Sarraute, *L'Ere du soupçon*. She takes the phrase from Stendhal's *Souvenirs d'égotisme*, where he writes: 'Le génie poétique est mort, mais le génie du *soupçon* est venu au monde' (p. 430).

2 Love and the wayward text

1 See note 7 on p. 414 of Martineau's edition of *De l'Amour*. Martineau does not mention the similarity with *Romeo and Juliet*.

2 René Girard, *Deceit, Desire and the Novel*, first published as *Mensonge romantique, vérité romanesque*.

3 It is on seeing Count Altamira at the ball given by the Duc de Retz that Mathilde is struck by the thought about the distinctiveness of the death sentence: 'Je ne vois que la condamnation à mort qui distingue un homme ...: c'est la seule chose qui ne s'achète pas' (*Le Rouge*, p. 273). It is a

reflection of her own Don Juanesque attitude towards love that she doesn't see that the same applies to passion, as Stendhal explains in *De l'Amour*: 'Quoi qu'en disent certains ministres hypocrites, le pouvoir est le premier des plaisirs. Il me semble que l'amour seul peut l'emporter, et l'amour est une maladie heureuse qu'on ne peut se procurer comme un ministère' (p. 125).

4 Although Barthes makes barely any reference to *De l'Amour* in the *Fragments*, the two texts make illuminating companion volumes for each other.

5 Hence Barthes's unframed presentation of the lover's discourse in the *Fragments*: rather than subordinate it to some descriptive or analytic frame, he does no more than merely utter it.

6 Roman Jakobson, 'Closing statement: linguistics and poetics'. He uses the term 'conative' to describe utterances whose orientation is towards the addressee, the purest form of which are the vocative and the imperative. *De l'Amour* could be said to be written in the vocative.

7 See Victor Del Litto, 'Pourquoi Stendhal a écrit *De l'Amour*', p. 66. See also Anthony Purdy, 'De la première préface de *De l'Amour*: destinataire et intertexte'.

8 On this topic, see Geoff Bennington, 'From narrative to text: love and writing in Crébillon *fils*, Duclos, Barthes'.

9 I shall be returning to this comparison between opera and the novel in a later chapter.

10 On the *doxa* it seems best to cite Barthes himself: 'La *Doxa* (mot qui va revenir souvent [both in Barthes and in what follows]), c'est l'Opinion publique, l'Esprit majoritaire, le Consensus petit-bourgeois, la Voix du Naturel, la Violence du Préjugé' (*Roland Barthes*, p. 51).

11 See his four essays in *The Dialogic Imagination*, and in particular the essay 'Discourse in the novel'. I shall also be quoting from the opening pages of the essay 'From the prehistory of the novel', which provide a useful summary of Bakhtin's ideas on the novel. In this connection, see also my 'Realism reconsidered: Bakhtin's dialogism and the "Will to Reference"'.

12 This is the thrust of the argument of Shoshana Felman's stimulating *La 'Folie' dans l'œuvre romanesque de Stendhal*.

3 Unexpressing the expressible

1 The Castex edition of *Le Rouge* contains the newspaper reports of both trials in *le Dossier du roman* printed in the appendix. All references to the Berthet trial will be to this Dossier. There are two thorough and scholarly studies of these trials on which I shall be relying, Claude Liprandi's *L'Affaire Lafargue et 'Le Rouge et le Noir'* and René Fonvieille's *Le Véritable Julien Sorel*, which deals with the Berthet affair. I am grateful to Ruth Harris for information about the legal background to crimes of passion in the period.

2 The case would thus be a good example of what Jean-François Lyotard calls a *différend*, since 'J'aimerais appeler *différend* le cas où le plaignant est dépouillé des moyens d'argumenter et devient de ce fait un victime. Un cas de différend entre deux parties a lieu quand le "règlement" du conflit qui les oppose se fait dans l'idiome de l'une d'elles alors que le tort dont l'autre souffre ne se signifie pas dans cet idiome' (*Le Différend*, pp. 24—5). In this instance the idiom in which the conflict is to be discussed is the narrative idiom of the socially determined *histoire d'amour*. The repressed or silenced idiom is by definition impossible to characterise. The *différend* could be seen as one form in which dialogic conflict can take place, and as a means whereby monologic discourses of authority can silence alternative discursive modes.

3 This was evidently a man who didn't share Stendhal's enthusiasm for Shakespeare, and did not see the plot of *Othello* re-enacted five or six times a year in the crime reports of the *Gazette des Tribunaux*, as Stendhal himself did. See *Promenades dans Rome*, p. 1079.

4 See Liprandi, *L'Affaire Lafargue*, pp. 84—91 for Stendhal's interest in crime.

5 Roland Barthes, Préface, *Essais critiques*, p. 14.

6 On this theme, see Roland Barthes, 'On échoue toujours à parler de ce qu'on aime'.

7 Mathilde's (and Julien's) reading will be discussed in more detail in chapter 5 below.

8 Perhaps it is for the same sort of reason that Clélia's apparently in-explicable adherence to her vow made to the Virgin Mary goes unchal-lenged in *La Chartreuse de Parme*.

9 Roland Barthes, *Roland Barthes*, p. 171.

4 The speaking of the quoted word: authors, ironies and epigraphs

1 Victor Brombert, *Stendhal et la voie oblique*; Grahame C. Jones, *L'Ironie dans les romans de Stendhal*; Jean Starobinski, 'Stendhal pseudonyme'.

2 Wayne C. Booth, *The Rhetoric of Fiction*.

3 Geneviève Mouillaud, *Le Rouge et le Noir de Stendhal. Le roman poss-ible*, p. 30. *Rome, Naples et Florence* was published in 1817 as the work of *M. de Stendhal, officier de cavalerie*, whose travel diary it purported to be.

4 Cited in Gérard Genette, '"Stendhal"'. This is an indispensable article for anyone interested in the problems of authorial voice and writing in Stendhal. See esp. pp. 185—9.

5 See the passage entitled 'Le second degré et les autres' in *Roland Barthes* (pp. 70—1), where he coins this term: 'J'écris: ceci est le premier degré du langage. Puis, j'écris que *j'écris*: c'en est le second degré ... Tout discours est pris dans le jeu des degrés. On peut appeler ce jeu: *bathmologie*. Un néologisme n'est pas de trop, si l'on en vient à l'idée d'une science nouvelle:

celle des échelonnements de langage.' The passage is worth reading in its entirety, not least for what it has to say about '[les] maniaques du second degré', of whom Stendhal, surely, is one.

6 In his article on *La Chartreuse* almost the only negative comment that Balzac makes concerns Stendhal's style: 'Le côté faible de cette œuvre est le style, en tant qu'arrangement de mots, car la pensée, éminemment française, soutient la phrase. Les fautes que commet M. Beyle sont purement grammaticales: il est négligé, incorrect à la manière des écrivains du xviie siècle. Les citations que j'ai faites montrent à quelles sortes de fautes il se laisse aller. Tantôt un désaccord de temps dans les verbes, quelquefois l'absence du verbe; tantôt des *c'est*, des *ce que*, des *que*, qui fatiguent le lecteur, et font à l'esprit l'effet d'un voyage dans une voiture mal suspendue sur une route de France. Ces fautes assez grossières annoncent un défaut de travail' (Balzac, 'Etudes sur M. Beyle', pp. 1211−12).

In all three drafts of his reply to Balzac, Stendhal makes a point of defending himself on this charge: 'Enfin, tout en mettant beaucoup de vos aimables louanges sur le compte de la pitié pour un ouvrage inconnu, je suis d'accord sur tout excepté sur le *style*', and he describes his own aims in this matter as being the reverse of the polished effects achieved by Chateaubriand: 'Le beau style de M. de Chateaubriand me sembla ridicule dès 1802. Ce style me semble dire une quantité de petites *faussetés*. Toute ma croyance sur le style est dans ce mot' (*Correspondance*, III, p. 394).

7 My italics, p. 13. This reading is a correction proposed by Castex for what he considers 'une simple coquille du texte original' which gives 'fort inégal'. I do not, however, agree with his reasoning that 'le mot *inégal* ne saurait s'appliquer au caractère de cette héroïne', given that one must still account for the words 'en apparence'. See note 16 of the Castex edition, p. 524.

8 Brombert, *Stendhal et la voie oblique*, p. 54. Erica Abeel, 'The multiple authors in Stendhal's ironic interventions'.

9 Vladimir Jankélévitch, *L'Ironie*, p. 76. For further discussion of this citational view of irony, see Dan Sperber and Deirdre Wilson, 'Les ironies comme mentions'.

10 For a discussion of the salon as a Stendhalian ideal, see Leo Bersani, 'Stendhalian prisons and *salons*'.

11 See Claude Pichois, 'Sur quelques épigraphes de Stendhal'.

12 Antoine Compagnon, *La Seconde Main*, p. 30.

13 See Compagnon, *ibid.*, pp. 279−83. This distinction roughly corresponds to the English opposition between 'quotation' and 'citation'. However, under the influence of French the English word 'citation' is often used in the weaker French sense, and, if only to alleviate the monotonous repetition of the word 'quotation', I have tended to use it in this sense myself. Perhaps the academic format of the footnote would also be the

right place to point out that the traditional use of epigraphs is now largely restricted to the practice of academic writing.

14 I am indebted to Jean-Jacques Hamm's illuminating article, "Le Rouge et le Noir" d'un lecteur d'épigraphes', for these facts and figures.

15 Cited by Castex, *Le Rouge*, p. 515.

16 This point is made by Albert Sonnenfeld, 'Romantisme (ou ironie): les épigraphes de "Rouge et Noir"', esp. pp. 150–2.

5 The uses of reading

1 The ladies of Paris may regard themselves as above this kind of thing, but its importance for Emma Bovary is notorious. Stendhal and Flaubert seem to concur in their characterisation of these novels: 'Ce n'étaient qu'amours, amants, amantes, dames persécutées s'évanouissant dans des pavillons solitaires, postillons qu'on tue à tous les relais, chevaux qu'on crève à toutes les pages, forêts sombres, troubles du cœur, serments, sanglots, larmes et baisers, nacelles au clair de lune, rossignols dans les bosquets, *messieurs* braves comme des lions, doux comme des agneaux, vertueux comme on ne l'est pas, toujours bien mis, et qui pleurent comme des urnes' (*Madame Bovary*, pp. 34–5). Emma also reads Walter Scott. Another avid reader of *romans de femmes de chambre* is Molly Bloom, who asks Bloom to get her 'another of Paul de Kock's', but perhaps as much for the dubious connotations of his name as for any other reason (*Ulysses*, p. 57).

2 It was a snobbery that Stendhal himself was not unaffected by, since he was, apparently, proud of being published in octavo by Levavasseur, who also published a twelvemo edition of the novel. Balzac, who until 1830 had been published exclusively in the twelvemo format, was upgraded to octavo status with his *Physiologie du mariage*. See *Le Rouge*, note, p. 728.

3 Geneviève Mouillaud points out that although Stendhal's novels are ultimately addressed to the *happy few*, the only readers explicitly addressed in *Le Rouge* are contemporary and largely hostile. *Le Rouge et le Noir de Stendhal: le roman possible*, pp. 32–5.

4 The Parisian reader invoked at the beginning of *Le Rouge et le Noir* presumably shares the same liberal opinions as the author, with whom he is in every other way so strongly identified. Judging by the preface to *Lucien Leuwen*, the scrutiny on questions of political allegiance that readers subject authors to is a widespread practice.

5 From the Civita-Vecchia copy of *Le Rouge*, where Stendhal adds, by way of explanation: 'Les habitants du premier sont esclaves de l'affectation des rhéteurs. Les jeunes gens qui pensent au lieu de croire habitent le sixième' (p. 499).

6 'Je regarde le Roman comme la Comédie au xixe siècle', notes on the Civita-Vecchia copy, p. 495. See also p. 496.

7 Experience of life for a Parisian tends to be equated with experience of

fiction: 'On voit que Julien n'avait aucune expérience de la vie, *il n'avait pas même lu de romans*' (p.336, my italics). The author is slightly ambiguous about the extent of Mme de Rênal's reading experience, claiming at one stage that 'Mme de Rênal n'avait jamais lu de romans' (p.76), but speaking at another of 'le très petit nombre de romans que le hasard avait mis sous ses yeux' (p.42). (Castex draws attention to this discrepancy in a note on p.541, and I am grateful to Geoff Woollen for reminding me of it.)

8 For an account of the different statuses of different readers, see W. Daniel Wilson, 'Readers in texts'.

9 For an account of the accuracy of the representation of this world, see P.-G. Castex, 'Réalités d'époque dans *Le Rouge et le Noir*'. However, he makes no mention of the role of the Parisian reader in the authentication of this representation.

10 On his arrival in Paris this language of the salons 'était comme une langue étrangère qu'il eût comprise, mais qu'il n'eût pu parler' (p.245).

11 See Castex on 'L'accueil des contemporains', *Le Rouge*, p.691.

12 Julien's reading includes the *Mémorial de Sainte-Hélène*, St Jerome, Cicero, Horace, Virgil, Tacitus, Martial, Livy, a history of the Revolution, *Othello*, Rotrou, Voltaire, and La Fontaine. For a discussion of the reading of Stendhal's heroes and of its significance for them, see James T. Day, 'The hero as reader in Stendhal'.

13 In the course of the novel Mathilde reads 'huit ou dix volumes de poésies nouvelles' (p.269), *Le Contrat social*, Vély's *Histoire de France*, d'Aubigné, Brantôme, Pierre de l'Etoile's *Mémoires*, *Manon Lescaut*, *La Nouvelle Héloïse*, the *Lettres portugaises*, Voltaire, and some of the 'nouveautés un peu piquantes' from her father's collection. She is forbidden by her mother to read Walter Scott.

14 Addition in the notes of the Civita-Vecchia copy of *Le Rouge*, p.502.

15 Wolfgang Iser, *The Act of Reading*. See in particular chapter 8.

16 Shoshana Felman, *La 'Folie' dans l'œuvre romanesque de Stendhal*.

17 See *Le Rouge*, pp.445, 446, 450, 453, 454, 455, 472 and 482.

18 See Léon Cellier, 'Rires, sourires et larmes dans *Le Rouge et le Noir*'.

19 See Cellier, *ibid.*, p.278.

20 'Ce *rire-là* ne fait rien à l'affaire, ne doit pas entrer dans notre analyse', *Racine et Shakespeare*, pp.65–6.

21 See discussion above in chapter 1, pp.36–7.

6 The reader and the life

1 Philippe Lejeune, *Le Pacte autobiographique*, p.44. Lejeune is, of course, not the only critic and theorist of autobiography to bring the reader into this prominence. See also, for example, Elizabeth Bruss, *Autobiographical ·Acts: The Changing Situation of a Literary Genre*, and Barrett J. Mandel, 'Full of life now'.

2 A notable exception is Jonathan Loesberg, who argues very eloquently that the critical emphasis on the reader in autobiographical studies has not gone far enough. This claim is based on his view that 'the problems which are normally attributed to the writing of autobiography [are] problems more nearly attached to the reading of autobiography'. See his 'Autobiography as genre, act of consciousness, text', p. 172. His concerns are, however, chiefly with the critical apparatus that readers bring to bear on autobiographical texts, and his argument therefore follows a somewhat different tack from the one that I shall be developing here.

3 Emile Benveniste, *Problèmes de linguistique générale*, p. 260. His italics.

4 These issues are discussed in further detail in my article 'Beyond contract: the reader of autobiography and Stendhal's *Vie de Henry Brulard*'.

5 E.g. Michel Crouzet in *La Vie de Henry Brulard, ou l'enfance de la révolte*, where the 'monstre' accusation is the starting point for his Oedipal reading of the text.

6 It's worth noting that despite his avoidance of all self-judgements, and his ticklishness on the subject of the judgements that have been made about him by others, Stendhal seldom has qualms about passing verdicts of his own on other people who have figured in his life.

7 Candace Lang also comments on this similarity (although from a slightly different perspective to the one which I shall be emphasising here). See her 'Autobiography in the aftermath of Romanticism', esp. p. 15.

8 Roland Barthes, *Le Plaisir du texte*, p. 25.

9 E.g. Béatrice Didier, *Stendhal autobiographe*. Didier is one of the few critics to acknowledge the importance to Stendhal of the readers of his autobiography, and suggests that 'peut-être le prototype de cette lectrice idéale [Mme Roland] serait justement sa mère' (p. 297). The final chapter of her study, '"Lecteur bénévole"', is devoted to a discussion of Stendhal's treatment of his reader.

10 Louis Marin, 'The autobiographical interruption: about Stendhal's *Life of Henry Brulard*', p. 597. 'You may', he adds, 'call this declaration a projection, an identification, or a pragmatic effect of Stendhal's text on the individual reader that I am.' I would argue that the declaration is a pragmatic effect that Stendhal's text has on any reader, and moreover, that the production of this effect is one of the book's primary aims.

7 The representation of politics and the politics of representation

1 The metaphor is also used in *Racine et Shakespeare* and the *Promenades dans Rome* and with the same kinds of connotation.

2 It is true, however, that this suggestion could also function as a covert form of promotion. But for what exactly? See Roger Fayolle, 'Stendhal et la politique', or Richard N. Coe, 'From Correggio to class warfare: notes on Stendhal's ideal of "la grâce"', or Michel Guérin, *La Politique de Stendhal*, all of whom argue in one way or another that the political

in Stendhal spills over into so many other issues that it is impossible to reduce it to the dimensions of the historically determined ideological alternatives of his day. In its own way, this chapter is attempting to show how and why this spilling over happens in Stendhal.

H.-F. Imbert has taken issue with Stendhal's reputation for political indifference, as his book *Les Métamorphoses de la liberté* seeks to demonstrate. I remain, however, unconvinced by the argument.

For other useful discussions of politics in *La Chartreuse*, see Bersani, 'Stendhalian prisons and *salons*', which stresses the absence of ideology in Parma's political parties; and Alison Finch, *Stendhal: 'La Chartreuse de Parme'*, esp. pp. 40−51.

3 Roland Barthes, *Le Grain de la voix: entretiens 1962−1980*, p. 206.
4 I borrow the term 'style' with reference to politics from Peter Brooks's discussion of *Lucien Leuwen* in *The Novel of Worldliness*, pp. 219−78.
5 Page 104. For discussion of some of the implications of the game-playing metaphor in *La Chartreuse*, see C. W. Thompson, *Le Jeu de l'ordre et de la liberté dans 'La Chartreuse de Parme'*. The chapter on Mosca deals with the political dimensions of this view.
6 Harry Levin, *The Gates of Horn*, p. 130.
7 This is a point also made by C. W. Thompson, *Le Jeu de l'ordre*, p. 17, where he writes 'la politique consiste à savoir manipuler les images trompeuses'.
8 I owe this point to Toril Moi.
9 Page 305. Gina is the source of this accolade, but there is nothing in Stendhal's depiction of Mosca's political skills to suggest that it is not merited.
10 Benjamin's phrase comes from the end of his essay on 'The work of art in the age of mechanical reproduction'.

8 A hero without qualities

1 If one accepts R. A. G. Pearson's persuasive reading of *Armance* as a 'comédie de la mélancolie', one sees at once that no one in their right mind could possibly want to be like Octave, the central figure in this 'entertaining critique of the attitude of mind known as the *mal du siècle* [which] presents its sufferers as engaged upon a wilful ''chasse au malheur'' in defiance of the real happiness which life, and particularly love, may have to offer'. See R. A. G. Pearson, 'Stendhal's *Armance*: the comedy of ''une chasse au malheur'' ', p. 245.
2 There is some doubt about whether Stendhal was actually the author of the 'Jeunesse d'Alexandre Farnèse', but on balance it seems pretty likely that he was. See the comments on the issue in the introduction (p. xii) and notes (p. 568) to Antoine Adam's edition of *La Chartreuse*.
3 Nathalie Sarraute, *L'Ere du soupçon*, p. 77.
4 Leo Bersani, *A Future for Astyanax*, p. 61. Chapter 2, 'Realism and the

fear of desire', gives an excellent account of the role of character in nineteenth-century realism, but Bersani's argument that the self is eventually fragmented by desire is rather different from the one I am proposing for the case of Stendhal. Fabrice's characterlessness is not designed to illustrate any belief that Stendhal may have had about the nature of the self. Rather, Fabrice's peculiar status in the novel is the consequence of a certain logic of realist fiction to which Stendhal was particularly sensitive; it is primarily a novelistic strategy designed to mitigate the corruptions brought about by readerly imitation.

5 See Gilbert Durand, *Le Décor mythique de 'La Chartreuse de Parme'*, esp. chapter 1.

6 See Elisabeth Ravoux's excellent article, 'Effet de réel et vraisemblable psychologique dans *La Chartreuse de Parme*': 'Comprendre la conduite de quelqu'un – dans le roman comme dans la vie, Stendhal le montre avec une perspicacité extraordinaire – c'est pouvoir la référer à une maxime admise ... Une fois ramenée à une conduite déjà observée, cette façon d'être n'échappe plus au langage commun – on sait *quoi dire* de ce caractère – ni à la classification' (p. 90).

7 Barthes, *Fragments d'un discours amoureux*, pp. 25–8. See also my discussion in chapter 2 above.

8 Alain Robbe-Grillet, *Pour un nouveau roman*, p. 31.

9 For a discussion of Stendhal's pseudonyms, see Jean Starobinski, 'Stendhal pseudonyme'.

10 Bersani has a nice account of Fabrice's political motives as a desire to defend the cause of the happy family and an 'impulse to find a congenial little group' ('Stendhalian prisons and *salons*', pp. 104–5).

11 I couldn't, therefore, disagree more with Stirling Haig in his article 'The identities of Fabrice del Dongo', where he argues that the masks adopted by Fabrice are 'essentially related to self-knowledge' (p. 173), a line which leads him to the conclusion that 'in love Fabrice has found his identity; he has also found self-knowledge' (p. 176). It seems to me that if Fabrice's experience of disguise culminates in the experience of love, then it is as a *liberation* from the vulgar and confining questions of identity and self-knowledge.

12 Michel Guérin is one of the few critics to have commented at any length and with any insight on Fabrice's disguises. He remarks that Fabrice 'est condamné au costume parce qu'il vit sous la protection des femmes' and stresses the role of disguise as a means of dissimulation rather than self-discovery (*La Politique de Stendhal*, p. 202).

13 Although one might concede that on a symbolic level, at least, Fabrice is 'mieux adapté qu'on ne le croit à ce métier de marchand de baromètres' because, says C. W. Thompson, 'personne ne mesure la pression de l'air plus attentivement que Fabrice, et Stendhal ne sera satisfait de lui que lorsqu'il pourra "voler de ses propres ailes"' (*Le Jeu de l'ordre*, p. 170).

14 Balzac seems to fail totally to appreciate this strategy when he attributes

some of the 'errors' of *La Chartreuse* to an excessive concern with the details of objective reality: 'il [Stendhal] a commis dans l'arrangement des faits la faute que commettent quelques auteurs, en prenant un sujet vrai dans la nature qui ne l'est pas dans l'art. En voyant un paysage, un grand peintre se gardera bien de le copier servílement, il nous en doit moins la Lettre que l'Esprit. Ainsi, dans sa manière simple, naïve et sans apprêt de conter, M. Beyle a risqué de paraître confus' ('Etudes sur M. Beyle', pp. 1208–9). It is extraordinary to see Stendhal of all people, who so loathed the trivia of 'la prosaïque réalité', being accused in these terms. Balzac seems to have been thrown off the rails by not finding the one thing that his own writing so amply and richly provides, namely, the revelation of the spirit that lies behind the letter of things. For reasons which this chapter has been devoted to explaining, Stendhal could not possibly follow Balzac along these lines; and Balzac presumably could see no alternative other than the choice between the spirit and the letter of representation.

9 Forgery, plagiarism and the operatic text

1 For some fairly schematic but interesting evidence about the variety of letters and the different kinds of activity associated with them in *Le Rouge* and *Armance*, see Suzanne Pons-Ridler, 'Recherche linguistique préalable à toute étude sur la communication écrite dans *Le Rouge et le Noir* et *Armance*'.

2 This link between forgery and poetry can also be found in a slightly more squalid version at another point in *La Chartreuse*: the author of the satirical sonnet about La Fausta, 'l'excellent poète Burati, de Venise' (p. 235 – Burati really existed and was known and admired by Stendhal), has the same name as the rather shady 'galérien' whom Raversi hires to counterfeit Gina's writing in the letter that finally traps Fabrice. See pp. 274–5.

3 E.g. Vivian Kogan, 'Signs and signals in *La Chartreuse de Parme*', William J. Berg, 'Cryptographie et communication dans *La Chartreuse de Parme*', and Peter Brooks, 'L'invention de l'écriture (et du langage) dans *La Chartreuse de Parme*'. My own reading of this rediscovery and re-evaluation of language is, however, rather different from those proposed in these articles.

4 James T. Day, in his article 'The hero as reader in Stendhal', remarks on the structural similarity of the St Jerome episode in *La Chartreuse* with the forged letter episode in *Armance* (p. 418).

5 For an interesting account of plagiarism in Stendhal, see Jean-Jacques Hamm, 'Stendhal et l'autre du plagiat'.

6 I take it that the Madame P... who sings so movingly at the Princess's reception in *La Chartreuse* (p. 498) is none other than Stendhal's exemplary singer.

7 Barthes's essay on singing, 'Le grain de la voix' (in *L'Obvie et l'obtus*), is indispensable reading for anyone interested in the relations between music and language. His interest in the voice has to do with 'la *friction* même de la musique et d'autre chose' (my italics), which constitutes its significance, and makes of it a kind of writing. See *L'Obvie et l'obtus*, pp. 236–45, and p. 241 in particular.

8 See note 11, p. 699. The discovery of the correct authorship of the two lines quoted in the novel was made by M. Veyne. It appears too that the poem is quoted in *La Nouvelle Héloïse*.

9 In the case of *Armance* the original inspiration was an unpublished novel, *Olivier ou le secret*, written by a Mme de Duras, whose hero was impotent. Octave was called Olivier in the first drafts of Stendhal's novel. *Lucien Leuwen* is a rewriting of a more obvious kind, having its origins in a manuscript called *Le Lieutenant*, whose author, Mme Gaulthier, asked Stendhal for advice. The fruits of this advice were another novel, *Lucien Leuwen*. For a very thorough account of Stendhal as an improviser of other texts, see Jean Prévost, *La Création chez Stendhal*.

10 See p. 651.

11 See Balzac's 'Etudes sur M. Beyle'; Maurice Bardèche, *Stendhal romancier*; Gilbert Durand, *Le Décor mythique de 'la Chartreuse de Parme'*. The conflicts between 'connaissance' and 'tendresse' in Jean-Piere Richard's account of Stendhal could also be seen in this perspective ('Connaissance et tendresse chez Stendhal').

Conclusion

1 For an excellent account of the place and importance of the concept of 'la grâce' in Stendhal, see Richard N. Coe, 'From Correggio to class warfare: notes on Stendhal's ideal of "la grâce" '.

BIBLIOGRAPHY

Unless otherwise stated, the place of publication is Paris for French titles, and London for English ones.

Works by Stendhal

Armance, in *Romans et nouvelles*, vol. 1, ed. Henri Martineau, Pléiade, Gallimard, 1952.

Le Rouge et le Noir, ed. Pierre-Georges Castex, Classiques Garnier, 1973.

Lucien Leuwen, in *Romans et nouvelles*, vol. 1.

La Chartreuse de Parme, ed. Antoine Adam, Classiques Garnier, 1973.

Chroniques italiennes, in *Romans et nouvelles*, vol. 2.

Lamiel, in *Romans et nouvelles*, vol. 2.

Romans et nouvelles, in *Romans et nouvelles*, vol. 2.

Journal, in *Œuvres intimes*, vols. 1 and 2, ed. Victor Del Litto, Pléiade, Gallimard, 1982.

Souvenirs d'égotisme, in *Œuvres intimes*, vol. 2.

Vie de Henry Brulard, in *Œuvres intimes*, vol. 2.

De l'Amour, ed. Henri Martineau, Classiques Garnier, 1959.

Promenades dans Rome, in *Voyages en Italie*, ed. Victor Del Litto, Pléiade, 1973.

Racine et Shakespeare, ed. Roger Fayolle, Garnier-Flammarion, 1970.

Chroniques 1825–1829. Tome I: Lettres de Paris 1825. Tome II: Esquisses de la société parisienne, de la politique et de la littérature 1826–1829, ed. Henri Martineau, presented by José-Luis Diaz, Le Sycomore, 1983.

Correspondance, 3 volumes, ed. Henri Martineau and Victor Del Litto, Pléiade, Gallimard, 1962–8.

All other titles from the *Œuvres complètes*, ed. Victor Del Litto and Ernest Abravanel, Cercle du Bibliophile, 1972–4:

Mémoires d'un touriste, vols. 15–17.

Vie de Rossini, vols. 22–3.

Histoire de la peinture en Italie, vols. 26–7.

Vie de Napoléon, vol. 39.

Mémoires sur Napoléon, vol. 40.

Bibliography

Vies de Haydn, de Mozart et de Métastase, vol. 41.
Mélanges. Tome II. Journalisme, vol. 46.
Mélanges. Tome III. Peinture, vol. 47.

Works devoted wholly or in part to Stendhal

Abeel, Erica, 'The multiple authors in Stendhal's ironic interventions', *French Review*, 50:1, pp. 21–34.

Adams, Robert M., *Stendhal: Notes on a Novelist*, Merlin Press, 1959.

Balzac, Honoré de, Etudes sur M. Beyle (Frédéric Stendalh [sic])', in *L'Œuvre de Balzac*, ed. Albert Béguin, Le Club Français de l'Art, 1952, tome XIV, pp. 1151–216.

Bardèche, Maurice, *Stendhal romancier*, La Table Ronde, 1947.

Barthes, Roland, 'On échoue toujours à parler de ce qu'on aime', *Tel Quel*, 85 (1980), pp. 32–8.

Berg, William J., 'Cryptographie et communication dans *La Chartreuse de Parme*', *Stendhal Club*, 78 (1978), pp. 170–82.

Bersani, Leo, 'Stendhalian prisons and *salons*', in *From Balzac to Beckett*, Oxford University Press, New York, 1970, pp. 91–139.

Birnberg, Jacques, 'Le lecteur narrataire des romans de Stendhal', *Stendhal Club*, 100 (1983), pp. 464–73.

Blin, Georges, *Stendhal et les problèmes du roman*, Corti, 1954.
Stendhal et les problèmes de la personnalité, Corti, 1958.

Brombert, Victor, *Stendhal et la voie oblique*, Yale University Press, New Haven, Conn., 1954.

Brooks, Peter, 'L'Invention de l'écriture (et du langage) dans *La Chartreuse de Parme*', *Stendhal Club*, 78 (1978), pp. 183–90.
Reading for the Plot: Design and Intention in Narrative, Clarendon Press, Oxford, 1984.

Castex, Pierre-Georges, 'Réalités d'époque dans *Le Rouge et le Noir*', *Europe*, 519–21 (1972), pp. 55–63.

Cellier, Léon, 'Rires, sourires et larmes dans *Le Rouge et le Noir*', in *De Jean Lemaire de Belges à Jean Giraudoux: mélanges d'histoire et de critique littéraire offerts à Pierre Jourda*, Nizet, 1970, pp. 277–97.

Coe, Richard, 'From Correggio to class warfare: notes on Stendhal's ideal of "la grâce"', in *Balzac and the Nineteenth Century: Studies in French Literature Presented to Herbert J. Hunt*, ed. D. G. Charlton *et al.*, Leicester University Press, Leicester, 1972, pp. 239–54.

Crouzet, Michel, *Stendhal et le langage*, Gallimard, 1981.
Stendhal et l'italianité. Essai de mythologie romantique, Corti, 1982.
La Vie de Henry Brulard, ou l'enfance de la révolte, Corti, 1982.
La Poétique de Stendhal: forme et société. Le sublime, Flammarion, 1983.

Day, James T., 'The hero as reader in Stendhal', *French Review*, 54:3 (1981), pp. 412–19.

Bibliography

Del Litto, Victor, *La Vie intellectuelle de Stendhal: genèse et évolution de ses idées (1801–1821)*, PUF, 1959.

'Pourquoi Stendhal a écrit *De l'Amour*', *Première journée de Stendhal Club*, Editions du Grand-Chêne, Lausanne, 1965, pp. 61–6.

Del Litto, Victor, ed., *Stendhal et les problèmes de l'autobiographie*, Presses Universitaires de Grenoble, Grenoble, 1976.

Stendhal–Balzac: réalisme et cinéma (Actes du XIᵉ congrès international stendhalien), Presses Universitaires de Grenoble, Grenoble, 1978.

Didier, Béatrice, *Stendhal autobiographe*, PUF, 1983.

Durand, Gilbert, *Le Décor mythique de 'La Chartreuse de Parme'*, Corti, 1961.

Elster, Jon, 'Deception and self-deception in Stendhal: some Sartrian themes', in *The Novelist as Philosopher: Modern Fiction and the History of Ideas*, ed. Peregrine Horden, Chichele Lectures, 1982, All Souls College, Oxford, 1983.

Fayolle, Roger, 'Stendhal et la politique', *La Pensée*, 131 (1967), pp. 67–78.

Felman, Shoshana, *La 'Folie' dans l'œuvre romanesque de Stendhal*, Corti, 1971.

Finch, Alison, *Stendhal: 'La Chartreuse de Parme'*, Arnold, 1984.

Fonvieille, René, *Le Véritable Julien Sorel*, Arthaud, Paris and Grenoble, 1971.

Genette, Gérard, ' "Stendhal" ', in *Figures II*, Seuil, 1969, pp. 155–93.

Gilman, Stephen, *The Tower as Emblem*, *Analecta Romanica*, vol. 22, Klosterman, Frankfurt, 1967.

Gormley, Lane, ' "Mon roman est fini": fabricateurs de romans et fiction intratextuelle dans *Le Rouge et le Noir*', *Stendhal Club*, 82 (1979), pp. 129–38.

Guérin, Michel, *La Politique de Stendhal*, PUF, 1982.

Haig, Stirling, 'The identities of Fabrice del Dongo', *French Studies*, 27:2 (1973), pp. 170–6.

Hamm, Jean-Jacques, '*Le Rouge et le Noir* d'un lecteur d'épigraphes', *Stendhal Club*, 77 (1977), pp. 19–36.

'Stendhal et l'autre du plagiat', *Stendhal Club*, 91 (1981), pp. 203–14.

Hemmings, F. W. J. *Stendhal: A Study of his Novels*, Clarendon Press, Oxford, 1964.

Imbert, H.-F., *Les Métamorphoses de la liberté, ou Stendhal devant la Restauration et le Risorgimento*, Corti, 1967.

Jefferson, Ann, 'Beyond contract: the reader of autobiography and Stendhal's *Vie de Henry Brulard*', *Romance Studies*, 9 (1986), pp. 53–69.

Jones, Grahame C., *L'Ironie dans les romans de Stendhal*, Editions du Grand-Chêne, Lausanne, 1966.

'Réel, Saint-Réal: une épigraphe du *Rouge* et le réalisme Stendhalien', *Stendhal Club*, 98 (1983), pp. 235–43.

Kogan, Vivian, 'Signs and signals in *La Chartreuse de Parme*', *Nineteenth-Century French Studies*, 2:1–2 (1973–4), pp. 29–38.

Bibliography

Levowitz-Treu, Micheline, *L'Amour et la mort chez Stendhal; méta-morphoses d'un apprentissage*, Editions du Grand-Chêne, Aran (Switzerland), 1978.

Liprandi, Claude, *L'Affaire Lafargue et 'Le Rouge et le Noir'*, Editions du Grand-Chêne, Lausanne, 1961.

Marin, Louis, 'The autobiographical interruption: about Stendhal's *Life of Henry Brulard*', *MLN*, 93 (1978), pp. 597−617.

McWatters, K. G., *Stendhal lecteur des romanciers anglais*, Editions du Grand-Chêne, Lausanne, 1968.

Merler, Grazia, 'Connaissance et communication chez Stendhal', *Stendhal Club*, 61 (1973), pp. 13−34.

Mossman, Carol A., *The Narrative Matrix: Stendhal's 'Le Rouge et le Noir'*, French Forum Publishers, Lexington, Kentucky, 1984.

Mouillaud, Geneviève, *Le Rouge et le Noir de Stendhal. Le roman possible*, Larousse, 1973.

Pearson, R. A. G., 'Stendhal's *Armance*: the comedy of "une chasse au malheur"', *Forum for Modern Language Studies*, 19:3 (1983), pp. 236−48.

Pichois, Claude, 'Sur quelques épigraphes de Stendhal', *Le Divan*, 285 (1953), pp. 32−6.

Pons-Ridler, Suzanne, 'Recherche linguistique préalable à toute étude sur la communication écrite dans *Le Rouge et le Noir* et *Armance*', *Stendhal Club*, 77 (1977), pp. 37−45.

Prévost, Jean, *La Création chez Stendhal*, Mercure de France, 1951.

Purdy, Anthony, 'De la première préface de *De l'Amour*: destinataire et intertexte', *Stendhal Club*, 85 (1979), pp. 25−31.

Ravoux, Elisabeth, 'Effet de réel et vraisemblable psychologique dans *La Chartreuse de Parme*', in *Stendhal−Balzac: réalisme et cinéma*, ed. Victor Del Litto, pp. 89−94.

Reader, Keith, 'Fabrice à Waterloo: une confluence d'histoires', *Stendhal Club*, 89 (1980), pp. 4−10.

Richard, Jean-Pierre, 'Connaissance et tendresse chez Stendhal', in *Littérature et sensation*, Seuil, 1954.

Simons, Madeleine Anjubault, *Sémiotisme de Stendhal*, Droz, Geneva, 1980.

Sonnenfeld, Albert, 'Romantisme (ou ironie): les épigraphes de *Rouge et Noir*', *Stendhal Club*, 78 (1978), pp. 143−54.

Starobinski, Jean, 'Stendhal pseudonyme', in *L'Œil vivant*, Gallimard, 1961, pp. 191−240.

Strickland, Geoffrey, *Stendhal: The Education of a Novelist*, Cambridge University Press, 1974.

Talbot, Emile (ed.), *La Critique stendhalienne de Balzac à Zola: textes choisis et présentés*, French Literature Publications Company, York, South Carolina, 1979.

Thompson, C. W., *Le Jeu de l'ordre et de la liberté dans 'La Chartreuse de Parme'*, Editions du Grand-Chêne, Aran (Switzerland), 1982.

Bibliography

'Expression et conventions typographiques: les notes en bas de page chez Stendhal', in *La Création romanesque chez Stendhal*, ed. Victor Del Litto, Droz, 1986, pp. 35–45.

Tillett, Margaret, *Stendhal: The Background to the Novels*, Oxford University Press, 1971.

Valéry, Paul, 'Stendhal', *Variété II*, Gallimard, 1930, pp. 75–139.

Winegarten, Renee: 'Stendhal: the enigmatic liberal', *Encounter*, 65:3 (1985), pp. 26–33.

Wood, Michael, *Stendhal*, Elek, 1971.

Other references – explicit and implied

Abrams, M. H., *The Mirror and the Lamp: Romantic Theory and the Critical Tradition*, Oxford University Press, New York, 1971. (First published 1953.)

Alter, Robert, *Partial Magic: The Novel as a Self-Conscious Genre*, University of California Press, Berkeley, California, 1975.

Amossy, Ruth and Rosen, Elisheva, *Le Discours du cliché*, Sedes, 1982.

Auerbach, Erich, *Mimesis: The Representation of Reality in Western Literature*, translated by Willard Trask, Doubleday Anchor Books, New York, 1957. (First published 1946.)

Bakhtin, Mikhail, *The Dialogic Imagination*, ed. Michael Holquist, translated by Caryl Emerson and Michael Holquist, University of Texas Press, Austin, 1981.

Balzac, Honoré de, *La Comédie humaine*, ed. Pierre-Georges Castex, Pléiade, Gallimard, 1976ff.

Barthes, Roland, *Le Degré zéro de l'écriture, suivi de Nouveaux Essais critiques*, Seuil, 1972.

Essais critiques, Seuil, 1964.

S/Z, Seuil, 1970.

Le Plaisir du texte, Seuil, 1973.

Roland Barthes, Seuil, 1975.

Fragments d'un discours amoureux, Seuil, 1977.

La Chambre claire, Gallimard/Seuil, 1980.

Le Grain de la voix: entretiens 1962–1980, Seuil, 1981.

L'Obvie et l'obtus. Essais critiques III, Seuil, 1982.

Le Bruissement de la langue. Essais critiques IV, Seuil, 1984.

Baudelaire, Charles, *Œuvres complètes*, ed. Claude Pichois, Pléiade, Gallimard, 1976.

Bellanger, Claude, *et al.*, *Histoire générale de la presse française. Tome II: de 1815 à 1871*, PUF, 1969.

Bellos, David, *Balzac Criticism in France 1850–1900. The Making of a Reputation*, Clarendon Press, Oxford, 1976.

Bénichou, Paul, *Le Sacre de l'écrivain*, Corti, 1973.

Benjamin, Walter, *Illuminations*, translated by Harry Zohn, Fontana/Collins, 1973. (First published 1955.)

253

Bibliography

One Way Street and Other Writings, translated by Edmund Jephcott and Kingsley Shorter, NLB, 1979.

Bennington, Geoffrey, *Sententiousness and the Novel: Laying Down the Law in Eighteenth-Century French Fiction*, Cambridge University Press, Cambridge, 1985.

'From narrative to text: love and writing in Crébillon *fils*, Duclos, Barthes', *Oxford Literary Review*, 4:1, (1979), pp. 62–81.

Benveniste, Emile, *Problèmes de linguistique générale*, Gallimard, 1966.

Bersani, Leo, *A Future for Astyanax: Character and Desire in Literature*, Marion Boyars, 1978.

Booth, Wayne C., *The Rhetoric of Fiction*, University of Chicago Press, Chicago, 1961.

A Rhetoric of Irony, University of Chicago Press, Chicago and London, 1974.

Borgerhoff, E. B. O., '*Réalisme* and kindred words: their use as terms of literary criticism in the first half of the nineteenth century', *PMLA*, 53:3 (1938), pp. 837–43.

Bourgeois, René, *L'Ironie romantique*, Presses Universitaires de Grenoble, Grenoble, 1974.

Brooke-Rose, Christine, *A Rhetoric of the Unreal: Studies in Narrative and Structure, especially of the Fantastic*, Cambridge University Press, Cambridge, 1981.

Brooks, Peter, *The Novel of Worldliness*, Princeton University Press, Princeton, NJ, 1969.

Brophy, Brigid, *Mozart the Dramatist*, Faber and Faber, 1964.

Bruss, Elizabeth, *Autobiographical Acts: The Changing Situation of a Literary Genre*, Johns Hopkins University Press, Baltimore, Maryland, 1976.

Cave, Terence, *The Cornucopian Text: Problems of Writing in the French Renaissance*, Clarendon Press, Oxford, 1979.

Champfleury, *Le Réalisme*, Michel Lévy, 1857.

Charlton, D. G., *The French Romantics*, 2 vols., Cambridge University Press, Cambridge, 1984.

Compagnon, Antoine, *La Seconde Main, ou le travail de la citation*, Seuil, 1979.

Comte, Auguste, *Cours de philosophie positive (première et deuxième leçons)*, ed. Charles le Verrier, Garnier, 1949.

Constant, Benjamin, *Adolphe*, ed. J.-H. Bornecque, Classiques Garnier, 1966.

Diderot, Denis, *Œuvres esthétiques*, ed. Paul Vernière, Classiques Garnier, 1959.

Flaubert, Gustave, *Madame Bovary*, ed. Edouard Maynial, Classiques Garnier, 1961.

Correspondance, Conard, 1926–30.

Foucault, Michel, *Les Mots et les choses*, Gallimard, 1966.

L'Ordre du discours, Gallimard, 1971.

Bibliography

Girard, René, *Deceit, Desire and the Novel*, translated by Yvonne Freccero, Johns Hopkins University Press, Baltimore, Maryland, 1965. First published as *Mensonge romantique, vérité romanesque*, Grasset, 1961.

Hobson, Marian, *The Object of Art: The Theory of Illusion in Eighteenth-Century France*, Cambridge University Press, Cambridge, 1982.

Howe, Irving, *Politics and the Novel*, Horizon-Meridian, New York, 1957.

Hugo, Victor, *Théâtre complet*, ed. J.-J. Thierry and Josette Mélèze, Pléiade, Gallimard, 1963.

Iknayan, Marguerite, *The Idea of the Novel in France: 1815–1848*, Droz, Geneva, 1961.

The Concave Mirror: From Imitation to Expression in French Esthetic Theory 1800–1830, Anma Libri, Saratoga, California, 1983.

Iser, Wolfgang, *The Act of Reading*, Routledge and Kegan Paul, 1978.

Jakobson, Roman, 'Closing statement: linguistics and poetics', in *Style in Language*, ed. Thomas Sebeok, MIT Press, Cambridge, Mass., 1960, pp. 350–77.

Jameson, Fredric, *The Prison-House of Language*, Princeton University Press, Princeton, NJ, 1972.

Jankélévitch, Vladimir, *L'Ironie*, Flammarion, 1980. (First published 1950.)

Jauss, Hans Robert, *Toward an Aesthetic of Reception*, translated by Timothy Bahti, Harvester Press, Brighton, 1982.

Jefferson, Ann, 'Realism reconsidered: Bakhtin's dialogism and the "will to reference"', *Australian Journal of French Studies*, 23:2 (1986), pp. 169–83.

Joyce, James, *Ulysses*, Cape, 1949.

Knight, Diana, *Flaubert's Characters: The Language of Illusion*, Cambridge University Press, Cambridge, 1985.

Lang, Candace, 'Autobiography in the aftermath of Romanticism', *Diacritics*, 12:1 (1982), pp. 2–16.

Leavis, Q. D., *Fiction and the Reading Public*, Chatto and Windus, 1932.

Le Breton, André, *Le Roman français au dix-neuvième siècle I: avant Balzac*, Société française d'Imprimerie et de Librairie, 1901.

Lejeune, Philippe, *Le Pacte autobiographique*, Seuil, 1975.

Levin, Harry, *The Gates of Horn: A Study of Five French Realists*, Oxford University Press, New York, 1966.

Loesberg, Jonathan, 'Autobiography as genre, act of consciousness, text', *Prose Studies*, 4:2 (1981), pp. 169–85.

Lough, John and Muriel, *An Introduction to Nineteenth-Century France*, Longman, 1978.

Lukács, Georg, *Studies in European Realism*, translated by Edith Bone, Merlin Press, 1972. (First published 1950.)

Lyotard, François, *Le Différend*, Minuit, 1983.

Mandel, Barrett J., 'Full of life now', in *Autobiography: Essays Theoretical and Critical*, ed. James Olney, Princeton University Press, Princeton, NJ, 1980, pp. 49–72.

Bibliography

Martin, Henri-Jean, and Chartier, Roger (eds.), *Histoire de l'édition française*, Promodis, 3 vols., 1982–5.

Maynial, Edouard, *L'Epoque réaliste*, Les Œuvres représentatives, 1931.

Muecke, Douglas, *The Compass of Irony*, Methuen, 1969.

Mylne, Vivienne, *The Eighteenth-Century French Novel: Techniques of Illusion*, Manchester University Press, Manchester, 1965.

Newhall, Beaumont, *Photography, Essays and Images*, Museum of Modern Art, New York, 1980.

Nori, Claude, *La Photographie française: des origines à nos jours*, Contre-jour, 1978.

Poétique. Special issue on 'Le discours réaliste', no. 16 (1973).

Special issue on 'Ironie', no. 36 (1978).

Prendergast, Christopher, *The Order of Mimesis*, Cambridge University Press, Cambridge, 1986.

Prévost, Antoine-François, *Histoire du Chevalier des Grieux et de Manon Lescaut*, in *Œuvres de Prévost*, ed. Jean Sgard, vol. 1, Presses Universitaires de Grenoble, Grenoble, 1978.

Reed, Walter, *An Exemplary History of the Novel: The Quixotic versus the Picaresque*, University of Chicago Press, Chicago and London, 1981.

Ricœur, Paul, *Temps et récit. Tome I*, Seuil, 1983.

Robbe-Grillet, Alain, *Pour un nouveau roman*, Coll. Idées, Gallimard, 1970. (First published 1963.)

Romance Studies, Special issue on 'Realism in the French novel', no. 1 (1982).

Rougement, Denis de, *L'Amour et l'occident*, Plon, 1939.

Sand, George, *Indiana*, ed. Pierre Salomon, Classiques Garnier, 1962.

La Mare au diable. François le Champi, ed. P. Salomon and J. Mallion, Classiques Garnier, 1981.

Sarraute, Nathalie, *L'Ere du soupçon*, Gallimard, 1956.

Scharf, Aaron, *Art and Photography*, revised edition, Penguin Books, Harmondsworth, Middlesex, 1974.

Schiff, Richard, 'The original, the imitation, the copy, and the spontaneous classic: theory and painting in the nineteenth century', *Yale French Studies*, 66 (1984), pp. 27–54.

Schöning, Udo, *Literatur als Spiegel: Zur Geschichte eines Kunsttheoretischen Topos in Frankreich von 1800 bis 1860*, Carl Winter, Universitätsverlag, Heidelberg, 1984.

Sperber, Dan and Wilson, Deirdre, 'Les ironies comme mentions', *Poétique*, 36 (1978), pp. 399–412.

Tel quel. Théorie d'ensemble, Seuil, 1968.

Todorov, Tzvetan, *Poétique de la prose*, Seuil, 1970.

Tompkins, Jane P. (ed.), *Reader-Response Criticism*, Johns Hopkins University Press, Baltimore, Maryland, 1980.

Varin d'Ainville, Madeleine, *La Presse en France: genèse et évolution de ses fonctions psycho-sociales*, PUF, Grenoble, 1965.

de Vigny, Alfred, *Œuvres complètes*, ed. Paul Viallaneix, Seuil, 1965.

Bibliography

Waugh, Patricia, *Metafiction: The Theory and Practice of Self-Conscious Fiction*, Methuen, 1984.

Weinberg, Bernard, *French Realism: The Critical Reaction, 1830–1870*, Modern Language Association of America, New York and London, 1937.

Wellek, René, *Concepts of Criticism*, ed. Stephen G. Nichols Jr, Yale University Press, New Haven, Conn., 1963.

Wilson, W. Daniel, 'Readers in texts', *PMLA*, 96:5 (1981), pp. 848–63.

Zola, Emile, *Les Romanciers naturalistes, Œuvres complètes*, ed. Maurice Le Blond, vol. 46, François Bernouard, 1928.

INDEX

Index

Index

260

Index

opinion publique, l', 22–4, 54, 59, 81,
　　88, 159, 239 n. 10

painting, see Stendhal on visual arts
Parent, Françoise, 235 n. 26
Pascal, Blaise, 93
Pasta, Mme Giuditta Negri, 148, 216,
　　220–1
Pearson, R. A. G., 245 n. 1
Pergolesi, Jean-Baptiste, 216, 225–6, 228
petit fait vrai, le, 34–6
Petrarch, 211, 213, 216–17, 219, 221,
　　227
photography, 27–31, 35–6, 237 n. 52,
　　n. 61
Picard, Louis-Benoît, 38–9
Pichois, Claude, 241 n. 11
Pingaud, Albert, 238 n. 66
plagiarism, xii, 25, 27, 207–17, 247 n. 5
pleasure, xiv, 8, 10–13, 22, 36, 38–40,
　　50, 61, 63, 117, 139, 147, 150,
　　156, 201, 206, 219–22, 224, 234
　　n. 14, 238 n. 70, 239 n. 3
　　see also Barthes on pleasure
plot, see narrative
Polidori, John William, 109–10
politics, see Barthes on politics,
　　Stendhal on politics
polyphony, 60, 63, 100, 107, 174–8,
　　201, 216–17, 229, 231
Pons-Ridler, Suzanne, 247 n. 1
positivism, xiii, 18–19, 22, 230
potin, le, 57, 86–92, 203
Poussin, Gaspard, 39–40, 132
Poussin, Nicolas, 199
pragmatics, xiii, 8, 11, 13, 20–1, 25,
　　244 n. 10
Prendergast, Christopher, 233 n. 1, 236
　　n. 40, n. 45
press, the, 28–9, 31–2, 67–75, 87,
　　109, 159, 161, 176
　　see also Stendhal on the press
Prévost, Antoine-François, 13
　　Histoire du chevalier des Grieux et
　　de Manon Lescaut, 12, 77, 243
　　n. 13
Prévost, Jean, 248 n. 8
printing, 27–30, 237 n. 55
Proust, Marcel, xi, 3
punctum, 35–7, 39
　　see also Barthes, Roland
Purdy, Anthony, 239 n. 7
Pushkin, Alexander, 60

quotation, 80, 92, 99–100, 104–6,
　　108–12, 241 n. 9, n. 13

Racine, Jean, 10–11, 26, 99, 150
Raphael, Raffaello Sanzio, 39–40, 131,
　　223–4
Ravoux, Elisabeth, 246 n. 6
rêverie, 61–3, 112, 128, 200, 232
Ricardou, Jean, 233 n. 2
Richard, Jean-Pierre, 248 n. 10
Richardson, Samuel, 12–13
　　Charles Grandison, 150
Ricœur, Paul, 238 n. 69
Robbe-Grillet, Alain, xi, 188
Roland, Marie-Jeanne Phlipon, Mme,
　　72, 80, 116, 131, 145–9, 151,
　　244 n. 9
romanesque, le, 53, 60–3, 100, 163, 230
Romanticism, 9–11, 16, 33–4, 74, 109,
　　149, 187, 234 n. 11
Ronsard, Pierre de, 227–8
Rosen, Elisheva, 237 n. 55
Rossini, Gioacchino, 34, 219–21, 226
Rousseau, Jean-Jacques, 13, 78–9, 82,
　　149, 216, 238 n. 69
　　Les Confessions, 76–7, 137, 140
　　La Nouvelle Héloïse, 46–50, 77–8,
　　124, 149, 182–3, 225–6, 243
　　n. 13, 248 n. 7
　　Emile, 62

Sainte-Beuve, Charles-Augustin, 30,
　　108, 110
Saint Jerome, 211, 213–15, 243 n. 12,
　　247 n. 4
Saint-Priest, Alexis de, 19, 123
Saint-Réal, abbé de, viii, 26, 111, 237
　　n. 48
Sancho Panza, 61, 164–5, 201
Sand, George, 19, 27–8
Saurraute, Nathalie, 40–1, 184
Saussure, Ferdinand de, xii–xiii
Scharf, Aaron, 237 n. 52
Schöning, Udo, 238 n. 63, n. 70
Scott, Walter, 17–19, 24, 106–7, 112,
　　115–16, 118, 148, 217, 242 n. 1,
　　243 n. 13
self-consciousness, xi–xiii, 14
Senancour, Etienne Pivert de,
　　Oberman, 15
Shakespeare, William, 10, 48, 108, 129,
　　149–50, 199, 240 n. 3, 243 n. 12
singularité, 121–2, 128, 186–8, 192,
　　216
Sonnenfeld, Albert, 242 n. 16
Sperber, Dan, 241 n. 9
Staël, Anne-Louise-Germaine, Mme
　　de, 8–10, 80, 93, 99
　　Corinne, 15, 62

261

Index

Cambridge Studies in French

General editor: MALCOLM BOWIE

Also in the series

MAY 9 1989
APR 1 8 1990